NUMEROLOGY
The Romance in Your Name

NUMEROLOGY
The Romance in Your Name

JUNO JORDAN

DeVorss Publications
Camarillo, California

Numerology: The Romance in Your Name
Copyright © 1965 by JF Rowny Press
Copyright transferred to DeVorss & Company, 1988

ISBN: 9780875162270
Seventeenth Printing, 2024

DeVorss & Company, Publisher
P.O. Box 1389
Camarillo CA 93011-1389
www.devorss.com

Printed in the United States of America

DEDICATED

to the teachers and students of Numerology,
who have proved the principles of Names and Numbers
through years of research and practice.

CONTENTS

PART TWO

PART THREE

INTRODUCTION

From time to time, magazines and periodicals present articles written by men and women who have changed their names and suddenly come into wealth, fame and recognition.

Reading these reports, you may have been skeptical about the new name having anything to do with it—but at the same time secretly wondered what you would be like if you had a different name. Would the same thing happen to you—would you really be different—would you show more talent—perhaps have married someone else—or made a fortune!

That our names are something more than a family relationship or just a means of identification, often surprises and shocks those presented with the precept that destiny and experience are written in our names given us at birth.

It has been recognized throughout the ages that names play a vital part in directing and influencing the destinies of mankind and that they represent character, human nature, experience and divine authority. The Bible teachings repeatedly bring out the importance of names. The days of creation were numbered according to the activity taking place, day by day. The Lord often changed the names of His chosen ones to represent the task or service to be carried out. At times, even before birth, a name was chosen as in the prophecy of the Christ.

Numerology also recognizes the potentialities and the spiritual command hidden in our names and the numbers comprising them. It applies numbers to names and determines the character, the life experiences and ultimate goal of the individual bearing the name. The scientist writes H_2O and understands the symbol. The Numerologist writes—Joe 165 or (12)3 and also interprets the nature and activity which the symbol represents.

Few people are conscious of the degree to which names and numbers influence all human communication and progress. *Everything* is named and numbered. Houses are numbered—streets—telephones—calendars—clocks—birthdays—contracts and statistics are written and tabulated in figures and numbers concerning every daily undertaking. We live in a mathematical world and do not realize it. In the same way, our names are numbered—for every letter of the alphabet has a number corresponding to its position and orderly relationship to the 26 letters forming the alphabet. Every poem, novel, love-letter, business communication, or expression of romance and emotion is transcribed through the means of the alphabet and its 26 letters. There is no other means of communication—nor escape from this mathematical tabulation of mankind's interests, desires and ambitions.

The dream of riches and of service to humanity lies deep in the heart of everyone. It is a natural and spiritual urge of the soul. Outstanding attainment and the best life has to offer are the rights of every man or woman—young or old. No one gets all the "breaks" all the time. They belong to all. Just *how* is hidden in each person's name. The *way* is there—it need only be discovered.

Character analysis through Numerology places everyone in their right place; it gives a blueprint of the opportunities they were born to accomplish and shows the way to success and the best life has to offer. Life brings everyone many tests and lessons to learn, but no one was born to struggle a whole lifetime through. Only lack of understanding of one's potentialities and soul's grace can bring this about. Happiness, success and the joy of living are rewards for the one who wisely follows the *Destiny* written in his name. All these promises are written there for you in *your* name. *You do not need to change it.* Understand it and put it to work for you.

THERE ARE FOUR REASONS FOR PRESENTING THIS BOOK

First—To help you know and understand yourself and gain confidence in your right to the best—in your way—not someone else's way.

Second—To help you prepare yourself for a successful career—to show you how to side-step possible pitfalls along the way, and how to have love and romance in your life.

Third—To present Numerology in its true worth and as a spiritual influence shaping the destiny of mankind.

Fourth—To train you to counsel others—if you desire.

THERE ARE FOUR PARTS TO THE BOOK

First—An all-embracing and vigorous explanation of the meaning of numbers; also the first rules for analyzing character, finding the personal opportunities—and the ultimate goal crowning the life. *(This is easy to learn.)*

Second—Explaining the peculiar personal traits of character which can make for outstanding success—or failure. Also indicating fixed attitudes of thought, likes and dislikes which may result in unhappy experiences in business, partnerships, marriage and social interests—or on the other hand represent talent and genius. *(This requires more study and practice.)*

Third—Instruction in how to interpret personal experiences month by month, year by year; and the prophecies of the four life-cycles experienced by everyone. *(This is easy to learn and is for guidance and protection in the affairs of the outside world.)*

Fourth—The meaning of the letters—called the "Table of Events"—revealing the experiences to be met year by year, to prove your worth and character. It tells of past experiences, what is happening at present and what is still ahead in the future. This is very revealing and shows when the pitfalls may happen—and how to avoid them. *(This takes a great deal of study but is very rewarding.)*

There are many other points of instruction in the last chapters of the book, given as in class instruction and answering the questions you will ask.

The Romance in Your Name is a complete course in Numerology. It is a textbook for beginners and a higher course of study work for advanced students. It is based on many years of experience and study. The instructions have been confirmed by twenty-five years of research by the California Institute of Numerical Research, Inc.*

*Publisher's note: Upon completion of the researches, the Institute was discontinued.

FOREWORD

"The students of the ancient Atlantis were taught the mysteries of numbers, handicrafts, poetry and sculpture."

"The Science of Numbers and the art of will power are the Keys of Magic that open the Gates of the Universe," said the Priests of Memphis.

Pythagoras formulated and made exact his teaching under the name *Science of Numbers.*

The Romans said "Nomen est Omen." The name is the destiny.

Names and numbers are symbols.

They do not of themselves *make* things happen.

Instead, they announce and broadcast the programs of thought, feeling and action being enacted on the television screen of human relations.

When found symbolizing a condition, circumstance or activity, they state without equivocation the nature of the happening, its character, its past, present and future. They are there as signposts to guide, protect and reward all who have the wisdom and foresight to observe and understand.

PART ONE

CHAPTER I

HISTORY OF NUMEROLOGY
How It Became a Means of Human Analysis

Pythagoras, one of the philosophers of ancient Europe, is generally accepted as the founder of the Science of Numbers. He was born about the year 590 B.C., and was named by the Oracle of Delphi who, it is said, prophesied his birth. When a young child he was placed in one of the Temples and grew up in a very spiritual environment. He learned the lesson of meditation and developed a great love of the stars. He is credited with having the idea that the world is a sphere or round ball.

Very little of his early life is recorded, but it is reported he won prizes for feats of agility at the Olympic games, that he was tall, beautiful, magnetic, dynamic, and everyone loved him. It is written he was given a new name after many initiations and was called Yarancharya, using the letter Y, a symbol he considered very mystical. He established a school of learning at Crotona, which was the center of culture of that day and where for nearly forty years he taught his pupils and exhibited his wonderful powers. His teachings, for the most part, were given in secret, and no student was allowed to put into writing any idea or subject given in the school. As far as is known, no one broke this rule until after his death, and for this reason his teachings were almost lost to the modern world.

Numbers—Their Occult Powers and Mystic Virtues by W. Wynn Wescott and the chapter "Pythagoras: the Mysteries of Delphi" in *The Great Initiates* by Edouard Schuré are wonderful books of reference on the life and teachings of Pythagoras.

THE TEACHINGS OF PYTHAGORAS

There were two phases to his teachings: The Science of Numbers, and the Theory of Magnitude. The first division included two branches, arithmetic and musical harmony; the second, geometry and magnitude in motion or astronomy. Pythagoras taught his students an exact mathematical precision. "The principles governing the numbers were understood to be the principles of real existence; the elements of numbers were the elements of realities." His instructions were given according to the law of mathematics and *this relationship of numbers to experience* is the divine law, the foundation of the modern system of analysis called Numerology.

Therefore, the instruction and teachings given in this course can be depended upon and used with full confidence as a means of character analysis and for lightening the burdens of those who suffer but have not found their way to success and happiness, or to their ultimate goal in life.

THE ALPHABET—ITS ORIGIN AND GROWTH

Records of many ancient alphabets have been found, dating as far back as 2400 B.C. The Egyptians are credited with the origin of the alphabet but were slow in the use of it, as it had little practical value. The Phoenicians, busy traders, made use of it and added many signs and symbols to advance its usefulness. Through their trading and travel, they introduced it to the Greeks, who put it into a more artistic form, adding curves to the straight lines. Later, the Romans introduced the capitals. As the alphabet traveled from country to country and nation to nation, and down through the dark ages, many changes were made and new symbols were added, until at present there are twenty-six letters in the alphabet which symbolize our modern-day thoughts and ideas.

Our modern alphabet is an entirely accurate and exact

mathematical arrangement and association of numbers and letters—a fact which is surprising to those who have given it little thought. This will be explained to you in the chart of figuring described below.

The numbers are commonly designated as being of Arabic origin, but were of little value until the introduction of the cipher, which made a place value called "decimal." Some historians give ancient Syria credit as being the ancestor of the alphabet, and excavations in the region of Mount Sinai show that the children of Israel used a system of alphabet writing.

MODERN NUMEROLOGY

Numerology, as it is presented today, is based on the precepts presented by Pythagoras—that nature geometrizes, that divine law is defined and accurate, and that it can be computed and figured with mathematical precision as definitely as any statement in arithmetic or physics.

In the early times the Hebrew alphabet contained twenty-two letters or symbols. Our present-day alphabet, moving forward through the past ages of civilization, contains twenty-six letters. It will eventually contain twenty-seven letters, as mankind moves forward into a better understanding of the Brotherhood of Man.

Mrs. L. Dow Balliet of Atlantic City is the authority for the modern method of relating names, numbers and vibrations. She gave the world a spiritual and practical system of applying numerical symbols to the analysis of character, and wrote several books, which are to be found in the public libraries of many large cities.

For many years, Numerology was not a well-known subject. Through its presentation by Dr. Julia Seton, international New Thought lecturer, much was done to bring it to the public and into popular use. She presented it to the people of many countries—the United States, South Africa, Australia, and the

Hawaiian Islands—educating the public to the truths hidden in the scrolls, symbols, and numbers as interpreted by Numerology. She is credited with giving the Science of Names and Numbers the modern name "Numerology."

Many excellent teachers and lecturers, recognized for their knowledge, experience, books and research, are serving humanity through the teachings of Numerology, and much credit is due them for their work and good standing in the community.

My first studies in Numerology were based on the personal instructions by Mrs. Balliet. Later, to test the accuracy of the numbers and the significance given the meaning of numbers, I called together a group of teachers, students, and co-workers, and organized the California Institute of Numerical Research, Inc. For twenty-five years, we studied every phase of the science of names and numbers: testing, proving, disproving, until through records and statistics, we can say, "NUMBERS DO NOT LIE" but signify character and the events of human experience with dependable accuracy.

It has been my privilege to present four points of instruction to the teachings of Numerology: the Pinnacles—the Challenge—the Planes of Expression—and the Reality Number.

The instructions given in this book can be relied upon and used with full confidence as a means of character analysis, or of lightening the burdens of those who have not found their true way to success and happiness.

My name at birth was—Juno Belle Kapp, born June 8, 1884. Dr. Julia Seton was my mother. For many years I was a practicing dentist. In 1957 I was presented a Distinguished Citizens Award for Humanitarian Service. My first book, *Your Number and Destiny*, was written under the name of Dr. Juno Kayy Walton. My students call me Dr. Juno.

THE RELATIONSHIP OF THE NUMBERS
AND LETTERS

This is your first step in learning to read a name.

Make a copy of this chart. To make good progress in reading names, *learn* this chart by heart. It is not hard. Notice some of the groups make words—slightly rearranged: FOX = 6; DMV = 4.

1—A–J–S

2—B–K–T   This chart is not arranged by the Numerologists. It is the result of the growth of the alphabet

3—C–L–U

4—D–M–V   down through the ages. Numbers and letters are

5—E–N–W   one and the same thing. They are never separate

6—F–O–X   from each other.

7—G–P–Y   *Rule:* Always find the *single digit* for any

8—H–Q–Z   sum of numbers. Add any sum of numbers—two

9—I–R   or three or more—together and keep on adding until a final sum is reached. In other words, reduce any combination of numbers to a final total by adding its component parts, repeating the addition until a final number is reached. This final number is the *single digit*.

Examples:

23 equals 5 (2 plus 3 equals 5, the single digit).

111 equals 3 (1 plus 1 plus 1 equals 3, the single digit).

149 equals 14 or 5 (1 plus 4 plus 9 equals 14; add again: 1 plus 4 equals 5, the single digit).

1962 equals 18 or 9 (1 plus 8 equals 9, the single digit).

In the same way, each letter of the alphabet has its corresponding number, by addition.

Example:

The letter O has the value of six on the chart. It is the 15th letter of the alphabet. (1 plus 5 equals 6.)

The letter P has the value of 7. It is the 16th letter. (1 plus 6 equals 7.)

Each letter of the alphabet has its own number, a fact not

realized by many. *Every time a letter is written* in a name or used in any way, a *number is also written* and a mathematical statement is made.

FIGURING A NAME

First, let me advise you to keep good notes on your lessons and copies of the names you figure. This will help you to make comparisons as you go along and to relate the points of study to your names.

Examples:

```
H  a  r  o  l  d
8  1  9  6  3  4    Add these numbers together. They add up
   31               to 31. Add again. 3 plus 1 equals 4, the sin-
   4                gle digit. Therefore, 4 is the symbol and nu-
                    merical value of the name Harold.
```

Use the same method for figuring a full name.

```
F  r  e  d  a      M  a  r  y      N  o  r  t  o  n
6  9  5  4  1      4  1  9  7      5  6  9  2  6  5
   (25)7              (21)3            (33)6
```

Add each name separately.

Freda adds to . . . . (25)7
Mary adds to . . . . (21)3
Norton adds to . . . . (33)6
     Total . . . . (16)7

The numerical value of the full name of Freda Mary Norton is a 16 or 7. This represents her Destiny in life and her Field of Opportunity.

Play the game of NUMBER OBSERVATION. Become number conscious. Notice numbers as you go about your daily affairs. You will be astonished how much they influence your daily life. Observe the number of your house, your place of business, your automobile, your bank account, your telephone, your age, the day you were born.

The *Romance* in your name is in the letters and numbers that are written there.

INSTRUCTIONS TO STUDENTS

Take plenty of time to understand each point of instruction. Do not hurry through or neglect one or more lessons. If little time is given to the lessons on character analysis, your analysis of future experiences is apt to be incorrect. Many students hurry ahead to the fascinating lessons on personal experiences, failing to realize that the volume of the experiences depends upon the character of the individual. Be sure, also, to figure every point of analysis given in the instructions as you learn them chapter by chapter.

One time a student brought me the name of a man whose numbers, she thought, indicated fine character, but who in business was an unscrupulous man. She was discouraged and thought Numerology was going to fail her. We studied the name together and found she had failed to take into consideration the Planes of Expression, which revealed a complete lack of practical ability and an over-imaginative tendency. Numerology is one of the easiest methods of character analysis, but at the same time it takes study and time to relate all the different parts of the name to finally build up the whole personality and individuality. The best way to gain experience is to read many names. Even if you cannot go far in analysis at first, go as far as you have studied. You will help someone, for every point of analysis turns a light on the character and experiences of the individual.

If you decide to become a counselor, make your work warm and personal. Do not trust to chance or an inspiration.

Consider your client and his or her needs. However, do not give personal advice or opinions that are not written in the name.

Our names tell astonishing stories and reveal amazing experiences. They uncover unlimited possibilities, the romance of living, the drama of being born, the thrill of a career, the inspiration of companionship, the promise of usefulness to the end of life—all are written in each and every name, given at birth to the newborn soul.

CHAPTER II

THE SIGNIFICANCE AND MEANING
OF NUMBERS

As you become aware of the influence of names and numbers in all business and personal activity, what they stand for is next in importance. Naturally your own numbers—your house number, office number, your name number, your age number, your social security number—can only have significance as you are able to interpret them in terms of human experience.

As you become able to transcribe the meaning of the numbers, it will be like learning to read a "secret code," giving you an "in" not possessed by others.

When you read the story in your own name and discover what it has to tell, your affairs will no longer be left to chance or hit or miss. The lives of others will be open books for you to read, giving you the privilege of service and helpfulness to many who are groping for light and understanding in their own world. When you begin to read the story written in your name and others, no book, novel, mystery story, or autobiography will be so fascinating, thrilling, or inspiring. At the same time, it is important to realize that numbers do not set up conditions by themselves—they simply photograph and explain the circumstances behind their appearance. They do, however, contain within their symbols a hidden force of spiritual attraction, calling to themselves—like a magnet—the powers with which they were endowed in the days of creation.

Your name is an autobiography of your life and your experiences, past or yet to be. Nothing is hidden. It can unfold before you step by step as you delve into its intricate facts. It has many facets. It encompasses your talents, skills. It foretells of many experiences, many happenings; it advises you what to do and what not to do to accomplish your dreams and to find your successful place in life.

Just how will be explained in the following instructions. What the numbers mean must first be understood. They are the a-b-c's of Numerology and analyzing names. They are like the multiplication table in mathematics. Skilled analysis depends upon how well you know the meaning of numbers. You will not be able to remember each number fully at first. As you figure names and observe the names of others, their meanings will take on life and importance and become second nature to you.

The negative side of the numbers is given to help you gain the general idea about them. A number in itself is never negative, but at times when one number becomes involved or bound up with another, there may be a clash which can be straightened out only through the understanding of what each number stands for and is seeking to express.

The meanings of the numbers have been divided into four parts, as follows:

The Cosmic Pattern—giving their spiritual background.

Opportunities—for service and true self-realization.

Vocations—for business success and personal career.

Human Relationships—for marriage, social ties, romance, health, and human frailties.

MEANING OF NUMBERS

THE NUMBER ONE

Watchword: Courage. An Introvert Number.

Positive	Negative
Originality	Aggression
Individuality	Dominance
Creative thought	Wilfullness
Inventive ideas	Impulsiveness
Will, Determination	Boastfulness
Courage, Initiative	Knowing it all
Executive ability	Cynicism
Energy, Force	Contrariness
Leadership	Talkativeness, then reticence
Self-determination	Egotism, a boss
Strong opinions	
Masculinity	

COLORS: Flame, Copper, Lilac, Apricot.

COSMIC PATTERN

"In the beginning, God created the heavens and the earth. And the earth was without form, and void; and darkness was upon the face of the deep. And the Spirit of God moved upon the face of the waters."

Pythagoras affirmed—"that the mind of man or the intellect takes from God its absolute active nature."

The Science of Numbers deals with the living force of the divine faculties in action in man and in the Universe.

Number *One* is the number of action. It has the knowledge of what is to be, followed by the courage, daring, will and intelligence to move where all is dark and void. It fears no obstacles—exploring, inventing and creating with dynamic force and energy—and sets the pattern and outline for others to follow. It becomes the leader and head of broad undertakings.

In human affairs—without the number *One*—there would be no beginnings.

OPPORTUNITIES

Excellent powers of concentration, will, determination, and fine memory give the number *One* unlimited opportunity. Its natural executive faculties and desire for action place it in the professional and creative world of business. It is not a physical laborer—it is a thinker and planner and lives on the mental plane. Early in life a reticent side to the nature may cause it to turn aside from its opportunities and refuse to show its ability to energize and promote the undertaking in which it finds itself. Or, it may go from one thing to another, seeming to lack in application and concentration.

This is not the true expression of the number *One*. It is a number of leadership, position, and authority and was born to take its place at the head of worthwhile enterprises and undertakings. This may be brought about by many strange, sudden, and unexpected happenings which force the number *One* to stand on its own feet and to make use of its natural talents— sometimes early in life. Experience is a good teacher for the number *One* and it should take every opportunity which calls forth its creative orginality and its mental vigor and energy. The number *One* is the doer. It is the number of action. Others look to the number *One* to think up the plan and to start things going.

New ideas, new ways and means, new undertakings interest the number *One*. It likes to originate and support undeveloped projects, rather than old established methods or routine procedure. It is impatient and inwardly dissatisfied to work under others when its many fine ideas do not find outlet or expression. The number *One* is a better starter than a finisher and needs others to help it carry out its plans and ideas. It can plan and dream from the practical to the idealistic and can always "work up" in any line of endeavor if it takes time to train and cultivate its creative talents—even in old and long-established undertakings.

The number *One* has a fine financial attraction when its plans are for the good of others as much as for personal satisfaction and prestige. It is the one who says "let's go" when activities come to a standstill or obstacles stand in the way.

VOCATIONS AND TALENTS

The fields of endeavor open to the number *One* are:

As the engineer dealing with construction, building, mining, mechanics, real estate, irrigation, and water projects, ranging from outer space to the depth of the ocean; broad undertakings based upon knowledge, skill, training, and intelligence, touched with imagination.

As the designer—originator of fashions and creative designs—high-class salons, stores, or shops where beauty is the product, line of business, or is presented and originated.

As professors of colleges, presidents of groups having to do with education; composers and musicians—writers of books, keepers of libraries, art galleries, museums, and antique stores or shops.

As religionists and teachers of fixed opinions and convictions often outside the conventional or accepted line of thought.

The number *One* establishes many types of business which it heads—expressing its own particular creative idea, ingenuity, and originality—sensing the public interest in the odd, unusual, thrilling, and different. The number *One* can improve on all established methods.

HUMAN RELATIONSHIPS

The number *One* is a good companion and fine company, pleasant, good-natured, a good talker with a keen sense of humor, wit, and gift of repartee. It represents sterling qualities and outstanding character, but is different from all others.

Its feelings are expressed with dignity, sensitiveness and artistic taste. It enjoys social contacts and friends, but prefers well-liked associates of common interest, rather than the crowd of unrelated groups. It is attracted to the opposite sex but responds only to beauty, personality, character and self-confidence. It strongly dislikes dullness, the commonplace, or a demanding companion. Without realizing it, it wants to do the demanding itself, and generally does so, for it has great self-respect, deep pride and expects its importance to be recognized. It has great respect for others with wealth and abundance.

In business and marriage the number *One* must be understood and led into its own good. Since number *One* is very sensitive to the approval of others, criticism and disapproval may bring about resentment and anger, causing it to retire into a shell of silent unreasonableness—even inertia—or to react with hurtful opinions, cynical speech, and surprising temper, not the true nature of number *One*. At times this strong and capable one may appear shy, vacillating, self-conscious, afraid to express its opinion—anything but the forceful character it really is. This is overcome with good education, vocational training, and wise and understanding encouragement. The sense of insecurity and lack of usefulness which may fill the mind of the *One* when it does not understand itself disappears when it is placed into the right environment and association. Boastfulness and aggressiveness frequently cover up an inner sense of aloneness and self-distrust.

The number *One* needs a warm and patient mate, capable of standing on its own feet and strong in character. Love and affection are important to the number *One*, for with all its independence it does not reach its highest possibilities of success in worldly affairs without understanding at home and in the domestic life. The number *One* is apt to react in a negative manner when told what to do, or where it is wrong, if love and approval are lacking.

There is a very strict side to the nature, generally concerning obedience or cleanliness. It is offended by carelessness, indifference to order and principle, or vulgarity and unlovely speech. There is a spiritual force in the heart of the *One*, as it was the first step in creation in the beginning. Therefore, it will turn away or seek to escape from unattractive situations or environment when the finer nature is not understood, causing problems in marriage.

Vocational training when young, and understanding of the individuality, help to make the pathway of life easier and more successful. Often the number *One* is the non-conformist, being urged on by its love of the new, its desire to do something different and the feeling that the whole world is its own. But the number *One* can be the man or woman deeply loved and admired or highly successful when it loses itself in its desires to provide the new, the beautiful, and the wealth of the world for mankind as well as for its loved one.

The Number Two
Watchword: Peacemaker. An Extrovert Number.

Positive	*Negative*
Arbitration	Overconscientiousness
Meditation	Self-consciousness
Diplomacy	Timidity, Fear
Tact, Persuasion	Shyness, Slyness
Association	Unhappiness, Aloneness
Partnerships	Strife, Discord
Agreement	Negation in plans
Consideration	Sometimes the Extremist
Sensitivity—Esthetics	Too much detail and
Modesty—Sincerity	Loss of time
Culture—Graciousness	Femininity
Spiritual influence	
Extrovert, a gatherer of facts	

COLORS: Gold, Salmon, Prune, White, Black

COSMIC PATTERN

"And God said, Let there be light; and there was light." "And God saw that it was good; and God divided the light from the darkness."

"The primordial light, vibrating beneath the divine impulse, contains the essence of all souls, the spiritual type of all being."—Pythagoras.

The spiritual inheritance of the number *Two* endows it with powers not equally shared by the other numbers. It is the "Light-Bearer" from on High. It shall not grope in darkness. It has the "Light" within itself. The love of peace is its strength; its gentleness, its sensitiveness, its insight into right and wrong, the gift of persuasion, its talent for unity, are its never-failing reward. It is endowed with the faculty of true awareness of the relationship of God and man.

OPPORTUNITIES

The number *Two* "wins" its reward from life through a natural desire to live in peace with its fellow man. Its success is not gained through force, dominance and will. It seeks to gain results without discord. It is gifted with the ability to bring others together for a common purpose. It is not the outstanding executive, but through tact, diplomacy, and spiritual insight, of which it may not be aware, it persuades others to accomplish what no one could accomplish alone. It gives its talents, its keen perception, and its gift of mediation to the final goal for the good of the many, rather than for the few.

It can be depended upon to gather facts and place them where they belong—to strengthen and support any undertaking to which its accuracy and alertness are assets. It is capable of being impartial, and its goal is to find the harmonious way for all, that many may benefit and good be the result of its work and endeavor. To the more aggressive, dominant, and self-interested character the number *Two* appears to be too easy-going, too considerate of others, weak, a go-between; but in the face of criticism and opposition, number *Two* should always remain true to its own soul dictates and remember it was born to be the peacemaker, the mediator, and the light-bearer to all. Then continuing to gather facts, information, hidden or unknown statistics, to dwell in its love of beauty and the things of the spirit which represent peace, and harmony on earth—slowly but surely it becomes the leader of men—sought after by all, even those who condemned it. The number *Two* belongs to the masses.

"Blessed are the peacemakers: for they shall be called the children of God."

VOCATIONS AND TALENTS

Many fields of endeavor are open to the number *Two*. The ability to gather facts and statistics, its gift for accuracy, its ability to put two and two together, a fine sense of timing and rhythm, its appreciation of beauty and esthetic taste and its spiritual intelligence—all give it a wide scope of opportunity and financial success.

The finer or more technical fields of electricity, electronics, radio, television; dealing with the laws of sound, space, and light on both the material and spiritual planes are fields of opportunity.

Banking, financing, distribution, and control of monies for the welfare of the public are possibilities.

All lines of medicine, healing and health matters—brain surgeons, nerve specialists, laboratory technicians, as well as lines of healing which have to do with new or advanced methods, are open to the *Two*.

The ministry attracts many *Twos*—religious activities, the teaching and training of those who need spiritual guidance.

The number *Two* has musical talent, often neglected or untrained. Musical instruments, orchestra leaders, or group entertainment may be the outlet.

Artistic feeling and a fine sense of timing and rhythm give opportunity through dancing, instruction and the theatre.

There is opportunity through designing, and where good taste is of value.

Fraternities, organizations and institutions where others

are brought together for education, training, care, and good citizenship are places where *Twos* may be found.

All lines of diplomacy, governmental and foreign assignments where personality, charm, goodwill, and ability to bring others together for common agreement can use the *Twos*.

Art galleries, museums, and as the appraiser and connoisseur estimating the worth and value of what is presented give interest and opportunity.

Bookkeepers, accountants, secretaries, hostesses along any line of activity may be the *Two*.

Consultants in lines of endeavor where weakness, faults, or the undesirable must be discovered could successfully be the *Two*.

Should the number *Two* find itself limited by routine endeavor, finding little use for its skills and love of helping others, it should take up a hobby or many hobbies, until it finds that special thing which gives an outlet for its desire to bring beauty, peace, and comfort to the world.

HUMAN RELATIONSHIPS

When the deep inner sensitiveness of the number *Two* is not understood, much suffering and unhappiness results. Self-confidence and daring to be itself are the lessons the *Two* has to learn. The number *Two* is a strong character. It should remember this at all times. To want to please and to feel consideration for others is not weakness. The number *Two* is like a cosmic mother who, with intelligence, love and soul-like qualities, endows her children with faith in themselves and the knowledge of a better way of life. The need for someone to pour oil on troubled waters is always present out in the world of competitive affairs.

When not understanding this truth about itself, the *Two* may fall into self-depreciation, indecision, timidity, hurt feelings, dependence upon others, fear of failure, fear of what others think and say, and also into negative states of mind and action. It should change this attitude of thought and feeling and realize that its amiability, its desire to please, and its endless patience have as much commercial value as any other talent.

However, it is not advisable to push the *Two* too far. It can show quick and hot bursts of temper. Sharp and blunt speech in retaliation for criticism surprise those who thought the *Two* lacked spirit.

There is something of the "extremist" in the nature of the number *Two*. It may get so carried away by a plan or desire that it becomes argumentative and difficult to reason with. The gentle *Two* may develop strong likes and dislikes and unexpectedly bring confusion and discord from which it may have to be rescued if it is to go forward into better things.

The number *Two* is determined about little things, exacting about some things—food, clothing, cleanliness, personal appearance. It can build up a complex about some personal feature—its feet, nose, or an imagined lack of beauty—causing discord and misunderstanding in love affairs and marriage.

The number *Two* grows in a harmonious and refined environment. A dominant father, mother, or employer will fail to bring out the best in the *Two*. Vulgarity, coarseness, and lack of refinement should not surround the growing and developing number *Two* child. It should be brought up to be the lovely character it is.

Out in the world of romance and social activity, the number *Two* is very popular. Its courtesy, kindly nature, and charming ways cause it to be sought after as sweetheart and companion. It needs love and marriage for its happiness, for companionship and sympathetic understanding are very important to it. It can be most unhappy when alone or not loved. The mate of the number *Two* will need to provide a charming environment—an orderly and artistic home. The number *Two* is very fastidious, and can be offended, unconsciously, by lack of cleanliness, neatness, and beauty in its mate and in its surroundings. When living up to its finer nature, it is a gracious host or hostess, a refined, intelligent character, successful and in demand for its skill and knowledge out in the world of specialized endeavor.

THE NUMBER THREE

Watchword: Joygiver. An Introvert Number.

Positive	*Negative*
Imagination	Fads, Fancies
Inspiration	Extravagance
Emotion	Exaggeration
Creative talent	Gossip
Gift of words	Selfishness
Gift of the vision	Self-centeredness
Artistic feeling	Too much talk
Prophetic impressions	Lack of direction
Self-expression	Scattered energy and
Optimism	possessions
Happiness	Unfinished undertakings
Merriment	Moodiness, Criticism
Love of pleasure	Unforgivingness

COLORS: Rose, Ruby, Amber, Russet, Blood

COSMIC PATTERN

"In the beginning was the Word, and the Word was with God, and the Word was God. All things were made by him; and without him was not anything made that was made."

"And God said, Let there be—"

The number *Three*, the child of God, forever young, ever renewing, touched with the fire of enthusiasm, is gifted with the magic power of the word, turning the impossible into the possible—bringing into being that which has never been before.

The number *Three* dreams—visualizes in its mind's eye—speaks the word and dreams come true. Touched by the heavenly fire, a child of the infinite father and mother, the number *Three* is a "chosen one" and commands the gifts of the Kingdom of Heaven here on earth. Beauty rewards its efforts when it dares to speak of its inner sight and feeling and responds to the ever-flowing exuberance which floods its being. Never truly practical, it depends upon the other numbers to catch and put into form the prophecy which lives in its imagination.

OPPORTUNITIES

The number *Three* is at its best when the strong inner urge to create and beautify finds a channel for expression. A narrow or limited field of activity, which restricts or represses the use of imagination and demands constant practical application, or kills the impulse to take flight into fancy, may lead to a mediocre existence and little happiness. To deaden the enthusiasm for imagining is to kill the spirit of the cheerful, happy, merry and believing number *Three*.

The number *Three* likes to do things on a broad scale. Its vision of accomplishment travels over space and time and through the unfinished to that which will be there in the end. At times it may seem to live in delusions of grandeur, but the desire to add beauty, feeling, and emotion to its undertakings has commercial value.

The number *Three* has a keen mind, learns quickly and easily. It can be a brilliant student and clever businessman. It may even be practical at times, under pressure to accomplish and gain its desires, for it can do anything it makes up its mind to do. It wants the best life has to offer and will give its all to attain this. But unless it has something creative to work with, it will not feel the happiness it dreams about. If compelled to live under strict practical rules and routine, it should take up studies which train the imagination or develop the gift of speech and use of words. These will lead to wider accomplishments and personal satisfaction.

Three is a lucky number. It has a natural attraction for money. It possesses the talents and skills to attain its desires without hard work. It is not a laborer. It is a creator. Its enthusiastic way of talking about what it is doing and what it wants to do inspires others to help and to take part in its plans. Enthusiasm has a commercial value for the *Three*.

In the kitchen, the butcher shop, the road camp—or in the studios of the musician, artist, decorator, designer, writer, inventor—the number *Three* finds scope, expression and successful use of its special, God-given endowment—creative imagination.

VOCATIONS AND TALENTS

All lines of endeavor expressing the arts and crafts give business opportunity: The entertainment field as actor, actress, musician, singer, and the theatre. Success through illustration, decoration, designing. Creation of books—authors of fantasy and unreality, appealing to the emotions of young and old. Opportunity through the desire for luxury on the part of humanity and for the extravagant things which fill the home and environment, beyond the commonplace.

The gift of words, one of the number *Three's* outstanding talents, opens many doors for success and financial reward: Lecturers, speakers on any subject, commentators, salesmen, advertisers, teachers, and instructors.

Stocks and bonds, investments, real estate—especially where the design is to be developed or the outline to be created —big business, having to do with toys, fashions, amusements, travel, and all lines of commercial art.

Gift shops, clothing and cosmetics, beauty parlors, libraries, kindergarten teaching, rest homes, care of the aged and young, restaurants, bakeries (as chefs and fancy cooks) often interest the number *Three*.

The number *Three* has a strange gift of prophecy. Being inwardly sensitive and intuitive, it often senses events before they happen. Presentiments, when not colored by fear or personal feeling, guide and protect the number *Three*. It possesses a natural psychic ability as the medium or clairvoyant. It is often found in the ministry where the spiritual feeling is combined with the gift of words and inspiration.

Should the number *Three* lack in opportunity or financial success, it should overcome moods, criticism or strong dislikes and return to its natural happy nature and dare to believe in its wonderful power to attract what it desires by its natural gift of imagination.

The number *Three* often finds opportunity in the Army, Navy, and in aviation.

HUMAN RELATIONSHIPS

To be popular, to be loved, and to love is a basic part of the nature of the number *Three*. Without love, admiration and friendship, especially of the opposite sex, the number *Three* does not grow and develop into usefulness and a balanced emotional life. It is capable of a deep love, affection, and loyalty in marriage, home, and family—sometimes giving with lasting self-sacrifice for love's sake. It is generally called upon to meet this experience sometime during its lifetime—through friends, relatives, brothers and sisters, husband or wife—imposed upon by those it loves and trusts.

The number *Three* meets many interesting experiences and the happenings are so many, odd, and emotional that a story book or novel could be written about its life, the eternal triangle, the plot of the story. More than one love, more than one interest, more than one admirer keeps the emotions deeply stirred. Its desire for popularity and admiration, its awareness of its charm, beauty, and attractiveness, linked with great self-confidence add to the possibility of many emotional experiences.

The enthusiastic number *Three*, having many talents and filled with the joy of living, follows its own interests fully— many times to the exclusion of the interests of others. What it thinks and feels, what it desires to do are of the utmost importance to it. To the more serious-minded person the number *Three* may seem self-interested, self-centered, and lacking in consideration for others, since it's a good talker and is never lacking in something to talk about. When the number *Three* is living only for ease, luxury, pleasure, and social ambitions, not making constructive use of its creative talents, it is possible for it to become lost in thoughts of self and self-interests to the point of selfishness.

The number *Three* is very conscious of what is said to it or about it. Words spoken in criticism can change the whole life. It may say very little, but it will always remember and may not forgive. Number *Three* children should not be told of weakness, unlovely features or handicaps. They should be encouraged to grow and develop the imaginaton.

The number *Three* can talk too much and lose friends and opportunity in this way. It should remember it has the gift of words and make each word a talent and means for success. If hurt, it can be reticent, retiring, and aloof, turning away from the person or situation which hurt it—learning only through loneliness to turn back again into the world and to take its place, filled with creative endeavor.

The number *Three* is easily influenced by environment. It likes nice things, fine clothes, and pretty accessories. Even the masculine number *Three* has a desire for the colorful in living, dress, and attire. The number *Three* can be a pleasing host or hostess, entertaining with generosity and extravagance— sometimes even in the midst of its own sorrow. Whatever its faults, the number *Three* can be readily forgiven, for its natural sweetness, its inner beauty, and its bubbling interest make the world a happier place to live in.

THE NUMBER FOUR

Watchword: Construction.   An Extrovert Number.

Positive	*Negative*
Concentration	Lack of imagination
Application	Extreme seriousness
Form, Method	Great detail
Management	Contrariness, Stubbornness
Construction	Opposition, Slowness
Sense of values	Exactness
Practicality	Argumentation
Science	Very fixed opinions
Seriousness, Determination	Confusion from change
Relationship of facts	
Foundation for accomplishment	

COLORS: Green, Blue, Indigo, Emerald, Coffee, Silver, Maroon

COSMIC PATTERN

"And God said—Let the earth bring forth grass, the
herb yielding seed, and the fruit tree yielding fruit after its
kind, whose seed is in itself upon the earth; and it was so!"

The number *Four* holds the key to all arrangement and interpretation of form, plans, dreams, ideas, and patterns from
the material, mechanical, and mathematical to the artistic, esthetic, religious, and spiritual levels of thought and feeling. It
provides the foundation upon which all things stand to sustain
life and entity.

"It is the number of rational exposition of principles and
ideas. It explains, arranges, constructs, builds, maintains, carries out, and makes exact the system and formulas which provide the matrix for lasting and tangible results."

It turns raw material into particular forms, shapes, and
moulds them into harmony with each other. It demonstrates
the cosmic order of growth and attainment, and with a powerful and firm hand brings time and space down to earth. It arranges that which has been imagined and dreamed of and
makes it concrete and applicable to human living.

OPPORTUNITIES

The number One conceives ideas and presents them for
form and use.

The number Two draws the blueprint and gathers
information.

The number Three sees the beauty and envisions the possibility of the plan.

The number Four finds the material and builds the form
into which the idea is shaped, moulded and made concrete.

There is an urge in the heart of the number *Four* to make
all things real. It finds opportunity through undertakings
which require patience, perseverance, determination, careful
and expert attention to detail. It sees things in a common-sense

manner and likes to establish system and permanent and lasting form.

It is not an originator, but when the idea has been provided, the form outlined—and the number *Four* is convinced of its practical worth—it has a way of getting things done, establishing practices, rules and regulations, even traditions which may carry on long after the work of the number *Four* has been accomplished. Emotion and imagination, even impulse may touch the mind of the number *Four*, but it is not apt to be carried away—at least for very long—by fancy, or dreams which have no apparent foundation or practical aspects.

The number *Four* has high standards of honesty, courage, the gifts of concentration, application, the ability to appraise and evaluate worth and value. It gains through hard knocks, responsibility, and its own mistakes. Experience is a good teacher for the number *Four*. Through this it gains the "know how" which is its place of power out in the world of business accomplishment.

The number *Four* is a steady, industrious worker. It likes to keep busy and is not at its best without something to build, construct, fix, mend, organize, or arrange according to rules and regulations. Because of its ability to evaluate and conform to patterns, systems, and established order, it generally finds it slowly but surely becomes the head, the manager, and the authority in many undertakings.

During its lifetime, the number *Four* finds it cannot work for selfish purposes. It will always be called upon to take care of others: to attend to the work left undone by those who have failed to complete and accomplish what they have promised to do. It is often called upon to give more than it receives, because it is so capable and does many practical things easily. It manages its own affairs carefully with thrift and practical judgment. Sometimes the *Four* gives too much to those it loves, and may be dominated by relatives and associates. Until it finds and evaluates its own worth it may lead a very ordinary, workaday life. When the number *Four* makes use of its active energies, its strong capable hands and mind along constructive lines, it finds everything it touches becomes successful. It eventually, too, takes its place among those who do life's important work.

VOCATIONS AND TALENTS

The number *Four* is a natural mechanic and can succeed in all endeavors having to do with machinery and mechanical construction from the most intricate device to heavy industry. All types of engineering come naturally to the number *Four* as it understands form and procedure. Manufacturing, and the production of fabrics, clothing, furniture, and public utilities give opportunities.

The number *Four* has a scientific mind, is interested in natural law and order. It finds opportunity through research, discovery, investigation, and delving into the hidden relationships of material form and being—the geologist, biologist, archeologist, research chemist, and explorer of nature's hidden secrets.

The number *Four* is a lover of nature and willing to work hard; so farming, cattle-raising, dairies, horticulture, landscaping, and real estate give it useful work for success and satisfactory accomplishment. All lines of construction, from the building of its own home to world-wide construction projects, call to the number *Four*.

The number *Four* being careful, cautious, and not inclined to take too many chances with money, succeeds in banking, the management of money, savings, and practical investments along all business lines where money is managed. It is put to work as the economist or authority on ways and means.

Legal matters, dealing with contracts, agreements, mortgages, buying and selling; plus the ability to evaluate worth and security, to estimate price and appraise, give the number *Four* a wide range of business opportunity.

Pomp and ceremony or where protocol and conventional procedure are "according to Hoyle" are avenues of expression for the number *Four*.

The ministry attracts the number *Four*, having fixed opinions on right and wrong. The military—where adherence to rules, regulations, and discipline are required, also attracts the *Four*. The number *Four* has the ability to become the commander. In fact, the number *Four* can become the head of any undertaking when it trains and develops its talents for rules and regulations.

Education is an open field of endeavor—professors, heads of schools, and educators where knowledge has been proved and certified. The general work of the world is done by the number *Four*—stores, shops, offices, and where routine work must be carried out day by day, and results must be depended upon.

The number *Four*, having a deep desire to establish, construct, or build something in its own way, often establishes its own business or shop. It may work in a small way, but through application, steady endeavor and good and dependable service, may become the head of a very successful business, with many employees.

The number *Four* enjoys a practical joke and may turn this into success on stage and in the field of entertainment.

HUMAN RELATIONSHIPS

The number *Four* is the salt of the earth—the wholesome, dependable, helpful, and straightforward human being. It likes people and desires to be liked by others. It seeks to be recognized as a useful citizen in its community and to take part in civic, religious, and political activities. It loves its family and enjoys life, simple pleasures, good food, a comfortable home; it is fond of animals, and is indulgent to those it loves.

It is fundamentally serious, conscientious, has strong opinions of right and wrong, and lives by these opinions. It does not like to have these contradicted, for without them the number *Four* loses self-confidence and ability to plan and work. First, last, and at all times, the number *Four* feels the need for security in business, in marriage, and in the right to be itself. It gives its time, energy, talents, and love to this end. It likes to plan, work, look forward, and wait until results are attained. When its mind is made up, it goes ahead and can therefore be confused by sudden changes or by demands of others which do not coincide with its desire.

This leads to many problems in association. The number *Four* is willing to perform any task when requested, if it feels this is right and needs to be done, but it can be suddenly aggressive, argumentative, irritable, stubborn, or show temper when "ordered." It does not like to be "told" without being consulted. It subconsciously feels the need of being in control over what it is doing. It may take the opposite side of the question, go off at a tangent, or express an unreasonable determination to have its own way until it is convinced or understands.

Those who work with and love this fine character should try to understand its seeming stubbornness and be willing to talk things over patiently—take a roundabout approach to gain agreement and cooperation, until the number *Four* thinks it out in its own way.

Family and in-laws are a responsibility for the number *Four* throughout its lifetime. Many domestic problems have to be met, with unfair responsibility or dominant opposition. The number *Four* manages to take care of these problems if it feels its efforts are respected and its own rights considered; otherwise the will of the number *Four* is weakened and the financial opportunity lessened.

The number *Four* should not allow resentment to build up into dislikes or moods. It should try to understand others also —then go ahead quietly and with perseverance, training and developing its true individuality. It is the duty of the number *Four* to place a foundation upon which others may stand, work, and be protected.

With self-control and self-understanding, the number *Four* makes money, saves, builds, and in the end gains a financial security not possessed by those of more impulsive and imaginative nature.

The number *Four* does not like to be hurried. It works

slowly, sometimes moves slowly. It may seem unlucky or miss opportunity even though it works hard, because it does not act, think, or work with quickness and speed. It will gain much through taking up public speaking or by taking part in sports and games and by going with those who think and act with directness. This will help to quicken its own adaptability and methods.

THE NUMBER FIVE

Watchword: Progress.   An Introvert Number.

Positive	*Negative*
Progression	Restlessness, Nervousness
Resourcefulness	Discontent
Versatility	Criticism
Action	Moods
Energy	Sharp speech
Investigation	Temper
Administration	A rolling stone
Promotion	Dissatisfaction
New ideas	Many irons in the fire
Freedom loving	Impatience, Hastiness
Quickness in thought	Impulsiveness—
Curiosity	lacking in application

COLORS: Cherry, Pink, Cerise, Raspberry, Claret, Wisteria

COSMIC PATTERN

"And God said unto them, Be fruitful, and multiply, and replenish the earth, and subdue it: and have dominion over the fish of the sea, and over the fowl of the air, and over every living thing that moveth upon the earth."

With this command government began—the right of action—the development of resourcefulness—the wonder of being alive—the stimulation of choice.

The number *Five* is life's field of action. It represents experience. It is at all times the administrator.

OPPORTUNITIES

Opportunity lies in all directions for the number *Five*. The command to be fruitful, multiply, replenish and subdue opens up an unlimited field of endeavor and choice for the busy, active number *Five*.

The number *Five* is not an originator, but its quick mind, excellent powers of observation, pep, speed, energy, wit, enthusiasm, desire to know what is going on in the world and to take part in public and worldly activities enable it to become a leader in activities of a progressive and forward-moving nature. It belongs to the public, promotes public interests, and, through its resourcefulness, can turn failure into success, and fire and stimulate big undertakings to broader usefulness. A prominent place in all business endeavor is given the number *Five*, who is a rapid thinker with a fertile mind and a gift of words and languages and perception as to the need of the public and the masses.

Being a natural law-giver, it can govern and control from the legal and political to the religious, philosophical, and even the odd and mysterious in thought, feeling, and aspiration.

The curious number *Five*, unafraid of experience and enjoying worldly interests, has brought the stigma of "wine, women, and song" to the reputation of the freedom-loving number *Five*. The number *Five* abhors dullness and tiring routine. "Don't fence me in" and "Let's go" sum up the worldly side of the number *Five*. Freedom of thought, freedom of action, and freedom of worship emphasize the finer spiritual qualities coloring the activities of the seemingly worldly number *Five*.

The number *Five* not only supports but understands the law of change. In its own personal experiences change often comes suddenly and unexpectedly. Opportunity is always to be found through changing events. The number *Five* needs to extract from experience the value it represents, and should weigh and balance each experience, practically, emotionally, and spiritually. However, too many changes, too many interests, too many irons in the fire lead to lack of application and lack of discipline and can bring failure and loss. To be the "rolling stone that gathers no moss" is the clue that, even though the number *Five* is "smooth," it is not fulfilling its destiny of the original command. After all, even in the midst of many plans, ideas, and opportunities, the number *Five* should keep roots down to the substance of life which promotes growth, stability, dependability, and the permanent and lasting.

VOCATIONS AND TALENTS

The number *Five*, being the number of progress and growth, finds happiness and success through lines of work or business that deal with the public and its interests. Any line of endeavor that calls for long hours of routine work or confinement without variety or contact with people does not give the number *Five* the chance to grow or develop. Monotony is death to the number *Five*.

The number *Five* loves to travel, to be active, coming and going from one thing to another. All lines of business having to do with transportation give opportunity—railroads, tourist bureaus, sightseeing guides, and management of public entertainment. Advertisement is an open field of endeavor for the number *Five*. All lines of entertainment, sports, games, amusements, and activities which interest the fun-seeking crowd and pleasure-loving public are a challenge to its resourcefulness and administrative ability.

The number *Five* is often an entertainer on its own, enjoying the applause and approval of the crowd as well as being a versatile actor or even being something of the clown. The challenge or obstacle which can be overcome through quick action, wit, and cleverness appeals to the number *Five*. It learns easily, but it is not naturally the deep student, gathering much information but often changing its interest before lasting results are gained.

Because of its innate and sometimes not recognized respect for law and government, the *Five* finds success and opportunity in the legal profession and in all lines of civics and government, from the clerk in the office to the judge or high official. It is a natural stickler for the law and likes activities which formulate and regulate the legal side of any undertaking.

The number *Five* is a natural salesman and can sell anything from a silk stocking to a new religion. In fact, the number *Five* is always selling something—a product, a method, or an idea—and being a good talker, is also a good speaker or lecturer. The number *Five* likes to help others, to show them how to do this or that and has many ideas of improvement. The basis of its desire is to influence others.

Clothing stores and dress shops, which present the new, different or unusual, are managed by the number *Five.*

Newspapers, reporters, columnists dealing with the news in any manner interest the number *Five,* especially when responding to the public's desire to know, and fulfilling the public's right to freedom and advancement.

Number *Five* has the ability of the administrator, and becomes the head of companies and organizations, not because it is the true executive, but because of its ability to keep affairs moving forward, to get others to act. It gathers information and can handle or keep several lines of endeavor going at the same time. However, the number *Five* needs rest and relaxation often to avoid tenseness and nervous and mental strain.

The number *Five,* being observing, can be the critic and the judge as to methods and good procedure in any line of work, business, or professional activity. The number *Five,* having the ability to find out things, can uncover and reveal crime and wrongdoing.

Even though the number *Five* appears to live in worldly interests, because it is an introvert number and reticent within itself, it finds interest in occult, mystical, and religious presentations. The number *Five* seems to grasp the meaning and usefulness of these studies and is able to bring them down to the level of those seeking the higher or soul side of living. It finds opportunity as the teacher, as the psychologist, and along lines of progress having to do with health, diet, and emotional disturbances. The number *Five* is happiest when it has a feeling of usefulness through promotion of individual and public welfare.

The number *Five* is found in lines of business having to do with speculation and money-making endeavors which get quick results. There is a touch of the gambler in the number *Five*, liking to take a chance. Also the number *Five* can be gullible and be taken in by the fast talking of another salesman. The law of change and the unexpected which operates in the life of the number *Five* makes it doubtful for it to speculate, and it should find ways and means of growing into sure and lasting success. The number *Five* can turn change into success through understanding that all progress comes through change and through building its life on a work or vocation that, even though dealing with the changing interests of the public and life itself, has a permanent and growing usefulness.

HUMAN RELATIONSHIPS

The number *Five* has more extremes of temperament and more ups and downs than any other number.

The restless inner nature, the natural curiosity, the venturesome spirit, and the desire to be part of and to know what is going on in the world result in many experiences and sometimes knowledge and success the hard way. However, this makes the number *Five* an interesting and entertaining companion. Life is never dull when the number *Five* is on the scene. The life of the number *Five* is shaped and directed by its independence, demand for personal freedom, and its desire and sometimes unconscious determination to escape from routine.

A touch of the Bohemian and the unconventional colors its moods and action. In fact, the unexpected and the law of change always follow the number *Five* wherever it goes, for change is the keynote to progress for all *Fives*. It is natural for the *Five* quickly to lose interest in the old, the dull, or "the same old thing" and "to enter in where Angels fear to tread," causing the *Five* many problems, often blamed on others or the environment. However, having great resourcefulness, clever wit, and quick perceptions, it can just as easily get itself out of the same deep waters. Also that inner and natural respect for law and government gives it fine qualities which redeem it from its careless or hasty actions at any time it desires—lifting it to a place and position of worth, even controlling and regulating the actions of those who fail to respect the law of the land. These traits and characteristics make *Five* a complex personality.

There is a social side to the number *Five's* nature. It likes to be one of the crowd or the gang and to know many people. It generally has many friends and acquaintances, assets in business as well as socially. It is fond of the opposite sex, but may hesitate to marry for fear of losing its freedom; or it may break up its marriage or companionship if it finds it dull or binding. Also the *Five* is not a truly domestic type nor too interested in repeated or binding responsibility. All this makes it an outstanding type of individual and should be taken into consideration by anyone marrying or going into business with number *Five*.

The progressive spirit keeps those with whom it works "on the ball" and up-to-date. The marriage partner of the *Five* should recognize this and adjust to its desire to be active and doing something all the time. The husband or wife who tries to reform the *Five* and to restrict its activities without understanding, or to curb its forward-moving spirit, is likely to lose in the end and find sorrow and unhappiness instead of the loyalty which is really there underneath the restlessness. The news stories of the daily papers and the divorce courts tell this story of these misunderstandings. The *Five* needs an active, eventful, entertaining, and useful life. Then it is a happy and protecting companion.

Without training and good education the *Five* can go to extremes, show hurtful temper, haste and undisciplined impulse, bringing accidents, quarrels, and legal matters. Legal problems often beset the number *Five* in spite of right living, for problems in the environment can cause irritation and impatient action and speech.

A lack of appreciation for all it has received or for all that has been done for it may seem unfair to others. The *Five* may even claim as its own that which belongs to others because it has helped to make improvements or to guide another in business or personal projects, again leading to great sorrow or loss. A critical manner of the *Five* temperament is also one of its trying traits, when used to hurt others. The *Five* is more dependent upon others than it wishes to allow and may resent this within itself without realizing it. It should recognize this and learn to share more honestly.

All other numbers depend upon the *Five*, for it represents civilization. It has a flair for living. Its money comes and goes, but it is the "administrator" of the common wealth, which gives it a very important part to play in the affairs of the world.

THE NUMBER SIX

Watchword: Humanitarian Service.   An Extrovert Number.

Positive	*Negative*
Artist	Sympathy
Idealist	Duty
Humanitarian	Others' troubles
Service	Self-righteousness
Truth, Justice	Obstinacy
Righteousness	Outspokenness
Unselfishness	Family ties
Harmony, Approval	Slowness in decisions
Domesticity	Self-sacrifice
Love of home	Stubbornness
Conventional influence	Dominance
Fixed opinions and beliefs	Complaint
Welfare worker	Egotist, Falling for flattery

COLORS: Orange, Henna, Mustard, Leather,
Scarlet, Heliotrope

COSMIC PATTERN

"And God said, Behold, I have given you every herb bearing seed, which is upon the face of all the earth, and every tree, in which is the fruit of a tree yielding seed; to you it shall be for meat.

"And to every beast of the earth, and to every fowl of the air, and to everything that creepeth upon the earth, wherein there is life, I have given every green herb for meat; and it was so.

"And God saw every thing that he had made, and, behold, it was very good. And the evening and the morning were the sixth day."

Therefore, the rewards of creation are provided for and are at hand for the number *Six*. Divine inheritance is its blessing. Having been given the seeds of all life, it becomes the storehouse, the provider, and the caretaker of all mankind. The fruits of its labor give comfort, happiness, protection, abundance, and richness to all people. Harmony, usefulness, beauty, and the privilege of service should follow it all the days of its life.

The "humanitarian" establishes the place of the number *Six* in all human and spiritual affairs. Its crowning glory is the good it has done for others. Intelligent, capable, and practical, yet it is a dreamer of dreams, living on a high plane from which it senses and expresses the grandeur and beauty of life and living.

OPPORTUNITIES

The number *Six* is wise and conscientious. It lives from the precepts and guidance of the heart. It has deeply ingrained principles and strong convictions, even from childhood, concerning religion, right and wrong, truth and justice—demanding fairness in all things and for all people. It will fight for these ideals and principles if deeply concerned; however, always according to its own beliefs and ideals.

The number *Six* prefers to act in a conventional manner and according to established standards and seeks the harmonious way of adjustment rather than discord; it is deeply disturbed and confused by the unlovely and sordid in relationships or situations. It seeks to right wrong at all times and in a kindly, generous way, thus giving it its place as the humanitarian.

Responsibility follows the *Six* all the days of its life and in all its undertakings, but it is capable of taking this, for it is motivated by a high sense of duty. It finds pleasure in doing good and worthwhile things for friends, family, and community. It can give to the point of exhaustion and act without reason. On the other hand, to fail to give is to fail to receive the rewards given the number *Six* for its service and helpfulness.

Responsibility becomes a pleasure and privilege when the *Six* understands the beauty of service and gives of its abundance in reverence and wisdom. Four opportunities await the *Six*. It may choose one or all of them:

the standard bearer   the provider
the humanitarian   the entertainer.

The number *Six* has only to choose which pathway of service it will follow for it has a real attraction for wealth, luxury, and the good things of life and has the ability to make these good things possible for others as well as for itself.

It may choose to teach, minister to others, and to guide and protect mankind against evil and wrongdoing.

It may choose to heal, to be the welfare worker and to find a better and happier way for those in distress.

It may go into business and provide the means and sustenance which make life worthwhile.

It may choose to sing sweet songs, write music, plays, opera, illustrate, paint, decorate and color the activities of every day with beauty and the music of the Spheres.

The number *Six* is called the cosmic mother or the cosmic father. It gives its devotion to God, its fellow man and to its country.

VOCATIONS AND TALENTS

When gainfully and usefully employed, the number *Six* loves to work, and it likes to be well paid. It generally insists on full value for its efforts. It is not a laborer or a drudge. It is physically strong and can, if it desires, do the hardest of day labor, but generally works into positions of authority due to its intelligence and ability to learn. If the *Six* finds itself continuing in hard physical work, it is not making use of its talents or has not discovered them.

The number *Six* is always a teacher and sometime during its experience finds itself teaching and instructing others. Its love of truth and justice places it as the minister, the educator, the philosopher, the historian, the theorist, the professor, the scientist in theory apart from practice. Its strong principles give it interest in reform ideals and movements. It may be the religionist, writer of books (often for children), philosopher, teacher, and instructor along all lines of interest based upon the emotions and spiritual longings of man's soul.

All lines of welfare work such as nurses, physicians, hospitals, institutions, health and healing methods are generally part of the life of the *Six* to some degree. Being born the humanitarian, if not doing humanitarian work, the number *Six*, quietly or secretly, does generous and helpful acts. The *Six* likes to help others and finds business opportunity as a result.

The *Six* has excellent business ability. Many lines of endeavor call for its talents: providing products for the home, its comfort and ease, and to beautify the surroundings; manufacturing and marketing of commodities—wearing apparel, cosmetics, accessories, perfumes, and articles of personal adornment.

The *Six* likes good food and abundance of everything—is often the chef, succeeding through restaurants, high-class night clubs and luxurious apartment houses and inns.

All methods of service through healing—health stores, rest homes, and care of the weak and helpless—give financial reward.

The number *Six* is interested in nature and is found as the mining engineer, the horticulturist, geologist, zoologist, bacteriologist; and the *Six* is interested in boats, shipping, irrigation, ranching on a large scale.

Art, beauty, cultural interests are part of the makeup of the number *Six*. The *Six* often gains through marriage and family inheritance. The care and education of children, where love and understanding are needed, give wide opportunity for *Six*.

HUMAN RELATIONSHIPS

Six is the lover.

To love and be loved is a deep desire in the heart and mind of the *Six*. Its happiness, its sorrows, from childhood to old age, swing around this need, and, without love, the *Six* does not reach the heights of success or the soul satisfaction it is capable of attaining. In human relationships—to those who do not understand this—it may appear as a desire for approbation, or as egotism, even a weakness, but it is the nature of the *Six*, for it is the number of the heart.

Home, family, children necessarily form the background of the *Six*, and its ideals give it loyalty and generosity to those it loves. A natural love of luxury and the good things of life make it indulgent to its own needs and to family and friends, so it is capable of being completely blind to the faults of others where its heart and affections are given.

The desire to protect its loved ones, and its overflowing generosity, can at times bring about weakness, even frustration, rather than helpfulness; and, as a father, mother, or sweetheart, it can "smother" rather than help, bringing about a desire to escape on the part of child, husband, or wife. It is capable of sacrificing itself in giving and loving and yet failing to realize its own lack of understanding.

The *Six* may surprisingly remain unmarried because of the high ideals it holds regarding love and marriage, or because of a fear of not being equal to the generosity and support it would love to give. This can be a mistake, for growth and development come to the *Six* through companionship and home life.

The *Six* may fail to marry because of an early disappointment in love affairs or its loyalty to a father, mother, or family, born of its fine sense of duty and responsibility. Now and then true love comes late in life as a reward for a life of service and sacrifice.

The firm convictions, religious principles, and sense of truth and justice (when the *Six* has led a sheltered life) may bring many problems into the life of the *Six* and its family. It can be hard, unrelenting, dominant and unforgiving, very stubborn and unresponsive to reason. Even though naturally sympathetic and kind, it can be very set in its ways and methods, and demands for discipline. Feeling itself the head of the family, it does not like to be crossed or contradicted. It is slow and deliberate in thought and action and retreats into a shell when crowded or hurried into action or promises.

Always anxious to do worth-while work in the world and having deep pride, the *Six* can be influenced by others through approval and praise and give foolishly or be taken in the wrong direction, which may cause it to fail in giving where it is really needed, even at home and to loved ones. This strange contradiction of character may bring difficulties, and the *Six*, not understanding itself, may speak of "lack of appreciation" on the part of others. (The *Six* should learn to strike a balance between giving and receiving.) Not receiving the appreciation it feels it deserves, it may seek companionship or work elsewhere.

The honest, straightforward *Six* can speak "the truth" very bluntly when disturbed by what it thinks is a wrong done to others or to itself. It can be narrow in beliefs and difficult in association at times. Dishonesty for money's sake means eventual failure for the *Six*.

The *Six* is a wonderful person. It was born to do good, to comfort, and to provide for humanity. The world is its child.

The Number Seven

Watchword: Understanding   An Introvert Number.

Positive	*Negative*
Investigation	Shrewdness
Research	Hidden motives
Calculation	Too much pride
Analysis	Reservedness
Observation	Misunderstanding
Specialist	Silence or sarcasm
Technician	Suspicion
Science	Repression
Invention	Unreasonableness
Discovery	Lack of powers of
Detection	self-expression
Skill with hands	Over-positiveness
Discrimination	Over-analysis
Thinker	Argumentation
Meditation, Occult	Cynic
Dignity, Pride	Temper
Perfectionist	Independence
Charm of manner and	Hidden thoughts
personality	The best
Intelligence	Lack of generosity
Love of solitude	

Colors: Old Rose, Purple, Magenta, Brick, Pearl

COSMIC PATTERN

"And God blessed the seventh day, and sanctified it: because that in it he had rested from all his work which God created and made."

The number *Seven* had been born to have the rewards of the number *Six*, but commanded to discover the inner knowledge and the Laws of Divine Creation. It had already gained the abundance of its past labors. Now calm, serene in meditation and contemplation, it looks out upon established facts and beholds in visions and dreams the realities of unseen power, thus becoming the possessor of the wisdom of the ages.

Having the blessings of the most High, it may reach out for greater vistas of learning and discover that which has not before been perceived.

Standing in the midst of material things, the number *Seven* finds something of the soul in all things. Not of a religious nature, it still makes holy the facts of mankind's existence.

OPPORTUNITIES

The number *Seven* is primarily a law unto itself. It does not find its success in ordinarily established situations or conditions. It seeks to appraise, evaluate, and to test the worth of all activities on all planes of life.

It does not accept any idea, plan, information, or even accepted fact at its surface value. At all times it asks the "reason why," ultimately leading to discovery beyond the scope of the average mind.

The number *Seven* is the thinker, the student of life's finer relationships, and is never satisfied until it links the known with the unknown. It is constantly urged on by its analytical mind to discover hidden facts. Thus it becomes the discoverer, the scientist, even the occultist, the inventor, and ultimately finds its success along a specialized and outstanding line of work or undertaking. Knowledge is power for the *Seven* and its quick, keen, and observing mind adds to its ability to gain position and success.

The *Seven* does not always find life simple, as it is naturally reserved, quiet, reticent, finding it difficult to express its thoughts and ideas, sometimes confused by its inability to be part of the activities of the everyday life. However, when the *Seven* trains and finds its place in the world, it is never inarticulate or alone as it sometimes feels itself to be. It is called from the background to the foreground. Mankind beats a pathway to its door to partake of its wisdom and understanding.

The *Seven* has little interest in frivolous or foolish waste of time or extravagant imagination. It seeks knowledge above all else. But underneath its seemingly cool, dignified manner there is another side to its nature. A mystical quality lies underneath its reserved and dominant manner. It has need to be alone to seek the quiet places: for intuition guides it more than it may wish to acknowledge. It feels and responds to the occult and metaphysical, dreams dreams of beauty, romance and heavenly things, and senses the wonder of its own soul and its relationship to the Creator of heaven and earth.

The number *Seven* is a lucky number; the law of attraction governs its accomplishments, giving it an inner force which draws unexpected help and assistance in surprising ways. In spite of its cautious and calculating mind it likes to take a chance. To gamble is a dangerous game for the *Seven*, (especially when formed by the number 16—a karmic number demanding payment in full). However, when it depends upn that inner guidance to lead it to knowledge and skill, the *Seven* always wins life's reward. Training, education and wise use of its excellent mental powers lead to true and lasting success.

VOCATIONS AND TALENTS

The number *Seven* should always endeavor to become the skilled worker. With application to the task, it generally gains this distinction. Education and training should always be the goal.

A number *Seven*, claiming lack of opportunity and education, has not made use of the public libraries of the country or dared to be true to its longing for knowledge and to know the reasons of things. To drift—due to restlessness or the feeling the grass is greener on the other side of the fence—brings delay and unhappiness. The *Seven* normally loves to read and study and should surround itself with books and scientific periodicals. Even if placed in the most ordinary circumstance, feeling deeply the lack of education, it can always find broader opportunities if it applies its mind and hands to the present task, even if seemingly beneath it, until its natural ability eventually leads it to better positions and a higher level of activity.

The vocational field is wide and unlimited. The number *Seven* finds success through research, calculation, observation, and analysis. It should endeavor to excel and to be expert in what it is doing. The *Seven* is the "specialist" with the ability of synthesis as well as analysis. When it gains skill, its intuition and soul power add color to its endeavors. The *Seven* can enter the fields of science, investigation, technical research, and finds opportunity through laboratory and statistical work. Chemistry, invention, history, old and ancient subjects open avenues of interest and business success.

The *Seven* can succeed through insurance and mathematical lines of business—is generally quick at figures, charts, and graphs. Law is a splendid field for the *Seven*, often the criminal law and the technical rather than the general practice. Medicine, medical research, the surgeon, often the brain specialist, or some outstanding line of specialization in the field of healing and health can be the *Seven's* career.

The *Seven* deals successfully with books, literature, and all lines of education, for, even with all its talents, it is fundamentally the educator. Professors of universities and schools give wide interest and success. The *Seven*, due to its powers of observation and hunches, makes a good detective, criminologist, secret service man; and the ability to be silent and self-controlled helps in these fields.

The *Seven* is artistic and is often the connoisseur of literature, sometimes of food—giving opportunity through high-class restaurants. Having skill with its hands, it can develop skill in carving, etching, and the use of finer tools and instruments. The *Seven*, living in its mystical side, finds interest and opportunity through occult teaching and secret societies and religion, not in blind faith, but as a seeker after the truth. It is not uncommon to find the *Seven* a reformer at some time during its lifetime, endeavoring to present an idea or principle it has discovered to change the world. The *Seven* likes to have a plan well in mind before it undertakes its accomplishment and sometimes hesitates or wastes time because it cannot find the perfect and exact method it senses and wants to bring forth. The *Seven* should not fear to take a step at a time, gaining perfection as it goes along. Fame and fortune can follow when the *Seven* has gained knowledge and found itself and its purpose. It can be an engaging and compelling speaker.

HUMAN RELATIONSHIPS

The well-adjusted *Seven* is a most charming "gentleman" or "lady," poised, dignified, gracious, proud, a good companion, quick of wit and repartee, somewhat exclusive and reserved, normally kind and helpful, and greatly admired for its talents and accomplishments.

However, there is something of the "lone wolf" in its nature, giving the impression of being distant and hard to meet and talk to. Being a perfectionist and selective in all things, the *Seven* does not mix well and always waits to know better or to find real interest in those with whom it comes in contact. The need of the *Seven* to retain its poise and dignity is always present and, if forced to live in uncertainty or confusion in work or human association, it loses its power of attraction so important to its success.

The *Seven* often builds a protective wall of silence and reserve around itself until it is sure it is on familiar ground. As to friends and environment it is selective, but when well-acquainted it reveals all the charm of its inner nature.

The *Seven* is not an adaptable person generally. It is rarely changed or reformed, and attempts to influence it cause withdrawal into a shell of silence and untouchable manner. It is, however, more sensitive in feeling and emotion than it cares to acknowledge and, like all other people, it needs love, sympathy, understanding and is responsive to approval and appreciation.

The *Seven* is extremely averse to being asked questions, especially point-blank, and will seldom answer or may express its irritation through sarcasm or contradictory speech. Even bursts of temper may mar the moment, out of tune with qualities of the "gentleman." It is always best to wait until the *Seven* is ready to tell or answer on its own accord—then the full story will come out. This is true for children as well as the adult *Seven*. The *Seven*, nevertheless, does not hesitate to ask questions and can be very disturbed by an evasive answer. It sometimes shows itself as the doubter or skeptic and demands proof and, while this is the keynote of its success in business or research, in domestic relationships this can be a source of difficulty and unhappiness. It may be surprisingly suspicious and secretive, leading to negative habits and repression. It should give the same confidence to others that it demands for itself and take time to talk things over. Understanding is the watchword for the *Seven* and, being hard to understand and realizing it, the *Seven* gains much by trying to understand others and endeavoring to make itself, its feelings, and its actions clear to others.

The *Seven* likes and needs a good environment. It always wants the best. A good home, well-furnished, elegant and well appointed is what it will strive for, especially the feminine *Seven*, with all details correct.

The *Seven* does not like to have the house filled with many people, only those who have a common and intellectual interest. It is the head of the house, and, in marriage, which is not always an easy adjustment for the *Seven*, it should select one of the opposite sex who also seeks knowledge, books, and the finer things of life. If, by chance, the *Seven* marries into a large family, its lack of true domesticity is revealed and it may express many strange moods or likes and dislikes. The number *Seven* needs to be alone from time to time and should be allowed to have its moments of quiet, rest, and time to read, think, and study.

The emotional and sex nature of the *Seven* is strong, but the fine qualities of self-control and the tendencies of the stoic enable the *Seven* to live alone or even to retire into the priesthood or ministry. Many strange expressions of character may be demonstrated because of the repression of the feelings or again as an unbridled play of emotional nature. A marriage based on the deeper attractions of the soul and mind brings the happiest and most rewarding experiences of the *Seven* life.

Being selective and fussy about food is characteristic of the *Seven*. The *Seven* should always follow rules of diet and corrective eating. Rest combined with directed exercise are very fine rules for the *Seven*. The spine, glands, and spleen are sensitive parts of the body.

The number *Seven*, careful in regard to money, is often considered close in many ways. It is extravagant regarding its own wants but sometimes thoughtless or careless about the needs of others. The *Seven* is not destined to be the world's caretaker, but is instead its educator. However, if thoroughly convinced, it will give abundantly to a worthy cause or real philanthropic need.

The *Seven* should find something of the soul and divine in all things and keep a warm heart as well as a keen mind.

THE NUMBER EIGHT
Watchword: Judgment.   An Extrovert Number.

Positive	*Negative*
Power	Straining to attain
Authority	Too much energy
Efficiency	Overaction
Supervision	Tension
Executive ability	Ambition
Direction of business activity	Love of display
Recognition gained	Repressing others
Character analysis	Demanding recognition
Judgment	Lacking true humanitarian
Organization	feelings
World affairs	Money difficulties
Strenuous action	Impatience with others
Strength	Forcefulness
Capability	Few illusions
Demanding of others	
Seeking power	
Working for a cause	

COLORS: Tan, Canary, Bronze, Buff, Opal, Ivory

COSMIC PATTERN

"And the Lord said, If I find in Sodom fifty righteous people, within the city, I will spare all the place for their sakes."

To bring the infinite and the finite into harmonious relationship is the purpose and divine inheritance of the number *Eight*.

"Thy kingdom come. Thy will be done in earth, as it is in heaven."

Armed with divine awareness, learned through many past lifetimes, the number *Eight* plunges into the depths of experience; touched by the knowledge of the great mysteries of Being and the secrets of occult art and science, it presents to the people of the earth the reality of the divine dream of creation.

The number *Eight* is a double number. It is the masculine and the feminine—the masculine, strong, demanding, active; the feminine, passive and capable of being molded. Together they express the celestial in material form. Separated, they bring sorrow and destruction—heaven and hell.

The number *Eight* represents authority and can guide and direct mankind—not as the humanitarian but as the arbitrator, controller, the judge who weighs and balances with wisdom and without prejudice. The number *Eight* must not allow the seven days of creation to fail. It has charge of the expansion of the works of creation. It provides the order, the knowledge, the supervision and the stability to cement the dreams and visions of all the other numbers, that growth and progress may be even greater than before.

Its task is great; it has many burdens. As its righteousness remains true to divine command, it becomes the noble and greatly respected judge and is rewarded from on high. It is the Solomon of numbers.

"Judge not, that ye be not judged. For with what judgment ye judge, ye shall be judged: and with what measure ye mete, it shall be measured to you again."

OPPORTUNITIES

When awakened and developed, the number *Eight* becomes the Master Mind working for the cause of humanity and finds its perfect reward in the great accomplishment.

Often it does not understand itself or the great power within, awaiting birth, to bring forth fine deeds and broad attainment. Personal ambition may throb within; love of money and power may color its plans and dreams, only to result in loss and long periods of frustration, because it has failed to listen to the higher command: "on earth as it is in heaven."

When a balance through moral integrity, spiritual feeling, and material gain has been found, unusual opportunity and worthwhile authority is given, bringing success in any undertaking with the power, influence, recognition, and financial reward so deeply desired.

The rewards of life are not easily attained, however, for it is the destiny of the *Eight* to give "its all" to whatever it undertakes. Repeated effort is often necessary to get results, accompanied by mental strain and long periods of frustration. At the same time, repeated effort and patience, until the work or dream is accomplished, are part of the strength and character of the number *Eight*.

The number *Eight* finds its greatest opportunity through a real purpose or goal: something to plan for that has usefulness, beauty, and wide service to the community or nation. It is always called upon to plan, supervise, lead, and to take up the reins of the plans and dreams of others in order to bring them to lasting and permanent accomplishment, not as the humanitarian, but as the one who loves the work and the thrill of the successful attainment of a worthwhile goal. Money comes to the *Eight* through its efficiency, excellent mental powers and good judgment—which is impartial and for the good of all concerned. It does not have the natural and easy attraction for money like the *Three, Six,* and *Nine.* Success is the result of work well done, outstanding ability, its own unceasing effort, mental attainment, combined with fine character and right action.

There is a philosophical trend to the nature of the number *Eight.* It likes to theorize, to discover the motives and feelings behind human action. It is clever in relating feeling and facts, due to the feminine side of its masculine nature. Often it is the wise counselor, guiding and directing without prejudice or illusions, an ability gained only after many experiences and a few hard knocks by life itself. When the energies are spent striving for wealth and grandeur, the will may be broken by strong outside forces and a new start must be made. Through these struggles, an inner awareness of higher purposes is finally gained; and a calm unprejudiced management of affairs and fine powers of leadership enable the number *Eight* to rise to emergencies, to become the outstanding character and the "Master Mind," the reward granted from the beginning.

VOCATIONS AND TALENTS

Industry, commerce and organization on a large scale give the *Eight* broad opportunity to make use of its natural talents. The *Eight* is the supervisor, director, controller, one who has charge of the business affairs of others. It is successful in building up run-down business activity of firms, corporations, and organizations; able to spot or uncover the weakness and to guide those in association to the goal to be accomplished. A natural efficiency expert, it impartially places facts, both as to cause and effect, in proper relationship.

Governmental affairs, civics, and political management interest the *Eight,* giving opportunity to direct affairs of State. Statistical departments and all lines of research are fields of success, as the *Eight* likes to gather facts and to relate them to the goal or undertaking to be developed. Civil engineering or building on a large scale, world-wide contracts and agreements are possible, linked with general improvement for many people and combined with education and instruction.

Real estate is a broad opportunity, or loans and trusts dealing with the buying, selling and management of property and estates. Even in a small way, the *Eight*, at some time during its life, is concerned with the management and maintenance of property, land, buildings, or homes.

The literary field attracts the *Eight*, and success can be gained through printing, publishing, newspapers, magazines, correspondence, more in the nature of the reporter, educator or traveler than along lines of drama and romance.

Business having to do with transportation, travel by land, sea, or air are fields of endeavor. The *Eight* enjoys having more than one iron in the fire and likes to know what is going on in the world; it is always seeking, digesting, and adjusting information.

The intelligence service is a natural field, as the keen mind, powers of observation, courage, and strong self-control make the *Eight* adaptable to many situations.

As the two loops of the number *Eight* give it a desire to be fair and to see both sides of a question, it makes a fine judge and counselor and when trained, takes its place among those holding high positions. Recognition for dependability and trust generally crowns the work of the *Eight*. Even in a small way, the *Eight* has a way of being known in its locality for its outstanding character and good works. The number *Eight* does not like subordinate positions and generally seeks important contacts. When the command from its spiritual nature for righteousness is carried out, it gains power and influence. The number *Eight* should always train and educate its hands and mind. It should never trust to luck.

As nurses, physicians, heads of institutions of health, the *Eights* find opportunity to manage and direct. The *Eight* has an outstanding ability to control others, even the insane. This ability to direct and lead is sometimes only discovered when an emergency arises, forcing the *Eight* to make use of its inner strength, will, courage, and executive skill.

Sports, games give pleasure and success. Hotels and summer resorts, especially in the country can lead to desirable business success.

The philosophical side of its nature, as natural to its character as its executive ability, gives the *Eight* interest in secret societies where there is form, organization and mystical training. It is often found reading, studying or teaching all lines of the mental sciences and ancient philosophies and is interested in studies of character and vocational analysis. This is brought about because of its desire to know about life and its relationship to divine purposes. The *Eight* has the ability to be a public speaker and is more direct than flowery.

The *Eight* has musical talent, not always trained. It is attracted to musical instruments, finds interest and success through antiques, museums, art galleries.

The *Eight* makes money, works with money-making activities, but others may often receive more than the *Eight* that has given the effort, the brains, and the "know-how." However, as the *Eight* continues to make use of its mental powers and its wise judgment, it never lacks for right compensation. It is a mental worker, not a physical laborer.

HUMAN RELATIONSHIPS

The number *Eight* is always busy. Its strenuous driving force may make it try to be all things to all people, to take part in a variety of activities, wearing out its health and overwhelming its more plodding associates. Its intensity of action now and then defeats the very purpose for which it is working. It should learn to take time to rest and relax and to find an inner peace which will take away the sense of strife, strain, and frustration which accompanies "too much" effort.

Being a strong character it is naturally a doer and others

depend upon it; but it is part of the *Eight's* lesson in life to strike a balance between doing and resting for lasting results.

, The *Eight* has a strong personality and is a good companion because of its many interests and varied activities. It gets on well with others, likes important people but associates with persons in all walks of life. It enjoys big houses, good clothes, and to make a good appearance with a touch of showmanship.

It is a number of honesty and frankness and may, at times, speak out bluntly and severely, for it is annoyed and may even show temper over repeated blunders and inefficiency on the part of others. Its anger is soon over and it is more likely to feel condemnation for itself than for others. The *Eight* has a tendency to indulge in repeated self-analysis and self recrimination. It should not carry this too far, especially in times of seeming difficulties and problems.

In love, marriage, and romance it is loyal and true, but with so many plans and ambitions it can be too busy for sentiment or love-making even though it may be deeply in love. It needs love and admiration to soften its nature, and should find time to express love, beauty, and sweetness to those it loves. Life becomes happier when the *Eight* learns to deal more patiently with others and to realize its own sometimes overwhelming driving force.

There is a contradiction in the character of the *Eight*. Filled with purpose and capable of seeing great possibilities in a plan, business activity or worth-while endeavor—supervising with great skill, and generally correct in its prophecy of final success—still the *Eight* may hesitate to take its rightful position and surprisingly stand aside to allow others to gain the reward and recognition. A little more self-confidence at the right moment would give the *Eight* its rightful reward and the great satisfaction in accomplishment which it has desired above all else.

THE NUMBER NINE

Watchword: Forgiveness.   An Introvert Number.

Positive	Negative
Perfection	Too much love of self
Love, Compassion	Jack of all trades
Ideality	Personal interests
Impressionability	Impulsive action, Taking
Charitable ways	no blame
Brotherhood of mankind	Changeableness in love affairs
Impersonality	Possessiveness
Forgivingness	Demanding approval and
Leaders in philanthropic	appreciation
endeavor	Moods and depression
Artists, Writers	Failure to use talents for
Religionists	good of world
Having big opportunity in life	Dissipation of higher forces
Capacity for living by	Carelessness in financial
Divine Standards	affairs
Money attraction	Seeking an easy time and
Leaders in art or good works	approval
Dramatic talent	Wrong habits
	Wanting to be hale fellow

COLORS: Red, Carmine, Lavender, Olive, Straw, Smoke

COSMIC PATTERN

The number *Nine* represents the Beginning and the End of all human experience.

It is the Force of the outgoing number *One*,
the Light and the Peace of the number *Two*,
the Imagination of the number *Three*,
the Form and Order of the number *Four*,
the Life and Progress of the number *Five*,
the Responsibility of the number *Six*,
the Intelligence and Perfection of the number *Seven*,

the Judgment of the number *Eight*,
the Compassion and Benevolence of the number *Nine*.

The number *Nine* represents mankind's last earthly lesson: *"Forgiveness."*

"Then said Jesus, Father, forgive them for they know not what they do."

The number *Nine* is the heart and harmony of God's Plan: it is also the Law and the Principle of Love that maintains, supports, and fulfills the promise of Eternal Life.

"Wherefore I say unto you, All manner of sin and blasphemy shall be forgiven unto men: but blasphemy against the Holy Ghost shall not be forgiven unto men."

Many disappointments may color the experiences of the number *Nine*. However, awakened to the "Music of the Spheres" and to the great Harmony of Being, it is finally redeemed out of all peoples, all religions, all creeds into the One Self which is in all and through all.

Then life becomes a glorious experience to the number *Nine*. All who touch its life are warmed by the Divine force of compassion radiating from its heart.

OPPORTUNITIES

The opportunities of the number *Nine* may span the whole world, ranging from the center of local activity to foreign contacts and foreign businesses. The affairs of the number *Nine* naturally move in wide circles and great achievements. When the desire is awakened to promote civilization, to educate, comfort, and protect mankind, its possibilities are unlimited.

So all-embracing is its scope of service, life's gifts seem to be handed it on a silver platter, placing it in command of the greatest good life has to offer, as it keeps the Law of higher purposes as its goal. Only in this way does it keep and hold its reward—love, money, and philanthropy.

The number *Nine* is a number of imagination, intuition, sympathy, and generosity of such power and high voltage, that it can warm the heart of all mankind when this is poured forth without personal motive and desire. It must be bigger than all others in all situations and in all motives. It must grow in compassion, tolerance, forgiveness, and the understanding of true service to reap the fullness of its promise of greatness and to gain its goal.

Early in life it is hard for the number *Nine* to understand many hurtful experiences of loss, sorrow, and disappointment which may occur until the great love which pervades its soul is turned from the personal to the impersonal. To plan its goal or achievement as a means to personal gain alone, to desire love, money, and power for personal satisfaction only, is to wreck its life, destroy its power to accomplish, and to suffer personal pain and crucifixion.

The number *Nine* is divinely protected. It has every power within itself to succeed nobly. When it finally learns to love life, success, and people in unison with the great universal "good" rather than for personal prominence or favor, it receives greater love, personally and impersonally, than it may have ever dreamed of.

The number *Nine* attracts:

money	and	fortune
4 6 5 5 7 = (27) 9		6 6 9 2 3 5 5 = (36) 9

It may make a fortune and just as easily lose it more than once during a lifetime. "Easy come, easy go," for it is generous, impressionable, and idealistic. It can be influenced and imposed upon because of its generosity, giving where it should not or without reserve, until, eventually, it learns to serve, to promote, and to help without personal loss and without taking from others the responsibility of their own growth and development. Number *Nine* must give to sustain usefulness and not from generosity alone.

The number *Nine* has been blessed with the ability to restore its position, to redeem itself from failure, and to re-establish its success at all times. As the *Nine* goes forth into life, conscious of the brotherhood of man, serving all people, all races, all nations, not in self-sacrifice, but in the realization that God has given it a heart of gold, silver bells of many talents, and a shining faith in the highest good for all, its life becomes great and wonderful.

VOCATIONS AND TALENTS

The number *Nine*, being endowed with imagination, vision, and artistic feeling, is naturally the dramatist, and showman, and succeeds through plays, theatres, and all lines of endeavor which appeal to the emotions of others.

The literary field—books, novels, publications—give opportunity, for the number *Nine* can express moods and feelings with force and appeal, ascending from the heights of exultation to the depths of despair. The *Nine* can be the actor, actress, the painter, the designer, the architect, or along any line calling for feeling, dash, and the use of color in bold and unusual manner; sometimes the mimic and comedian.

Creative ability, artistic talent, and an underlying practical ability enable the *Nine* to turn objects of little worth into something useful and original. In the more practical fields, the number *Nine* may be the cabinet maker, upholsterer, technician repairing works of art. The number *Nine* is not happy in a menial position and need not remain there if it keeps its standards of usefulness and service to all. It can rebuild and reconstruct human lives as well as material objects and become the lecturer, orator, religionist, and educator along lines of corrective living and charitable inspiration.

The number *Nine* may be a fine lawyer with appeal to the heart or a surgeon with the skill of perfection, as the *Nine* is a perfectionist in all things.

All lines of business having to do with foods and health

matters, and businesses which appeal to the comfort and luxury of people in general appeal to the number *Nine*. The number *Nine* likes the best and has a splendid ability to attract the best in living conditions and surroundings.

The number *Nine* can deal with the unusual and has an appreciation of sound and its influence and value as well as of color and beauty. Being able to ascend to the heights of intuition, it may become the inventor or composer and bring into being that which has never been known or experienced before.

All lines of industry which have a broad scope of usefulness give opportunity, for the *Nine* adds finer qualities and something of the soul even in business. Travel means much to the *Nine*, and through this it finds many chances for success and use of its talents. To be broadminded is a fundamental required of the *Nine*.

HUMAN RELATIONSHIPS

The number *Nine* has charm of personality. Its sympathy, understanding, and warmth of feeling give it popularity and ability to influence others. It is generally well liked and is a good companion, enjoying life and the fun of living.

Early in life, the number *Nine* seems to have two sides to its nature, leading to many experiences, even to sorrow and loss until these are blended together for a true purpose in life. The personal and the impersonal, acting together, tend to make it seem inconsistent and difficult to understand. At one time it will be warm, helpful, tolerant, and wonderfully generous, giving without thought of self and to its own detriment. Or again it may be cold, hard, distant, and very self-interested, keeping its money and its affairs to itself, although reaching out for personal gain, even sacrificing those it loves to gain its desires. Then again it may be lost in dreams, living in a world of abstract plans and visions, while failing to be practical or to listen to advice. These changing moods cause delay and appear as defeat to the number *Nine* and its loved ones until it awakens to its higher possibilities and seeks to find its right place among those who promote the welfare of peoples.

The number *Nine* is very idealistic and loves its home, family, and friends. Its ideals are very high and it is attracted to beauty in others. It falls in love with great intensity, although romance may fade as quickly if the ideal of its dreams fails to live up to the ideal of perfection and beauty of character, as well as personality. It has contempt for small actions or unlovely responses to conditions and surroundings. It has strange experiences in love, marriage, and friendship until it realizes that true love is not sacrifice or possession, but is the reward of service based on strength of character and dependence upon the higher laws of being, not on personal attachment alone. True love is inner growth and development.

It is well not to drive the number *Nine* too far, or to impose upon it unreasonably. The number *Nine* has strength of character, inner wisdom, and intuition, and its consciousness is supported and rounded out by the qualities of all the other numbers. It is human, however, and like the number *Six*, asks for love and approval, for it needs these to do its best work. It is not a number of sacrifice and renunciation. When it falls into temptation and "plays the field" it is set for eventual loss and sorrow. Being the highest number on the scale of human experience, it cannot transgress the principles of inner grace and spiritual living.

When undeveloped it may appear to be meek, shy, and vacillating, looking on the dark side of things, restless and fearful, longing for something—it hardly knows what. It needs a helping hand and good education. The *Nine* should make every effort to develop its talents and to cultivate its individuality. It need not try to be like others and should not be afraid of life, for the number *Nine* has unusual ability to attract assistance, opportunity, and the necessary ways and means to enter upon a successful and useful life.

The number *Nine*, being a number of high potency, should avoid habits of drink and wrong stimulation. It is very hard for the *Nine* to break habits or for anyone else to reform it. This must come about by its own desire and faith in God.

The father is often a strong influence in the life of the number *Nine*, both for great happiness and love and for great misunderstandings.

The health is generally good. However, unhappy emotions such as temper, jealousy, or antagonistic feeling, also hard menial work, can disturb the circulation and general health.

Faith and confidence in itself, faith in the great spiritual plan of creation, love of its fellow man, form lasting foundations for the number *Nine* to stand upon.

LET'S TALK IT OVER

When you first begin to analyze names, you will be able to read only the "digit" or final sum of the name or group of names. However, as you figure many names, you will gradually observe the numbers behind the digit, and realize that names having the same total or digit are different in construction.

A student said to me one time, "My name is Mary and I am a *Three*. My sister's name is Jane and she is a *Three*, and we are not a bit alike." It is true—both are *Three*, and this total is first in importance in reading the name. However, the numbers making up the *Three* in each case give a slightly different slant on the way the talents will be expressed. Do not allow this to confuse you at present; later this will come naturally as you relate the numbers and character.

For example, observe the names:

Ann	Margaret	John
1 5 5	4 1 9 7 1 9 5 2	1 6 8 5
11	38	20
2	2	2

Each of these names has the digit *Two*. All three have its fine sensitive feeling and spiritual color. John will be more personally sensitive than the others, due to the intensification from the cipher.

Another example:

David	Joyce	Thomas
4 1 4 9 4	1 6 7 3 5	2 8 6 4 1 1
22	22	22
4	4	4

These names have the spiritual force of the *Two* channeled through the practical endeavor of the *Four*.

Surprisingly enough

Heaven	Hell
8 5 1 4 5 5	8 5 3 3
28	19
1	1

This is one of the reasons the number 19 is considered a test in human experience.

Reducing all sums to a final digit is the correct procedure for all names, even the 11 and 22 which are sometimes left standing alone in some teachings of Numerology. In the teaching of Mrs. L. Dow Balliett, a very sweet and spiritual character, a great deal of importance was given to these two numbers. They are both endowed with high spiritual potency—and this should be recognized—but unless reduced to a final digit, the true reasons for the power of the numbers is overlooked and not rightly interpreted.

Observe these charts:

11	or 2	13	or 4
20	or 2	22	or 4
29	or 2	31	or 4
38(11)	or 2	40	or 4

All these groups have different backgrounds but the same digit.

Why, then, are the 11 and 22 given special qualifications? During the many years of research by the California Institute of Numerical Research, we gained a clearer understanding of these numbers, backed up by statistics and experience. Through these studies we cleared away much misunderstanding and misuse of the correct application of the 11 and 22.

THE 11 AND 22

The number 11 has the will and determination of the two 1's supporting the digit 2. Therefore it is much stronger than the 20 which has only the 2 value. The number 1 gives the gentle 2 courage, strength, and purpose. The word "Spirit" (figured) digits to a 1. The word "Light" digits to a 2. It is through the 2 that the healing and deep sensitive feeling is given the forceful 1's, causing the number 11 to be called a "spiritual messenger."

This combination gives outstanding qualities—the inner power to influence the masses and to bring Light to humanity. It is, however, often found in the names of political leaders, artists, and scientists as well as religionists. Discovering its ability to become a leader, very frequently it may allow personal ambition to enter in and a downfall results. Both Hitler and Mussolini had the 11 prominent in their names. Rightfully lived up to and expressed, the 11/2 rules the masses, but spiritual living is demanded.

The number 22 is considered the "spiritual master in

form.'' You can readily understand how the Light of the spiritual 2, intensified by repetition, gives thought and feeling on the higher levels of consciousness. However, spiritual qualities of the 2 are held down to the practical and material level of the 4. This often results in strange inner conflicts for the 22: the 2 finds it difficult to bring its thoughts and desires down to the ordinary everyday activities, and to put into *form* and *order* its concepts and finer attributes. The 22 often needs the help and support of others and must learn to cooperate with circumstances—not pull *against* them. Often there is a dominant person in the environment to test the peacemaking qualities of the 2, causing the 22 much unhappiness and sorrow. The 22 finds its victory in helping others and in working with large undertakings or groups. When you find these two numbers on any of the four major positions of the name (the following four lessons) give the individual help in understanding the power with which he is endowed by the spiritual force the numbers represent.

THE 16 AND 19

In these lessons it is my desire to help you and those you love or serve find the way to the greatest happiness and usefulness possible, to overcome any sense of failure, self-distrust, or lack of faith in yourself. There are always problems to be met and worked through, but it is not necessary to remain long in any unhappy situation. There are those who go down before any negative thought or suggestion. To avoid this, should you have been a student of Numerology and heard of the so-called Karmic numbers 16 and 19, I wish to explain them at this time for your future use and understanding. Many occult and philosophical teachings place great emphasis on ''karma,'' brought about by mistakes and wrongdoing in previous lifetimes, from which they learn there is no escape.

It is true that many wonderful men and women of fine

character accept heartbreaking experiences, sometimes a whole lifetime through, hardly to be accounted for by their own actions. Reading the names of these people, I have found this pattern of "experience" forecast by their names right from the time of birth. Through understanding and studying their ultimate goals in life, they have learned by overcoming the sorrow and loss, they may lead happy, useful lives and thus outlive retribution.

Has this "karma" been brought about by previous lifetimes? Is this an indictment by Divine Law? Reading the story the name reveals and finding no other reason for the strange and often peculiar experiences being taken, or why one fails and another succeeds, I have come to believe life is but a part of the Great Eternity in God's plan for His Own. There must be more opportunity for life than this one short earthly period, many wonderful lifetimes behind us to allow us to learn and grow in grace and beauty, and many lifetimes waiting where the "White Ones Go in Their Mystic Mating." We are children of the Most High, learning to express and grow in His Image and Likeness in the schools of life everlasting—here on earth or elsewhere in some Heavenly Mansion. It is not strange then that we make mistakes or find it hard to learn and must take the lesson over again until we come face to face with the Truth —that love is the fulfillment and the reward.

But remember, in every name is hidden the "way out." The "pattern of experience" written there also contains the pattern of success and "Destiny," the nature of the work to be accomplished in this lifetime. There are talents indicated, opportunities and spiritual forces for good and for "overcoming" running side by side with the events of so-called Karma —so strong, vital and positive that the old story is rewritten and a new life begun, free and inspiring, when the "way" is discovered.

In reading names, at no time do I dwell on the negative side of the life-story. It is my task as a Numerologist to find the true way, the new life for you or my clients. Only as I prepare the way to the best life has to offer can I really hold a respected place as a Numerologist and sincere counselor.

The number 16 is called a karmic number. When it appears as an experience, sudden happenings can take place. In the "Tarot" instructions it is represented by a lightning-struck tower. It has the power to disrupt and cause circumstances to fall apart with loss and some humiliation. However, the wisdom of the 7 (1 plus 6) and its intelligence, scientific knowledge, and skill soon bring about a recovery. If no effort is made to use this intelligence, the experience can be difficult.

The number 19, also called a karmic number, is less severe. It forces the individual to stand on his own feet and to take a stand for self-development and self-realization. It is a test of courage, initiative, and self-determination. The pressure and urge is felt within the individual's own mind and heart but not apparent to others nor understood by them. When the will is cultivated and combined with the tolerance and compassion wrapped up in the number 9 of the 19, fine progress can be made. If resistance and self-pity direct the actions, the road to success and happiness is difficult and trying. A well-developed individuality and successful use of the talents also overcome the test of the 19.

When the 16 or 19 are found as totals of the name at birth or on any of the major positions, understanding of the meaning of the numbers and right use of the principles for which they stand can lead to a rich, full life. Do not be afraid of these numbers. Misunderstanding by students and Numerologists has led to an overemphasis on the negative qualities.

THE NUMBER 8

Experience and research have proved that the number 8 is greatly misunderstood by Numerologists and students. It is a power number which gives success, recognition, and leadership qualities. Fine character, ability to weigh and balance, and seeing both sides of the queston give it position and authority. However it has more than its share of disappointments. But its success is *earned* by repeated effort, well-directed purpose, and giving its all to maintain and hold on to what it has rightfully earned. Just at the last moment others may receive the reward and the wealth when the goal was just at the fingertips of the number 8. The word *Karma* digits to the total 8. The word *Mystic* is also endowed with the qualities of the 8. A philosophical turn of mind helps the 8 understand itself and others, so that it takes its place as the counselor, having learned the problems of others through its own long, slightly defeating experiences.

READING A NAME

The following charts will help you later on when you begin to read names. They apply to character, experience and to any activity represented by a name and number.

Introverts 1-3-5-7-9 the odd numbers
Extroverts 2-4-6-8 the even numbers

The introvert is found in all walks of life and in all activities. It is characterized by a desire to accomplish something all its own and is capable of retiring from the public or the strenuous activities of the public. It needs people for success, but is selective and strong in likes and dislikes; it is reserved regarding itself and its activities. It may absorb itself in its own interests to the point of genius or become too shy to make use of its own talents. The introvert likes a few people, not the crowd.

On the other hand, the extrovert truly likes people, needs others to be happy, seeks to give of itself to loved ones, and has humanitarian interests. It is not shy or reticent. It brings life, fun, and joy to activities and is capable of giving the shirt off its back to those who need help or appeal to its emotions. It is not necessarily worldly nor is the extrovert always highly spiritual. The introvert can live alone; the extrovert cannot. Almost everyone is a mixture of both in character and interest.

First: 1–5–7 Go-getters: Keep things moving on their own level.

Second: 2–4–8 Carry-outers: Take care of activity, manage and direct. Earn their money.

Third: 3–6–9 Easy-takers: Like the best in life and believe in their right to it. Allow others to help them and need the help of others to reach success. Can make big money.

The following instructions give you the pattern for reading a name. As the contractor follows a blueprint for building, or a seamstress lays a pattern of many sections on a piece of material, reading a name must also follow a pattern before the character is fully revealed and experiences to be taken are outlined.

Some names are easy to read as they reveal the talents and temperament almost at once. Others are more difficult with many seeming contradictions when all the parts of analysis are read in order and position. The following chart shows the steps to be taken and are like an "autobiography" or photograph of the person whose name is being studied. I learned to read names step by step in this way, and it is interesting and amazing how the character, talents, and the peculiarities of the nature slowly but surely reveal themselves as the pattern is followed.

Some students, learning the meaning of the numbers, find it difficult to place them on the positions which are given in the following lessons. Remember that a number always means the same thing, but expresses its consciousness through the position on which it is found.

For example: If you find a 6 Destiny and a 7 Heart—the Destiny means the individual must work out to and express the qualities and talents of the 6; but having a 7 Heart, the 6 Destiny will be touched by the reserve, selectiveness, and scientific impulses shown by the 7 Heart number. This is what is meant by "synchronize"—blending the numbers and positions, one after the other, for the final characterization.

HOW TO READ A NAME

First: Read the *Destiny*—what you *must* be or do.

Second: Read the *Birth*—what you *have* or *are*.

Third: Synchronize these two numbers. Make them work together.

Fourth: Read the *Heart* Number—what you will *desire* to be or do.

Fifth: Synchronize this with the Destiny and Birth to balance the character.

Sixth: Read the *Personality*—what you will *appear* to be like and do.

Seventh: Read the *Reality*—the ultimate goal of all your life's experiences.

FOR MORE PERSONAL CHARACTERISTICS

Eighth: Read the *Planes of Expression*—for type and ways of looking at life.

Ninth: Read the *Points of Intensification*—for traits and outstanding talents; possibly genius.

Tenth: Relate these two divisions to the main characteristics—Heart, Destiny, Birth, and Ultimate Goal.

Eleventh: Read the *Challenge*—what you must cultivate to overcome a hidden weakness.

Twelfth: Read the *Point of Security*—talents you may not know about.

Thirteenth: Read vocation from all the above positions.

EXPERIENCES

Fourteenth: Read the *Pinnacles*—the four main cycles of life.

Fifteenth: Read the *Personal Year*. Yearly number.

Sixteenth: Read the *Race Consciousness*—(your age).

Seventeenth: Read the *Table of Events*—events of major importance throughout the lifetime.

Finally: Signatures and New Names.

How to put your name to music and other points of study and interest are given in the final chapters.

CHAPTER III

THE DESTINY NUMBER
The Prophecy in Your Name

"What does life hold in store for me?"—"What are my chances for success?"—are questions asked over and over again by intelligent and thinking people, seeking to find themselves and their right places in life.

Some have asked in desperation, others with the sincere desire to prepare for the future and a useful life; still others ask from an inner desire to reach spiritual perfection.

The story of what your life is to be, what you were born to do, and the part you are to play on the stage of life, now and in the future, are written in the scroll and symbols of the name given you when you were born.

With every birth a soul is born. Life is not a matter of uncertainty and chance. Our names are written in the Lamb's Book of Life—recorded and tabulated there by the letters and numbers designating our names in the same way our births are registered on legal records required by civic law.

Every name given at birth contains a Divine Command and a Divine promise of opportunity and personal privilege, but at the same time it demands a promise from everyone to keep faith with the purpose written on the Destiny scroll of the name. To know what your name means is a spiritual awakening.

To meet this Destiny requirement is not always easy. At times it will not be what you desire as it may bring experiences you do not understand; but, gradually, as you keep plugging along, these very experiences will tug, pull and push you until you finally swing out into the full tide of the accomplishment for which you were destined and the wonderful satisfaction which follows—that of fulfilling your purpose in life.

The name you were given at birth tells this story. All other names, nicknames, changes of names, signatures, or married names are but channels through which the destiny is worked out and expressed. At first you may not be one hundred percent in performance, but if you keep on trying you will find it easy and finally gain the love, success, and repeated rewards it has promised you.

Reading character from names and numbers covers many parts of the name given you at birth, as well as the month, day, and year you were born. Finding your Destiny is the first rule.

The *Destiny Number* is the sum of all the letters in the name given *at birth*. It means:

Your life's purpose.
What must be lived up to in this lifetime.
Your field of opportunity.
What you must give of yourself to others and to life.
The kind of people to meet and work with.
The environment and point of contact with others.
The spiritual mission to which you have been appointed.

It is read as what you *must do*. It is never read as what you *are*. The Destiny requirement remains the same throughout your lifetime. It can never be outlived, stamped out, or neglected. It is a subtle, commanding force to be constantly aware of in all of life's experiences. In fact, many of the happenings that test your willingness to be true to the purpose of your birth are brought about through your Destiny number.

FIGURING THE NAME

(According to instructions previously given. See pages 7–8.)

Example:

```
J o h n     H e n r y     J o n e s
1 6 8 5     8 5 5 9 7     1 6 5 5 1
  20           34            18
  2     +      7     +       9     = (18) or 9
```

Born to discover and remain true to the brotherhood of man.

Rules:

Give each letter its numerical value as shown by its position in the alphabet.

Add these numbers together. Add again, if necessary, until a single digit is reached.

Do the same with each name. A full name may be made up of two, three or four or more parts.

Add all these single digits together, finally reducing the sum to a digit. This is the Destiny number.

Never add the numbers of the letters straight through. It is important to get the value of each name. Each name has definite bearing on the way the Destiny will be expressed. The *first* or given name is the personal side of the nature and disposition which shows personal attitudes and feelings. The *second* or middle name is a reservoir from which latent powers can be drawn, and at the same time support the Destiny. The *third* or surname is very strong in its influence, indicating family characteristics, vocational histories and background. All the names comprising the name at birth indicate character and talents. However, they may pull against each other, making the Destiny harder to live up to.

It is the total number of all the names which represents the Destiny and is first in importance. Give this number its full meaning to discover why you were born and what your life means to you.

For anyone born in a foreign country—figure the name at birth as it is written in the native language. Later changes in spelling become as signatures, explained in Chapter 20. In case of *adoption*, if an original name was given, even temporarily, use this name to find the true *Destiny*. The adopted name shows how this Destiny will be worked out. Names given at *confirmation* are not part of life's destiny. They become part of the signature later on and are tools to be used if desired.

You will find your Destiny and why you were born among the following delineations of the Destiny numbers. Enjoy it and live up to it.

NUMBER ONE DESTINY

Your name destines you to LEADERSHIP. You must gain this position through your own initiative, independence, and originality of thought and method. If you live up to your name, you will become an outstanding character in some line of endeavor during your lifetime. Your life is destined to be an interesting one, with many odd and strange experiences; all for the purpose of developing your will and determination. Your success will come through your ability to stand on your own feet, think for yourself, and to individualize your character. This does not mean that you must be aggressive or dominant; but instead, to be strong, self-reliant, and determined to get on in the world by your own ability. Life will never let you down if you use a fine, constructive will-power in overcoming obstacles and meet your problems with courage and originality. Do not be afraid to get off the beaten track. Just be sure your plan is constructive and this will open the door to leadership and independence. Teach others true leadership.

FIELD OF OPPORTUNITY

There will be times when you need to broaden your opportunities. At such times investigate new ideas, new things and original and unique activities. If you are compelled to deal with old and established lines of work, put new and original methods into the undertakings. You are something of a promoter by destiny and must keep things from crystallizing. Undeveloped projects give you opportunity to show your initiative and executive ability. If you find yourself in, or remaining in, a subordinate position without hope of progress, it means that you are not making a consistent effort towards self-improvement or using your ideas to good advantage. Do not be different to be prominent. Just be strong, capable, intelligent, and your opportunities will come to you. Mix with people who are doing original things and have ambition to promote and engineer the causes of civilization; this will fire your ambition to use your own ideas. Live an active life. Dullness will defeat you. Make your home and surroundings artistic and interesting. Use your natural magnetic force to attract those who will help you and whom you can help. You have a fine Destiny. Keep life moving onward. When seeking opportunity wear becoming shades of flame, lilac, or crimson.

Number Two Destiny

You were destined by Life to play the role of "Peacemaker." Good will toward others is your magic power for success. You have fine powers of persuasion, diplomacy and cooperation, but they must be carefully cultivated and brought to a high point of perfection, along with your other characteristics, if you wish to attract the good things life has in store for you. In other words, you are one of Life's "trouble shooters" and will be called upon constantly to pour oil on troubled waters. You may not always want to do so, but you came into the world with this mission to fulfill, so it must be done, not only for the sake of success, but for your own peace and happiness. When things are not moving along smoothly, try tact, diplomacy and courtesy; for arbitration is one of your tools of trade. Avoid falling into the struggle for existence. Bring others together diplomatically; soothe, comfort, advise, counsel, and help people find peace, for this will give you great personal satisfaction and add to your commercial value.

FIELD OF OPPORTUNITY

Partnerships are important to you. No matter how independent an executive you are in other ways, cooperation is essential to your success. This does not mean that you should depend upon others for your success, but through fraternities, associations, groups, and in your personal and home life, you will find "sharing" a means to your own attainment.

Mix with people who are working for the refinement of the masses and who express the cultural standards of living. You have a fine power to influence people and it is a part of your mission as a peacemaker to encourage others to live by the higher principles of being. You are sensitive too, and should appreciate how others feel, and your understanding and persuasive manner give you ability to encourage and comfort others. Your own home, personality, character, and way of doing things should represent beauty, art, and loveliness. If at any time you find yourself living in inharmonious and unhappy surroundings, or there are jealousies and opposition in your home or business, you should make every effort to overcome this by being more cooperative and peaceful in your own actions; not weak or fearful, but willing to work for the good of your associates as much as for yourself. People who are interested in religion, politics, banking, science, statistics, higher mechanics, are in your field of opportunity. When seeking opportunity wear white, salmon, gold, or garnet.

NUMBER THREE DESTINY

You have a creative Destiny and are required to be the "optimist." Your mission in life is to help people realize the magic power of cheerfulness and inspiration. You must realize this for yourself too, for "laugh and the world laughs with you" is one of your slogans for success. "Weep and you weep alone" is equally certain in your experiences. Many people have lost the joy of living and it is your duty and mission in life to arouse their imagination and spirit, until their faith in people and in friendship has been rekindled, and they can laugh again. This may not always be easy for you to do, but this is a part of your success and you should make every effort to live up to it. You were destined to be popular, to have love, romance and money, but this will come to you only as you express beauty, art and inspiration in your own life. Dare to laugh at troubles. Mix sincerity with joy and you cannot fail. Also, if you are unable to express your ideas and character along some creative and inspirational manner, you should train your mind until you can do so easily and naturally. This will open opportunities to you which you could not gain in any other way.

FIELD OF OPPORTUNITY

There will be times when you will need to broaden your opportunities. At such times investigate some of the worldly activities which are more creative, fanciful and artistic than the ordinary, practical lines of endeavor. Study and engage in interests which will give you more ease of expression in words and feeling, whether in literature, drama, commerce, or business. You have a part to play, even a career, along the lines of imagination and creative undertakings. The art of words, constructively used, will take you far in life. Don't talk too much, or wear your heart on your sleeve, but enjoy life and help others enjoy life too. Keep optimistic and you will be the center of admiring groups. Friends are important in your life and you should cultivate the art of being a true friend. Mix with people who have a constructive philosophy and a comeback when things go wrong. Do not be afraid of the public; take an interest in the opera, theatre, charity, children, all the arts and crafts, religion, and all activities which amuse, entertain, and inspire the people. Through these you will find help, assistance and friendship and be able to do good in the world.

NUMBER FOUR DESTINY

You are destined by life to play the role of manager and "organizer." You are a builder, and it is your mission to make things permanent and lasting. You must make dreams practical and bring all imagination down to earth. Life will not permit you to take things easy and you may meet many serious problems until you become proficient in establishing system, order, form, and regulation in your business and personal problems. You may not always want to do this, but if you wish to get the best out of life, you must try at all times to establish unity between the idea and the result; for you were born to take responsibility, and others will ask you for support and protection. Your lasting success depends upon building from the ground up regardless of the kind of work you undertake. Or, at least you must strive for tangible results and give plans form and body. "Haste makes waste" in your affairs and carelessness can be your undoing. Any change or new plan must lead to better order, management and security. You were destined from birth to stand for the principles of honesty, sincerity, patience, perseverance, determination and faith. Keep these for your plan of life and your work will live after you.

FIELD OF OPPORTUNITY

There will be times when you will need to broaden your opportunities. At such times, investigate undertakings which have to do with buying, selling, exchange, building, engineering, regulation of ceremonies, education, administration, employment, and the maintaining of established order and system. Even if you deal with religion or abstract ideas, you must see that they are organized for others to use. Your own success depends upon your ability to establish system and order in your undertakings. Mix with people who are doing practical but worthwhile things. You can make lasting and helpful friends among scientists, organizers, lawyers, and promoters of the standards of living. Do not be careless in the selection of friends. Morals are part of your charm and attraction in friendships; try for a feeling of unity with all people. This will add to your success and popularity. Problems through relatives may come into your life and you may have to take a stand for your own rights. Do not be contrary; be willing to help them, but build your life after the pattern you feel is security for yourself and opportunity for your talents. You must be a strong character.

NUMBER FIVE DESTINY

Life will bring you many experiences and a good many changes, some of them forced upon you, others of your own making. You may find it hard to associate yourself permanently with the same people, work or undertaking, even though you may want to, for your mission in life is to promote "Freedom" and "Progress," and to keep Life moving forward. All progress comes through change, new ideas, new methods and renewal, and only by letting go of the old, can the new be realized. You must learn this lesson, for you came into the world to be one of those who stand for liberty for all as well as for the few. You must help people learn to live more fully and happily, and to know for yourself that lasting happiness cannot exist when the right to be free is not fully guaranteed. If your life is not free, cultivate the resourcefulness and versatility which is in your makeup and use your cleverness to keep up-to-date and in the stream of world progress. When changes come unexpectedly, do not fear them or cling to the old. Accept the new and make it a stepping stone to growth and greater attainment. To be free does not mean to break conventions deliberately. Progress is not rebellion. Instead, it stands for enlightenment, courage, ambition and willingness to learn. Keep your face turned towards the light and the best there is in the world. Refuse to be left behind in the race. Be a lawmaker, but combine charity and tolerance with instruction.

FIELD OF OPPORTUNITY

Your Destiny is a public one and you will find opportunity through people in general. You are likely to have more than one iron in the fire and must guard against scattering your energies. But you could lose your goal if not given frequent opportunity for exciting and interesting worldly contact. Broaden your life by going among people of all kinds, both religious and Bohemian. Mix with people who promote new lines of education and thought. Enter into the social activities of the public. Go among people who write, such as columnists, newspaper writers. The legal profession gives you opportunity and helpful friends. Publicity, advertising, and all fields of selling and public entertainment give you interest and development. Don't be a rolling stone gathering no moss, but be a part of what is going on in the world.

NUMBER SIX DESTINY

Service to the world is your Destiny. You are the "humanitarian" and it is your mission in life to comfort the suffering, weak, and unhappy. Duty will follow you down life's pathway, at home and out in the world, but your success and personal happiness depend upon how much good you can do, and upon the love and sympathy you have to give to those who need it or ask for help. You should not sacrifice your life for duty, for the world looks to you to maintain its ideals of charity, service, truth, and justice. You have an artistic Destiny too, and part of your life's work is to beautify this old world of ours. Harmony, beauty, and the ideals of love and companionship must be incorporated into everything you do if you wish to get the reward of honor which your name destines you to. Flowers, gardens, homes, nature, and mankind should spring into beauty at your touch. You must keep the Golden Rule of truth and justice before the minds and hearts of people, for you are a teacher too. Your ability to help the race is very definite and sincere, and you will be called upon to do so even though you might try to avoid it. Don't compromise with your ideals at any time. Give a helping hand when trouble knocks at another's door. Then in surprising ways, you will find yourself surrounded by love, luxury, and comfort, and a happy home life will crown your effort.

FIELD OF OPPORTUNITY

Because of your ideals and your ability to serve humanity, you should join with those who are working along the same lines. Religious activities, welfare work, all lines of race education, especially those dealing with children and the helpless give you interest and open a field of usefulness. Nurses, doctors, musicians, actors, singers, poets, and dreamers should be among your friends. Activities which have to do with art, flowers, music, gardens, furniture, interior decorating, radio, theatre, building of homes, and along the lines of literature awaken your own talents. Farmers, ranchers, horticulturists, miners, engineers should be on your list of acquaintances of those you can help and who can help you. You have a good earning capacity and if you find yourself without money, or drudging for others, it is because you have not been generous enough in your desires for the good of others or have failed to serve when called upon. In seeking opportunity wear becoming shades of orange, henna, scarlet, or heliotrope.

Number Seven Destiny

You are destined to be one of the "educators" of the world. You must study, prove, test, and make sure of facts, until you can write, teach, or demonstrate your knowledge to your fellow man. Your life should be an interesting one, for your search after knowledge will bring you many experiences and unusual associations, to teach you to discriminate between that which is true and false. You have been destined to discover, uncover, and understand the mysteries of life, to delve into the hidden, scientific, and occult. You may even be called strange, different, or hard to understand. You may often feel that you are alone, even in the midst of people, until you learn to live by your own soul's grace and not to depend upon the support or sympathy of others. It is your destiny to live by the realities of life and not by superficial standards; when you realize this, you will not be alone, for the world will then beat a path to your door for counsel, advice, and learning and to bask in the calm and certainty of your life. The affairs of your business, and even of marriage, may go to pieces, if you live too intensely in emotion and sentiment. Remember, you are the educator and you cannot take the easy pathway. It is through knowledge, science, skill, and wisdom that you take your place in the world. You may be out of the common class, but you will be loved and respected for what you have attained and know.

FIELD OF OPPORTUNITY

There will be times when you will need to broaden your opportunities. Travel, go into out-of-the-way places. Mix with people who are the thinkers of the world, such as scientists, investigators, historians, inventors, chemists, technicians, and those who are mathematically and analytically inclined. Writers, radio artists and technicians, lawyers, surgeons, and those who have specialized in work give you interest and can help you. Study religion and the sciences of being. Do research work as a hobby. Criminology, secret service, and the more subtle lines of endeavor will broaden your mind and help you understand life. The realm of scientific art should interest you and you could become the connoisseur of art, literature, and antiques. Invite to your home those who have brains. Make your home high-class and selective, but warm and helpful to all who seek knowledge and earnestly try to bring science and occult principles of knowledge to bear upon human experience.

NUMBER EIGHT DESTINY

You have a dynamic Destiny, giving you the right to position, authority, money, and recognition in the world. Your pathway will not be an easy one and your success will come through "knowledge of life and its spiritual relationships," as well as through financial effort and determination. Your reward will not always be in money, but in accomplishment; you must work for the love of doing things and find more satisfaction in the good work than in personal reward. To make money your chief ambition could mean to court failure and downfall from which it would be hard to recover. Money will come when you have learned to strike a balance between the material and spiritual forces of being and to work for the good of all concerned, rather than for yourself alone. You may be compelled to repeat your efforts again and again to reach your goal, but only until you fully realize that all attainment is based on the law of cause and effect, and not on chance or luck. Your lasting reward will come through your own efforts, strength of character, and mastery over self. Do not waste your energies struggling for wealth. Do something worthwhile, regardless of financial return. Train your mind to philosophical thought and always try to be an unprejudiced judge of the affairs of others. Manage and direct your activities with efficiency and meet emergencies with courage, and you will be pleased to discover that you are an outstanding and successful character in the community before you leave this old world of ours.

FIELD OF OPPORTUNITY

When seeking to enlarge your field of opportunity, join with people who are interested in civic affairs and the government. People who travel and get into out-of-way places should stimulate your mind. Writers, literary people, printers and publishers, correspondents should be your friends, and you may discover you can write too, if you want to. Take an interest in sports, games, and the general amusements of the public. Philosophical, mystical, and religious lines of thought should be studied for your mental growth. Big business men, who deal with large undertakings and control the affairs of the business world, should be among your friends and can help you develop your own talents for coaching, educating, and directing the affairs of mankind. Wear becoming shades of opal, canary, tan, or ivory, when seeking new opportunity.

NUMBER NINE DESTINY

You came into the world to stand for all that is fine, philanthropic, charitable, and beautiful. Music, art, romance, drama, color, ideality, and perfection should be the standards of your life, and even the most ordinary undertaking must be changed from the commonplace into the lovely, by your presence, thought, and ways of doing things. Your opportunities in life are so many, so all-embracing, and life will give you so many gifts, that in order to keep them for yourself, you must represent all that is fine, true and generous to the world. Love, tolerance, compassion, understanding, and generosity are the keynotes to your success and happiness. You may meet many experiences and tests; might even seem to fail, until you learn to express forgiveness for one and all. All that you desire in love and companionship will come to you when you learn that true love is service to the many rather than to the one. To cling to personal love, possessions, and power too tenaciously might be to lose all; but when you express love as a Divine Law, you will then receive greater love than you have ever dreamed of. There is a tremendous power wrapped up in your nature which you can turn on to warm the hearts of humanity and to awaken them to beauty, when you live true to your Destiny of love, service, and the brotherhood of man. Dramatize life—not the sorrowful, but the beautiful. This will put you in command of the best the world has to offer.

FIELD OF OPPORTUNITY

There will be times when you will need to increase your opportunities and to reach out into broader fields of endeavor. There is no real limitation of place or opportunity for you unless you make it so by careless living. People in all walks of life will help you and you can help them when you train your mind to universal thought. Physicians, lawyers, writers, artists, painters, orators, ambassadors and religionists should be among your friends; even those in the lower walks of life should know your generosity. Men and women in all walks of life will help and admire you as you give the dynamic force of your being to constructive opportunity. Do not allow popularity to go to your head at any time. Always be impersonal, for habit, weakness of purpose, or a too worldly life could cause you to miss the thrill of taking a hand in molding the hearts and minds of humanity. Make the expression of your personality colorful. Do not be drab or colorless in your dress or environment.

LET'S TALK IT OVER

It may seem to you that an overemphasis is placed on the name at birth. During my many years of teaching and counseling, I have read the names of men and women of all ages and in all walks of life. In every case, the true life-story was in the name given when the person was born.

A sweet elderly lady, 72 years old, came for consultation and asked me, shyly, if I could tell if she would live much longer. She said she had a little money left and if she was going to die soon she would spend it in a sort of final fling. If she had many more years to live, she would go on living quietly.

She was hoping, eagerly, that her time was short. Looking over her chart of experiences (which you will learn to use later) no radical change was shown, so I advised her to go on living quietly and to enjoy each day—glad that she was alive. You are wondering if I would have told her she was going to die, had I seen a crisis in her affairs. No! I would not; the time of death is in the hands of the Most High. It is not for me or any counselor to say. Our duty is to show people how to *live* and how to meet a crisis successfully and graciously. I told her of her Destiny and encouraged her to seek opportunity to help others.

Another woman, 65 years old, found herself in the midst of a thrilling but disturbing love affair. She wondered how this could happen to her, at her age. Her chart of experience definitely indicated the romance, timed for her at 65 years of age. Being a sensible woman, she freed herself from the attachment, but it left its mark. Telling her of her Destiny and its spiritual purpose helped her pull through.

A stepfather planning to legally adopt his wife's eleven-year-old son asked me to arrange a new name for the boy. When the name was finally decided upon, I told them to take good care of the boy's health as he neared his 14th birthday, as his birth name indicated a trying experience at that time but would be softened by his new name. At the age of fourteen a boyhood friend accidentally shot him, leaving a physical handicap. He has become a very successful man through the talents shown in his *name at birth* and the assistance of his new name.

All these cases and many more support the need of reading the *name at birth* (not any other name) if the true life-story is to be found. The blueprint of our lives and of what the future holds never changes, even to the end of life. All other names support or possibly detract from its fulfillment.

In cases where an adopted name was given after the birth of the child—if a name was given previously by the real parent or parents, even for a few hours, this must be considered for finding the Destiny. I, personally, figure the two charts, comparing the two names year by year. It is truly surprising how often the experiences are similar, showing the adopted name to be a support, but not an entirely new way of life. There is desire in the heart of every person who has been adopted to know his or her real name, as there is a slight feeling of insecurity from not knowing, even though successful and happy under the adopted home. This is the soul's spiritual determination to be true to itself. If records have been lost and the birth name is not known, this should not be a real problem, for the true life's purpose of the Destiny still runs through the adopted name and will gradually take over as life moves forward.

The use of an initial alone is a problem in reading names. Men, especially, use the initial of a middle name, sometimes for business reasons, or to hide a much disliked middle name. With a bit of probing this name will be revealed. In other cases men, sometimes women, use only initials for the first and second name, and claim they have no relationship to any name. They may say they just like the initials. These names cannot be read—at least I never try—but as much advice as possible is given from the month and day and year of birth. In every case, however, there is a subconscious relationship to the name behind the initial not acknowledged by the individual. One of our presidents used only a middle initial, claiming it did not represent any name. Later, however, it was revealed that back in the family there was a relative with the name which the initial represented.

There are a few laughs too. When I asked a woman for her name at birth, she answered me in disgust, saying she had been married so many times, she could not even remember her maiden name. Another client, a young struggling actress, had set her heart on playing opposite the leading movie actor of the time. She did not want me to know his name and asked me to read from the numbers she had written out. I told her I would know from the numbers, but she felt I would not be able to decipher it. She felt they had much in common and wanted it confirmed by Numerology. Talking pictures came in soon after and he went down and out, so her dream was not fulfilled. Letters and numbers are one and the same thing. Read this name: 3819351—(Charles).

Look back over your life. Did you live up to your *Destiny* during the times of stress or uncertainty? Every time you live true to your Destiny you build for the future and greater opportunity.

CHAPTER IV

THE BIRTH FORCE
Your Character and Natural Abilities

Many books have been written on "How to Be Successful."

The fear of being a square peg in a round hole is often lying low in the minds of even responsible men and women. To be assured of one's future in the business world—right from the start—is a dream almost too good to be believed in. This can happen for you, and right now. There is a way.

On the day you were born, a record of what you are like, what you have to depend upon to make your way in the world, your talents, abilities, your character, and your heritage from the past are outlined and transcribed by the numbers of the month, day, and year of your birth. Had your parents read this record and valued it, much uncertainty and anxiety could have been saved. They could have known exactly how to train, guide and direct you to your ultimate goal, wisely and with fine understanding. There could have been no hit-or-miss training.

THE BIRTH FORCE

The sum of the month, day, and year you were born is called the *Birth Force*. It is a positive vocational indication. It tells you what you are really like, what you are fitted to do, naturally and even without training. It is a source of power and energy to be depended upon and to be drawn upon as you go forth to meet the responsibility of your *Destiny* as shown by your name given at birth. It is what you *are* or *have*. It is read "you *are*" in contrast to the Destiny—"you *must* be."

There are many Johns, Marys, and Williams in all walks of life. They have some characteristics in common, but differ in talent, capabilities, and personal inclinations. A father and son may have the same name and still be very unlike in strength of character, even though working out the same Destiny. A different Birth Force number accounts for this.

The Birth Force and the Destiny may be compared to a man going into business but not yet established in trade. The *Birth Force* represents the stock on hand and the *Destiny* the business to be established. The numbers found on the Birth Force and Destiny, even though very different in meaning and purpose, work together at all times and belong together.

Have confidence in yourself and your natural abilities, and then move forward to do the work of your Destiny, whatever it may be. The feeling of insecurity which hangs over so many people will not be yours when you know yourself and dare to be what you were born to be.

The rule for figuring the Birth Force is simple.

Rule:

Add the numbers of the month, day, and year you were born and reduce to a single digit. Use the calendar order for the number of the month.

January	1	July	7
February	2	August	8
March	3	September	9
April	4	October (10) or	1
May	5	November (11) or	2
June	6	December (12) or	3

Example:

December   18th   1950
(12)3   +   9   +   (15)6 equals (18) = 9

December is the 12th month having the influence of the 3.
The 18th day reduces to 9.
The year 1950 added together reduces to 15 or 6.
The three digits added together equal 18.
Add again and the final sum is 9, the Birth Force.

Find your *Birth Force* from the following outline.

Number One Birth Force

TYPE

You are the leader type, strongly individualized, and demand the right to think and act according to your own ideas and convictions. You have a keen perception, good concentration, ability to get ahead, to direct and lead others and to establish your own business if you desire. You have executive ability, will power, courage, and are quite capable of overcoming any barrier to your success when you make use of your creative ideas. You are, or should be, selective in friendships, and have quite a sense of humor. You love the nice things of life and are sensitive to your environment and to what others think of you. Life should never be dull for you if you make the best of your initiative, executive ability and original ideas, for you have strong powers of attraction which will lead you into interesting work and experiences. Broad vision, magnetic force, and inspiration enable you to carry out your plans in a big way and for financial reward.

The negative side of your character is shown in the following ways, and you should keep this side under control; use your strong will and determination to avoid intensifying these qualities or allowing them to become "set" or "fixed" habits:

dominance; egotism; bossy manner; impatience with the opinions of others; over-confidence in yourself, or "knowing it all"; refusal to take advice or to be told; selfishness through too much interest in your own plans; and, at times, vacillation and indecision—all are to be avoided.

VOCATION

You have unlimited opportunity through active mental interests and undertakings. You can be very successful through developing new projects, for these bring out your initiative, originality and executive ability. New places, new situations, original and unique ideas are better than old and bring out your latent powers of invention, promotion, origination, designing, illustration, writing, and speaking. Governmental activities, engineering, mining, business of credit, bookstores, art and antique shops, health matters as well as the field of medicine and surgery are open to you. You could work as the head of departments, or as director and leader of creative industry, and in lines of business having to do with maintenance of social position; also the field of amusement and entertainment is your scope of activity, for you have a sense of humor and enjoy wit and comedy. Schools and colleges may claim your interest, and all types of business which are outside the established order of things.

Wear flame, lilac, copper, or apricot for a touch of color while you work.

Number Two Birth Force

TYPE

You are the diplomatic type, naturally sensitive, cooperative and considerate of others. There is a gentle side to your character and it is this which makes you more persuasive than forceful. You are a good mixer, able to influence others and to win them over to your way of thinking, especially when you realize the power there is in your quiet way. Your success depends very much on your ability to help others get what they want, rather than to be too selfish or self-interested. This is due to a spiritual quality in your make-up and you should not fail to value this even in business, for it is your peacemaking qualities rather than your attempts to dominate which win for you. Your natural sensitiveness when rightly directed becomes sincerity, graciousness, and esthetic feeling, and you should try to live according to high standards of culture and refinement. Your sympathetic feeling and consideration of others, ability to analyze, to be accurate and detailed, are fine business assets. An ability to associate with others, bringing people together for a common cause, is an attractive part of your nature.

There are a few faults in your make-up too. Sensitiveness could become a fault, making you negative, fearful, timid, and fretful, instead of strong and courageous even in a quiet way. Now and then you are uncertain, finding it hard to decide what to do for fear of being wrong, for you are naturally conscientious and want to do the right thing. Your accuracy makes you dislike mistakes, and you often hesitate for fear you may not do as well as you would like to. You should overcome this. Do the best you can at all times and gradually you will perfect your talents and make a success in the world. Even though you are courteous and kind, you can be surprisingly blunt in speech and exacting in your demands, expressing a great deal of nervous energy. You are something of the extremist too, strong in your likes and dislikes, and there is a touch of the reformer in your character. If you will cultivate the people who stand for the best in life, share what you have with others and then make use of your talent for doing things well, you will climb the ladder and stay at the top.

VOCATION

Opportunity comes through fine machinery and delicate instruments. Success may come through dancing, music, painting, literature, violin, harp, and other finer musical instruments. The ministry, religious activities, medicine, politics, and all lines of administration are open to you; also banking, as treasurer, teller, paymaster, accountant; and activities dealing with finance and money; radio, electricity, sending of messages, technical and mechanical pursuits; gathering of statistics, collecting art works, tapestries, papers, pieces of money; success through endeavor having to do with travel, liquids, and the moving public. Wear gold, salmon, garnet, or cinnamon while you work.

NUMBER THREE BIRTH FORCE

TYPE

You are the creative type, possessing a good imagination, power of inspiration, and deep emotional feeling. No matter how practical you may think you are, or try to be, you will find much of your success dependent upon the "vision" and creative imagination you add to your undertakings. You have the gift of words as a natural asset and this ability to express yourself in words, the gift of "gab," is a financial possibility. Socially, your ability to talk, entertain, and inspire others is the open door to friendship and social standing. However, you can talk too much and at the wrong time when you allow your emotions to get the best of you, so keep a guard on your speech and make it a vocation, not a scattering force. Your natural tendency to be obliging, to help those who are weak, and a cheerful, happy disposition are financial assets. You are capable of reaching great heights of attainment, even performing deeds of valor, when you live up to that inner feeling of power which comes to you at times. You like to do things on a large scale and have the intuition, or "hunch," which tells you what to do. This will always help you, but there may be times when you become too optimistic, scattering your forces and your money, thus failing when you should succeed. You should try to understand your own ambitions and carry them out, but avoid going too far or letting emotion get the best of you.

There is a reticent side to your character too, for you are very sensitive and can withdraw into a shell of silence when you are criticized or hurt. Now and then, too, you can be very critical of others and tell them of their mistakes or unconsciously become selfish and self-centered, causing problems in your love affairs. At other times you can be easygoing, seeming to lack in will, or to be too fond of ease and luxury. But you have the ability to supply yourself with the best there is in life when you use your creative powers successfully and can change your luck any time you put your imagination to work. You can be a very pleasing companion, admired by the opposite sex, and you are capable of enjoying life. You have splendid powers of attraction and if you are not getting the best out of life, it is your own fault, for you are unusually endowed with talent.

VOCATION

You may succeed in all artistic lines, both in business and in the professions, art stores, clothing, millinery, department stores, jewelry, candy, foods; all lines of entertainment, dancing, music, writing, and acting; stocks and bonds, printing, publishing, libraries, designing, illustration, drama, religious activities, and psychic pursuits; success in all lines of activity where feeling and emotion have financial value, and in making dreams come true.

Wear ruby, gold, amber, or russet while you work.

NUMBER FOUR BIRTH FORCE

TYPE

You are a practical type. You like to know just what you are doing and why, and do not take a chance unless you are sure. You are rather serious and quite fixed in your way, but are naturally honest, sincere and conscientious. You have a strong sense of what is right, and even though you are strong in your likes and dislikes, you have a natural friendliness, combined with a sense of dignity and self-importance. You like to feel sure, to have a nest egg, and have a very good sense of practical values which, if you cultivate it, will help you in the business world. You like to have a plan and are patient about the details when you can take time to work them out accurately and carefully. There is a fine ability too, in your make-up, to manage, systematize, and to establish order and routine. You like to have things done well and can be exacting about the details of personal items, sometimes neglecting the bigger things for the smaller details, even in business.

You are approachable in personality and in business are capable of helping everyone. At the same time you are rather selective in your personal friendships and associations. You are naturally careful with your possessions, competent, and a good manager, and have the ability to inspire confidence, for you are not easily carried away by fancies or fads and extravagant undertakings. You like the best in life, and are a good spender, but you can be very careful about money and demand return for value given. You are capable of working hard and show tenacity and perseverance when your mind is made up; and a few hard knocks are good for you as they bring out your natural courage, powers of concentration, honesty, and your good nature. You seem to do better when you have a hard problem than when things are too easy. Now and then you can be a little exacting, even a little bossy and dominant, and like to give orders rather than take them; and you may argue or be a little bit contrary when you do not have your own way; so watch out for this as it can make difficulties for you. But value your fine powers of management and of constructive endeavor, and these will take you far in the business world.

VOCATION

Number *Four* may find success through building, contracting, organization, and bringing plans into concrete form; success through buying and selling, administration, soliciting, hiring, employment, regulation of ceremonies, and management of well established business; success through scientific interests, educational matters, promoting campaigns, and in all lines of endeavor having to do with documents, papers, contracts, examination, legal activities, lending or exchange, and concerning property and real estate; store keeper, dealing with commodities, repairing, and supplying the public with its daily needs in practical necessities. Number *Four* is not good in "get rich quick" schemes, but in work that has background.

Wear green, silver, emerald, coffee or maroon while at work.

NUMBER FIVE BIRTH FORCE

TYPE

You are the independent type. You like your freedom and have a natural interest in what is going on in the world and are at your best when you can have more than one iron in the fire. You are an active individual, sometimes restless and impatient if things move along too slowly, or you have to do the same thing over and over too long at a time. You are versatile and clever, having natural resourcefulness and so much enthusiasm, that things do not stay the same for long where you are. You can keep things moving and are a rapid, quick thinker, charged with imagination and gift of words; you add pep and speed to whatever you undertake. This is one of your attributes of business success. Sometimes an inner restlessness causes you to act hastily and to burn your bridges behind you when you should have left them standing to cross over again. You can become discontented easily and change too readily for your own good when you allow the love of freedom and change to become too strong. You should seek the opportunity to travel, see the world, and to know life; but you should not be the rolling stone which gathers no moss.

You may be accused of lacking in application, because you like change and variety. It is true you do not like to spend unnecessary time getting things done, but your versatility and quick thinking give you power and authority in all progressive activities and lines of business. You can be bold and invincible when aroused to action and will challenge any obstacles in your way.

You can be very analytical too, sometimes unsympathetic,

and like to stir things up when expressing the negative side of your character; but the better side of your nature is charitable and helpful. Even though you are freedom-loving, you like to see the "law" fulfilled and do not lack stability. Without you the world could grow dull and get too fixed in its way for real progress. Many experiences will come to you in life. Extract the value from them and build your success upon the knowledge you have gained from much living and contact with all kinds of people.

VOCATION

The number *Five* may have opportunity through dealing with the public and its love of change and variety; opportunity through business which caters to the public's desire for life, travel and excitement; advertising, publicity, selling, newspapers, business of exchange, investment, and promotion, and all lines of work which call for energizing power rather than routine; legal matters, civil service, drawing up of contracts, transfers, distribution of material, law, politics, column and story writing, and the field of amusement; opportunity through mysteries, the occult and the unusual, scientific study and analysis.

Wear claret, wisteria, or strawberry while working.

NUMBER SIX BIRTH FORCE

TYPE

You are the humanitarian type and are capable of serving mankind and of doing worthwhile things in life. You are an idealist too, and have many strong opinions about what is right and wrong and cling tenaciously to your ideals of truth and justice. You are generous, kind, and sympathetic and have a loving, appreciative nature; much of your success in life, both in business and marriage, will come through the kindly, helpful, and protective things you do for others. Responsibility is the keynote to your activities, for your ability to do things in a big way and a natural tendency to serve and teach will keep you busy and help you attract money, love and admiration. Many will impose upon your good nature and take advantage of your generosity, even your family and loved ones; but as long as you do not become personal and resentful, but keep on serving humanity, you will always have money and opportunity in the world. Sometimes you give too much and sacrifice yourself for others, going to extremes because you love to help; and this must be guarded against, for it may cause unnecessary loss and emotional unhappiness. You are fond of your home, family, and relatives, have an artistic nature, love beauty, harmony, flowers, music, and the luxuries and comforts of life.

You should establish an artistic and harmonious environment. You need the same love and sympathy for your best growth which you give to others, and a chance to live an idealistic life. You are more controlled by your feelings than you care to acknowledge, so when you are not happy or appreciated you can become surprisingly stubborn, unreasonable, and unhappy and feel like giving everything up. And too, you can become dominant, exacting, and fussy. Don't be like that. You are too fine a character. Keep on giving and helping others, but sensibly, for after all, you are the one who serves, comforts, and teaches the race.

VOCATION

Business opportunity and luck come through lines of endeavor which serve humanity and make life more comfortable, easy, and luxurious. Doctor, nurse, teacher, rancher, cook, minister, welfare worker, restaurants, furniture stores, schools, select apartment houses, family hotels, and all commercial and industrial pursuits which combine art, comfort, and beauty, are in your life scope; fine opportunity through teaching and training children; animals and flowers give financial attraction; also interior decorating, gardens, pottery, and commercial art; possibilities as singer, story teller, and painter; boats, irrigation, ships, engineering, mines, horticulture, livestock; religious activities and all lines of reform and education. Should you find yourself drudging and lacking money you are wrong somewhere, or have forgotten to be generous, for you belong to those who should make money and have the comforts of life.

Wear orange, henna, scarlet, or heliotrope while you work.

NUMBER SEVEN BIRTH FORCE

TYPE

You are the scientific and thinking type. You have an observing nature and an analytical mind. It is not natural for you to accept things at their face value for you have a natural ability to relate facts, put two and two together, to size up situations and conditions from a technical and scientific standpoint. This is part of your financial success and gives you unusual opportunity if you use it well. You have a high type of mind, combined with an intuitive feeling and an ability to understand the hidden and non-apparent facts, making you a developer, discoverer, inventor, and specialist. Knowledge is power in your life, and the more you know, the farther you will go.

You are naturally reserved, thoughtful, silent, and selective, and while you like people and like to be with them, you do not care for the common crowd and select your friends and environment with respect for dignity and pride. However, when you are on your own ground and feel familiar and at home, you can talk well and interestingly. You have an inner magnetism which is an inspiration to others and a drawing card, both in business and friendship.

You are not a truly adaptable person and are averse to being asked questions outright, although you ask many and demand proof, making you seem to be a doubter, or cold and hard. This side of your character can make you difficult to understand and you may hardly understand yourself at times, but when you take time to listen to your inner guidance, you have nothing to fear at any time. You often need to be alone, to get close to nature, to think and read, for you gain your composure in this way and discover your true self, which makes you a most attractive and successful character. You are something of the stoic too, for too much emotion strips you of your power. Many times during your lifetime you will have to depend entirely upon your own ability and soul force; but just have confidence in your inner magnetism, your clear thinking mind, your technical and mathematical ability, and you will be called from the background into the luck you deserve.

VOCATION

All lines of business which call for calculation, analysis, fine deduction, scientific knowledge and technical ability; insurance, mathematical pursuits, chemistry, dietetics, history, research, criminal investigation and all business requiring skill and specialized ability; educational matters, technical and scientific art, medicine, law, engineering, invention, literary activities, laboratory and statistical interests, radio and cinema—are in your scope. The occult, mystical, and mysterious give opportunity; also music, pipe organs, and musical instruments; ability to do fine work with your hands, carving, etchings, and making of delicate objects of art and science; bookkeeping and accounting.

Wear purple, brick, or pearl while working.

NUMBER EIGHT BIRTH FORCE

TYPE

You are the executive type and have splendid powers of organization, placing you among those who organize, coach, supervise, direct, and govern affairs, at home and out in the world. You are capable of taking charge of things and are ambitious, energetic, efficient, and capable of judging people and situations with a fair mind. These talents should give you authority, recognition, position and power in the social, professional and business world. You have a natural ability to judge character, a philosophical turn of mind, and wonderful powers of self-control; you have the courage and energy to repeat your efforts until you reach your goal. You should be at the head of large undertakings and business and professional activities, for a small, narrow, routine life does not bring out your strength and efficiency. In fact, an emergency or need does much to bring out your real character and force of initiative. Your success in life comes from working for a goal or purpose through organizing work, endeavor, and plans helpful to many people. You are not exactly the humanitarian, but you do have the ability to inspire others to greater effort and to do things for yourself and the world in a spectacular and valuable manner.

There is a very fine side to your character, capable of mastering the hardest problems, through a faith in spiritual and philosophical law. Another side is often commercial, material in thought and interested only in financial gain. Your best success comes, however, as you strike a balance between these two, to give you the wise judgment which Life demands of you. Sometimes you strain, strive, think too much of money, and use so much energy doing things that you wear yourself out, driving love and business away instead of attracting them. Don't strive so hard. Just make sure your judgment is good and take time to do things well; then your natural executive ability will take you to the top. This judgment is the keynote to your position and authority and should place you at the head of business and broad professional enterprise.

VOCATION

The *Eight* finds success along any line of work demanding organization; opportunity through printing, publishing, correspondence, editing, exploring, civil government, supervising, coaching and regulating general business and finance; real estate, property, selling, exchange, games, sports, athletic activities, archaeology, drama, music, pipe organ, intelligence service, nurse, care of mental hospitals and institutions—for your abilities cover a wide scope; character analyst, judge, lawyer, historian, writer, and good in all lines of governmental activity, statistical and research departments, efficiency expert.

Wear opal, canary, or tan while you work.

NUMBER NINE BIRTH FORCE

TYPE

You are the philanthropic type. You have a deep feeling for mankind, sensing the heights and depths of life and the glory of existence. You are not always able to live in this high state of consciousness, but you do color your affairs with dramatic feeling. Your disposition is compassionate, generous, sympathetic, and tolerant, and you have a wide range of feeling, a sensitive nature, and a very vivid imagination. When you express your natural compassion you are capable of doing interesting and lasting work in the world, including art, philanthropy, religion, and business. You are impressionable and broadminded and eager to take on the responsibilities of life but sometimes meet disappointment because you do not find the perfection you seek in others or in yourself. You must rise above these disappointments and keep your generosity of purpose; and try to realize that perfection must be earned and cannot be reached all at once. Help others, counsel them and inspire them; but don't give to the point of weakness, for this only delays you and keeps you from doing the universal work which your talents permit.

You are idealistic, romantic, have a striking personal magnetism and a marvelous power to influence others for good or bad. You love deeply and passionately, and true love will remain with you always as you are more broadminded, tolerant, and compassionate than the ones you love. With all your beauty of character at times you can be strangely uncertain, timid, vacillating, even moody, and show weakness of character, because you cannot reach your ideal or attain the perfection you so deeply realize. But don't be that way. You have such marvelous power to turn the unlovely into the attractive, the worthless into the beautiful, to rebuild humanity and to promote civilization, that if you follow this goal, your success will be beyond your expectations.

VOCATION

Opportunity comes to the *Nine* along all dramatic, artistic and emotional lines of business; stage, literature, movies, education; dealing with foods, health matters, and lines of business which have to do with the broader phases of living; through travel, foreign people, or governmental activities and business dealing with and including many people; in ability to employ, place, train people and place them for success; in ability to beautify land, homes, property, and environment; as lawyer, teacher, physician; through mechanical arts and through use of knowledge of color, painting, designing. Religious and charitable activities give financial gain.

Wear much color while at work, especially pastel shades.

LET'S TALK IT OVER

During many quiet and confidential talks with my clients —they have told me of unusual and strange experiences, frequently occult or flashes of a spiritual nature—they have asked the questions: "What does this mean?" "Do you think I am an old soul?" These questions have been asked by intelligent people reaching out for the Truth of Life, and by those who have gone through the "long dark night of the soul" and the agony of losing everything held dear.

I have listened to love stories so strange and of such intensity, sometimes with such deep suffering, it has seemed these lovers must have been together before or have known each other in some distant lifetimes. "They have loved beyond the world."

Years of study and research have not shown me any method by which it is possible to tell, as a rule, if anyone is an old soul. We are all souls, divinely created, on a cosmic journey—some younger, some older—learning lessons according to our needs. However, as the date of birth of the newborn babe is known before the name is given, and never changes, to me it tells the story of attainment, character, talent, and capabilities built up in past lifetimes. It is like a report card—a cosmic report card—much in the same way a student, entering a new grade in school, presents his record and standing in past grades. The birth force may or may not tell the full story of previous attainment, but it relates what the soul brought in to support it in its new experience during the present lifetime. The Birth Force is *not* a *new lesson* to be learned: It is the needed support for accomplishing the new undertaking and experience shown by the Destiny Number. The two experiences work together to supply the necessary opportunities to reach the final and ultimate goal of this lifetime—the Reality Number.

There are times when I read names and study human nature and life's experiences that I feel a man or woman must be an old soul to have undertaken so much during one lifetime. I find, too, that in some intense love affairs both persons involved have the same Birth Force—love known in past lifetimes.

You now have two positions to read from. Analyze your own name and those of your family or business associates. Do not try to read beyond these two numbers at the present time. Only as you learn and understand these two can you become efficient in following the format of the following lessons.

CHAPTER V

THE HEART'S DESIRE
Your Secret Thoughts and Wishes

Perhaps, someone has said to you, "Why can't you think the way I do?" Instead of convincing you, the remark may have riled you to the point of wishing to do something entirely different.

If everyone thought and acted alike there would be no incentive to carry on—to create, to grow and develop; instead there would be complete boredom—no future, no progress, and no fun in living. The right to think and act according to one's own beliefs and concepts belongs to everyone. The right of constructive self-expression is a divine principle, man's link in the chain of divine activity. No one person, individual, sect, or regime has the right to prevent or destroy the urge within the soul for self-recognition and the right to live in tune with its own inner governing force and ideality. We are born free souls and must live and grow in ever increasing harmony and beauty from within; then we are true to our divine privileges and cannot be false to anyone.

The Heart's Desire is one of the most important numbers to be figured and analyzed. It is found from the letters a-e-i-o-u in the name at birth. It is read: You will *desire* to be or do—according to the number found there.

At times the urge of the Heart's Desire is so strong it subordinates all other traits of character, even those of the Destiny and Birth Force. Or again it will seem to lie dormant, repressed by circumstance until, suddenly awakened, it becomes active with startling force, changing all well-organized plans for work and success. Every person has this inner seed of yearning for self-expression. However, not all people hear the call of the soul's command or stop to listen to it, thus failing to gain from its life-giving energies.

The vowels in our names represent the "Celestial Harmonies."

At all times color your endeavor and Destiny with what your Heart's Desire number tells you. Make it part of your work and daily affairs; do not keep it separate from what you are doing day by day. Be true to your inner nature—described by the number there. This rounds out and beautifies your character.

If you are contemplating joining another in business or domestic relationships, make sure you know the inner nature of your associate or loved one. Even though you may have many things in common, at some time the inner nature of the other person (or your own) is bound to come to the surface. If you are not prepared, this may come as such a surprise as to cause many problems. Or it may bring deeper understanding and greater happiness.

Even though time and experience may seem to change a person greatly and circumstance mold the character, the nature of the Heart's Desire never changes; for somewhere, in the background, the urge of man's soul is quietly taking part in his affairs, interests, and desires.

By this time you should recognize that a number never changes its meaning. It expresses itself over and through the channel where it is found.

Always read the position first then the number found there. In this way you will analyze character with skill and meaning.

RULES FOR FIGURING

The Heart Number—sum of all the a's, e's, i's, o's, and u's in the name at birth.

Means—The inner urge. The individuality. The soul's longing. What the individual values most. Personal likes and dislikes. The ambition and incentive. Methods and ways of looking at things. The way the true character will be expressed.

It is read "You will *desire* to be or do."

In figuring the Heart Number use only the vowels: a, e, i, o, u. W and y are sometimes vowels, but are not correctly used in figuring the inner or soul urge. The Heart's Desire is found from the soft lip-sounds of song and harmony.

The w is a restless, difficult, and testing influence and not part of the inner nature.

The y is a crossroads, mystical, occult, wise, separate, and reserved, but very often stands for the unknown and what is to come. Its influence and power in the life of the individual or in your life is shown in the lesson *Points of Intensification.* It does not enter into the Heart's Desire. Some names have no other vowel but y. This indicates a spiritual development being made but not fully developed in this lifetime. Being a crossroads, the road to be taken must be selected.

Example:

6	+	1	+	(12) 3	= (10) 1 Heart's Desire
5	1	1		6 6	

F r e d a	M a y	N o r t o n	
6 9 5 4 1	4 1 7	5 6 9 2 6 5	
25	12	33	
7 +	3 +	6	= (16) 7 Destiny

December	19th	1940	
(12)	(10)	(14)	
3 +	1 +	5	= 9 Birth Force

From her Destiny (number 7) we find she came into the world to gain understanding: to delve into the secrets of Being and to educate others. Her Birth Number (9) reveals she is impressionable, artistic, generous, and filled with a desire to help mankind.

Still, we do not know what she is really like until we look into her heart and discover the number *One*. This gives a strong, courageous inner nature and ambition to be at the head of things. She will not accept a subordinate position over a long period. The number *One* gives her a desire to accomplish things in her own way, and from time to time she may show strong self-interests. But this is balanced by the philanthropic force of the number *Nine*. She will be strongly individualized due to the number *One* heart, but through training she can do splendid educational work and bring understanding and knowledge to many.

Figure the name of Henry Ford, born July 30, 1863. This will give you practice in synchronizing one position with another.

$$5 \quad + \quad 6 \qquad = (11) \ 2 \ \text{Heart's Desire}$$

H	e	n	r	y		F	o	r	d
8	5	5	9	7		6	6	9	4

$$\underline{34} \qquad\qquad \underline{25}$$

$$7 \quad + \quad 7 \qquad = (14) \ 5 \ \text{Destiny}$$

July   30th   1863

$$7 \quad + \quad 3 \quad + \quad 9 \qquad = (19) \ 1 \ \text{Birth Force}$$

Henry Ford had a Five Destiny. He was born to represent the new and to work for the public in some progressive way. He was destined to an eventful life, for the number *Five* does not like monotony and always brings changes, new ways, new contacts and many experiences. The watchword of the *Five* is Progress, and Mr. Ford definitely lived up to this. *Five* is often interested in transportation and travel, so he really fulfilled his

Destiny. Next we study his character and natural abilities for working out his Destiny. Having the *One* Birth Force, he had a strong character, positive, determined, with inventive ability, orginality of thought, feeling, and executive ability. Now we look into his heart and find the number (11) *Two*, just the opposite to his Birth Force. This revealed he was a man of gentle inner nature, shy and timid at times, very sensitive and not a forceful or dominant man at heart. He desired peace and harmony more than anything else, even though he had to make his way in the world of public competition. Also he was surprisingly dependent upon others and their good will, as the number (11) *Two* is the number of cooperation and partnerships.

At one time he outfitted a peace ship to go to Europe which did not turn out as he desired—perhaps because he depended too much upon others. His (11) Heart indicated his deep desire to help people and comfort them. He did this in a wonderful way—his Ford car.

Figure and read many names. Compare them. Read the names of well-known people, for this will help you make the relationships and realize how the main positions work together. Remember—there are no wrong names. Our names belong to us. We only need to learn how to live up to what we have and to follow the design of our lives, written in our names when we were born.

Find your Heart's Desire from the following outlines.

HEART'S DESIRE—NUMBER ONE

You are an independent character at heart, strongly individualized and courageous. You are ambitious too, and want to get on in the world, but by your own efforts and intelligence. You are not one to shirk your responsibilities, for you have much inner strength and determination, but you do like to feel independent and do things in your own way. You could never really be happy in a subordinate position. In fact, your ability would not allow you to remain there long, for there is too much inner power, determination, creative force and executive ability down deep in your heart to allow you to stay at the foot of the ladder of life. Should you find yourself remaining in such a position for some time, it would mean that you were not digging deep enough into your heart for the strength of character which is there. You have latent powers of executive ability, interesting and original ideas, and if you make use of them in a constructive manner, you will find you are making your way in the world with ease and satisfaction. The fulfillment of your Destiny depends a great deal upon the cultivation of this inner force of character and the innate strength and independence of your ambitions. But remember that in order to be the true leader, you must help others too and not think only of your own interests and desires. When you do this you will find others respecting and helping you; life will never hold a dull moment, but will open the way for outstanding position and opportunity.

There are possibilities of faults growing out of your inner will and determination. Now and then you can be headstrong, impulsive, willful; you do not like to be told to do things or to be bossed by those who are not in sympathy with your ideals or methods. This might make you appear contrary, or bossy, dominating and egotistical. This could lead to misunderstandings, unhappiness and quarrels at certain times in your life. You are not lacking in cooperation; in fact you often shrink from taking a stand or from doing the thing which will place you at the head of things, for fear of hurting others. You are reticent too and sometimes lack in self-confidence, except that something deep in your heart urges you forward. Stand for your rights, keep your self-confidence strong, be yourself, and maintain your pride in yourself and your accomplishments. But at the same time always express your ideas and plans with courtesy, graciousness, and sincerity, and then you will be a well-loved leader and character. At home, as well as out in the world, you feel your right to be recognized, or at the head of things; and you always will be as long as your nature is kind and generous.

So you see, there is much that is interesting in your

makeup; your pride, your sensitiveness, your moments of willfulness, impulse, and determination, combined with sudden reticence, shrinking, dependence, and wit are the things the one who loves you will see in you and admire. They are the lovely things about you and you should always keep them so.

Wear flame, copper, apricot, lilac, or shades of these colors when attracting love and friendship.

HEART'S DESIRE—NUMBER TWO

Deep in your heart there is sincerity, graciousness and consideration for others. You have an appreciation of the refinements of life, and when you are true to your inner nature you will express these qualities. Peace and harmony mean much to you and influence your actions in everything you do—business, studies and love affairs. You desire to obtain results harmoniously if possible; but you will fight if driven too far, although your tendency is toward persuasiveness rather than aggressiveness. Your almost unconscious urge for harmony may at times make you appear shrinking and even negative when you are really only trying to cooperate with others, or to avoid strife and disagreements. You do things for the sake of "peace" when you should not, and your gentleness and tendency to act in a non-resistant manner often make it difficult for you to stand up against a more willful or dominant person.

You are cooperative in your thoughts and actions; you love to share with others and to help those who are in need. You depend upon others too, even more than you care to admit, and you often fear to trust your own judgment. Consequently you often suffer periods of doubt and uncertainty, and sometimes are forced to subordinate yourself when you should be sharing equally with others. You have a natural dread of offending, but you should try to overcome this tendency to inner self-consciousness. It will make you unhappy and cause you to miss opportunities to use your talents and to carry out your Heart's Desire. Your gentle, sweet inner nature is your charm; quiet assurance, impersonal attitude, general friendliness, are your greatest assets; and if you will try to emphasize these traits, they will make you popular and help you win what you cannot force in life. Your sympathy and feeling for others make you appealing and attractive to the opposite sex, but it may result in many disappointments and problems until you learn to be self-determined and stand up for your own rights.

There is a spiritual quality in your make-up of which you may be unaware. From this quality springs your sensitiveness, love of beauty and culture as well as your gift of analysis and ability to understand the finer things of life. It causes you to shrink from everything coarse, crude and unlovely, but when you learn how to use this spiritual force, it will become a dynamic power, a magic key, enabling you to control and direct your affairs far more successfully than any material knowledge can give you. At times you may be indecisive and have difficulty in making up your mind. When you find yourself in this state, "snap out of it," and have more confidence in yourself. Forget your fears and worries and what others may think or say. Go after things in your own way, even though it may not be a forceful one. Appreciate the sincerity and cooperation in your nature. Transmute sensitiveness into artistic feeling and the refinements of life. Then you will be able to overcome the obstacles and problems of everyday life and get more "kick" out of existence. Your ability to "mix" should assist you in the business world, increase your Vocational assets and aid you in fulfilling your Destiny. Gentleness need not be vacillation or insincerity. Be true to your higher resolves. Share your success with others and you will find life very worthwhile.

People having the number *Two* at heart will be helpful and companionable. To attract sympathetic friends wear gold, salmon, garnet, cinnamon as part of your accessories.

HEART'S DESIRE—NUMBER THREE

You are something of a dreamer at heart. You would rather be happy than practical and have a strong desire to find the joy and romance in living. In fact, inspiration and imagination are your finest characteristics and when you learn how to use them intelligently they will be the means of your attaining the best that life has to offer. You love to do things grandly and on a large scale and like nice environment, protection, the comforts of life, and the elegance of living. But to what extent you realize these desires depends somewhat upon your Destiny and vocational talents. Should your artistic instinct and desire for self-expression in some happy, even fanciful, way be thwarted, you could become repressed, even unhappy or ill.

You love to talk and to express your opinions and ideas when you are with those you love and you will generally find yourself the center of activities because of your ability to liven things by your pleasant, friendly manner. You should specialize in making others happy. It is also true that there is a reticent side to your nature and you can shrink from the limelight and from becoming too conspicuous; and there is a tendency in your inner self to live in a world of feeling and emotion. You should try to express this emotion in some constructive manner —follow the dictates of your heart to create—and you will be easily successful in the world of finance and professional life. Sometimes you fret about small things and are inclined to be too exacting if things do not come up to the standard of perfection and loveliness you desire. You will do better in life if you follow your desire to do things on a large scale and do not try to hold yourself down to a limited scope of activity. Stick to your dreams and make them come true, but don't dream too much and fail to get down to earth.

Your natural urge is to be kind and obliging; you love to help those who are in trouble. You have a keen appreciation of friendship and your friends mean a great deal to you. You are capable of a deep love and of sacrificing yourself for those you love; and you want to have love and be loved. You see, you are a bit romantic at heart, as well as artistic and inspirational. You should be admired by both sexes when you remember to be reasonable in your demands and opinions; you can be a most entertaining and charming companion. You have so much ability to make others happy that you should never be alone or without love. Should you find yourself without admiration, it might be because you had unconsciously become self-centered or self-satisfied and so interested in your own affairs and activities that you had forgotten to think about the affairs of others; this could hurt those who love you and who are trying to help you. Now and then you talk too much and like to show off a little, but as long as you keep cheer, good will, and beauty in your heart, you will find no difficulty in carrying out your Destiny and working out your problems.

To win friends wear rose, ruby, amber, and gold as part of your accessories.

HEART'S DESIRE—NUMBER FOUR

You have a fine appreciation of law and order in your inner nature. When successfully used, this quality will be of value to you in the world of material success. You have a practical point of view and like to have affairs arranged with system and dispatch. You look at life in a wholesome way and you are very conscientious in your undertakings. You want things to be correct and "like they should be" and generally meet your problems seriously, in a matter-of-fact way. You like to look ahead, to plan carefully, and to apply yourself to your tasks with concentration and good management. Your Destiny and your Birth numbers may not give you the full opportunity to express this desire at all times, but you are happier when you can plan and lay a foundation of a permanent nature upon which to build your life. You can be very restless, unhappy, and inwardly disturbed when life is uncertain and lacking in security or when you have nothing to hold to, or for which to work.

In business, home, and love affairs, you are rather serious in thought and action. Your business or marriage partner should have a practical outlook too, because you want dreams to come true and desire real and tangible results. Loyalty, stability, dependability, mean much to you. You have many convictions and do not easily change your mind once it is made up. You are honest and sincere in your motives and have a fine inner determination. You can stick to things with tenacity and patience when you receive the right encouragement. Your ability to apply yourself to get things done enables you to overcome difficulties and to get definite results. Now and then you give too much time to details, for you like to have everything exact, correct, and just right. You may worry and fret if little things are not attended to. This conscientiousness is one of your good traits but if carried to extremes might be the cause of your missing some of life's larger opportunities. Greater happiness will come when you learn not to allow little things to count too much.

If I were to pick out a fault in your character, it would be an unconscious tendency on your part to take the opposite side of matters at the first approach. This is due to your desire to be right, to understand things, and to be sure. You may even argue and be hard to convince until you are sure. Friends and associates may accuse you of contrariness and slowness, but you really are not contrary. It is your inability to change your mind easily which makes you appear so. Plan your life according to your practical desires, but also put fun and inspiration into your undertakings, especially love affairs, so that you will find life more interesting. You should always follow your inclination to build and construct on all planes of life. Your soul urge is for constructive accomplishment which you can use to help humanity in many practical ways and also to make a success of your own life. Build your character and your life brick by brick and do not hurry. Take time to do things well and you will find your life built upon a rock of security, with success never failing you.

Wear blue, green, emerald, coffee, maroon, or silver in your accessories to attract friends.

Heart's Desire—Number Five

You are interested in what is going on in the world and desire to be a part of it in some way. You are enthusiastic, enjoy life, the new, the progressive, the unusual, and seek the opportunity to express yourself through groups or public activity.

The unexpected and exciting are more stimulating to you than the ordinary procedures of everyday existence. Independent in thought and action, you definitely claim the right to personal freedom; you do not permit people or conditions to interfere with your life or to limit your self-expression for any length of time. You are charitable and considerate of others, but at the same time you insist upon the right to follow your own ideals, and to live your own life.

Routine can easily become a bore to you regardless of your work or activities. You are not at your best when forced to do work or remain in a place which is always the same. Your attention may wander if there is not something new, different, or just a little bit exciting taking place to give variety and spice to life. Your Destiny or Vocational numbers may not allow you all the freedom you desire, but you will be able to express yourself better in a general way if you can change things from time to time to liven them up. Lack of freedom and variety may lead to a feeling of dullness, discontent, unrest, and dissatisfaction, causing you to act hastily and impulsively, and to do things which may lead to sorrow or regret later for others as well as yourself. If you will learn to recognize this unrest and turn it into worthwhile action and resourcefulness instead of impatience, you will develop an amazing power to accomplish things, influence people, and "go places" in the social, financial, and progressive world.

You are ambitious too, but you should avoid too many irons in the fire, scattering your forces and finances and undertaking more than you can successfully carry out. Too much change and variety may result in lack of proper application and concentration to the tasks at hand, so that you fail to accomplish anything. Watch out for this tendency. Be alive and active but in a very definite and useful manner. Your Destiny will help you decide how. There is a little of the "Bohemian" in your nature and you may become somewhat of a free lance in your religion, politics, or social life as you grow older and make up your mind in your independent way. Even in love affairs you are likely to keep things interesting or introduce the unexpected. Travel is good for you. When you feel yourself getting restless and critical or irritable, buy something new, take a trip, or make some constructive change which will improve your work and environment. Don't tear things down or criticize others. Your own restlessness and impatience may be at fault. Refuse to take from others more than is your due or than you can return. Claim your freedom but realize that freedom does not mean breaking the standards of living or being unconventional. It simply means living a fuller, richer life and helping others to do the same. Value your resourcefulness; make it pay you well and use it to bring joy to those you love. Keep in touch with what is going on in the world. You need to keep up-to-date.

Wear pink, strawberry, claret, wisteria, or cherry as part of your accessories to attract friends.

HEART'S DESIRE—NUMBER SIX

Deep down in your heart there is a fine sense of loyalty and a real desire to do good in the world. You are deeply sympathetic and sense the needs of humanity. You will always be somewhat of an idealist and much of your success, as well as many of your disappointments, will be the result of this quality. You are faithful to those you love, clinging to family standards and tradition, even to the point of sacrificing yourself for love, family, or some ideal of service. You are firm in your ideas of right and wrong, developing these convictions more positively the older you grow. You are apt to be frank, even bluntly outspoken when your sense of fairness and justice have been violated, but you will fight just as hard for others as for yourself. Your soul longs for beauty, harmony, and companionship, and when you follow your soul urge you are capable of living on a very high plane and inspiring others to do likewise. You should never permit life or experience to rob you of your ideals. Part of your work in the world is to help others, especially the young, to maintain ideals of love, beauty, and justice, and your whole life could be defeated if you allowed anything to darken your faith.

You are capable of a deep and lasting affection for those you love; but you want to be loved in return and you are not happy unless you have the full measure of love and appreciation which you believe is your due. At times you are overgenerous and indulgent to the extent that you give more than you should, more than is good for the other fellow. Many of your troubles result from this. You may even blind yourself to the faults of family, children, or friends, and then suffer when you find they are only human after all. Still, this very quality is part of your charm and is the reason why others love you. Keep a check on your kindness and do not give too much to one or two. It may not be right and end in unhappy experiences or lack of appreciation. Give some of your love to humanity and work for the good of the world as well as for those you personally love. A home and marriage mean a great deal to you and you will make every effort to establish yourself securely in a home and maintain your own comfortable place. Still you are capable of renouncing love for service, because your ideals are so high. You belong to those who beautify life, and your environment should be both artistic and beautiful. You should also surround yourself with friends who are making the world a better place to live in. Children, animals and those who are helpless appeal to you, and you will be loved by them.

Now and then you can be just a little stubborn about what you want and so determined to carry out your own ideas and plans that you forget to consider the viewpoint of others. Not that you mean to be stubborn, but you sometimes insist that others shall do what you think best because you believe your way is best. Your desire to help can be so strong that you almost smother those you love, who, in turn, are forced to free themselves to find their own good. Try to understand life a little more and realize that people differ in opinions. Learn to assist them to do what they want to do, not just what you think they should do; the more you do for others in a loving way the more popular you will be and the greater usefulness you will find.

Wear orange, henna, scarlet, heliotrope, or mustard in your accessories to attract friends.

HEART'S DESIRE—NUMBER SEVEN

You are naturally selective and discriminating, for deep in your heart there is a desire for the best life has to offer. A keen sense of perfection governs your life and all your undertakings. You aim high and strive for the perfect result. You should never lose sight of your ideals but sometimes you reach for a goal that is almost unattainable, thus making it difficult for others to understand you or to live up to your expectations of them. Your sense of the "fitness of things" is tremendously strong and you derive your greatest satisfaction from being sure everything is just right. You do not regard any effort to be accurate and certain as a loss of time. You greatly desire knowledge and want to know the reason why. You are not a person to accept things at their surface value, but seek to prove, test, and understand the motives, causes, and underlying principles before you accept them or make them a part of your life. Your ideals are well defined and, if possible, you refuse to accept anything—friendship, opportunity, or environment—if it does not measure up to your standards.

You have a deep intuitive feeling, and even though you may seem to be analytical and mental, you sense and feel hidden values, higher principles, spiritual and occult standards with which to measure life. You should accept them and use them in your everyday affairs. If you do they will make you outstanding, if not to the world, at least in your circle of activity, enabling you to uncover and develop the hidden laws of life for the improvement of humanity. Your desire for the best makes you particular about your associations. You are often very quiet in manner and have a great deal of pride. From time to time you experience the desire to get away from the jazz and excitement of the world, to live a life of solitude and serenity on mental horizons. No matter how active your life is, you should daily make it a practice to take time out to rest, relax and to be alone, to think, study and meditate, especially when you have a serious problem to meet. By so doing you will make fewer mistakes and discover your inner soul guidance.

Your natural reserve may cause people to consider you distant, proud and hard to meet. Your faculty of analysis may make you appear cool, calculating and suspicious. So be careful of your actions and allow others to discover the really generous spirit you have hidden beneath a seemingly cool manner, especially in love and marriage. You can be exacting and demand explanations from others which may bring about misunderstanding and separation. When others misunderstand you, conscientiously seek to overcome the misunderstanding. At heart, you are really a visionary person and you love the odd, the mysterious and the unusual. Keep a broad faith in life itself and in people, but do not permit your quiet, reserved nature to suppress you. Go forth with dignity and pride, but be kind and forgiving and value your urge to get the best out of life. Let the charm and distinction and cleverness which you inherently possess lift you to a specialized and outstanding position in life. When you realize your desires, be sure to share with others, if you want to find true happiness.

Wear purple, brick, or pearl as part of your accessories to win friends.

HEART'S DESIRE—NUMBER EIGHT

Deep in your heart there is a great deal of serious ambition. You want to get results and have such inner fire and force that you are not happy unless you are doing things in a big way. Human nature generally proves interesting to you, and while you are not exactly a humanitarian, you do try to improve life and conditions to get the best out of everything. You have the inner stamina and courage to overcome great difficulties and your latent ability to surmount obstacles is splendid. Life, however, will not always be easy for you, for you are apt to make it hard for yourself, striving for results until you overestimate your ability, or to aim so high disappointments are bound to follow. This courage and energy will eventually take you to the top in your chosen line, as you learn not to work for personal power alone, but for worthwhile purposes.

Your urge is to do big things and you are more interested in plans that can be carried out on a large scale, dealing with groups, organizations, etc., than through small activities and enterprises. You are somewhat of an organizer at heart, like to direct and supervise undertakings, do not find happiness in a subordinate position, and have a desire for money, or at least the authority it brings. You have the right to money and your ability should bring you success in the lines indicated by your Destiny and Vocation, but should you make money your only goal, you are likely to meet keen disappointment or experience ups and downs in life very difficult to control. When you follow your true soul urge, you will sincerely strive for mastery on all planes of life; deep within your heart there is a philosophical trend of thought and feeling.

You should study psychology and religion philosophically for you possess latent powers to analyze or to do research work in the field of human emotion and feeling. This will help you to overcome personal prejudices which otherwise might stand in the way of your real success in life. If you find your mind and heart filled with prejudice, resistance, or jealousy, strive for the impersonal point of view. Self-control will lead you to the front and give you the right to supervise and command other people. You should not expect too much appreciation from people. They may not possess the same powers of self-mastery you do. It is up to you to see both sides of the question. Your understanding of the laws of life and your ability to master your moods and to cooperate with others are the secret of your success in the business world. Life expects more of you than of the average individual. So search your soul for the standards which will not fail you.

Be careful that you do not take the lead too positively in your love affairs for you can unconsciously drive others and be too forceful. Sometimes you are too busy working out a plan or an idea to be a good "sweetie," or again you may be too self-sufficient, causing others to experience disillusionment.

Wear canary, buff, tan, opal, or ivory as part of your accessories to win friends.

HEART'S DESIRE—NUMBER NINE

You are deeply compassionate and impressionable. You love beauty and harmony and are capable of an impersonal attitude of mind. You can sense the Brotherhood of Man, and, if life permitted, you would love to help the whole world. Your ideals are high and you have a tremendous power to influence others for good when you make your ideals a reality in your own life. Your sense of perfection is so high that you are often discouraged if you cannot realize your ideals or find them in others. You should never allow these moods to continue, for there is something so fine, so warm and all-embracing in your soul that you can touch the cosmic mind and heart if you aspire to Divine love. Your deep, intuitive understanding enables you to reach the hearts of all people, and through expressing love, compassion, tolerance, and philanthropy you become one of the chosen of the earth. This means that forgiveness, patience, and sympathy, even for the lowest, should always flower in your heart.

Being essentially emotional, many times you will be torn to pieces by your feelings and the struggle between your higher self and your personal desires and ambitions. You will always strive to reach the goal of beauty, love, and service, but again the desire for human love, sympathy, and admiration will fill your mind, pulling you from your pinnacle of generosity and tolerance. You realize so keenly the glory of love and service that you sincerely seek to attain true perfection, but again you may allow yourself to become so involved in human emotions that you almost crucify your soul and cause confusion in the lives of those who love you. You can inspire ideals in others and lift them to great heights of perfection, but you need to control your own emotions, for they can ruin you or make you too sensitive for your own good unless turned to creative endeavor of universal nature. Follow the beauty of your own soul at all times.

You are a dreamer of dreams but you have a dynamic, inner force and can materialize your dreams of love and success when you remain true to your inner desire for beauty, harmony, and service. Never be disappointed, moody, or critical when you discover that you are only human like the rest of the world; for there is a timid, vacillating side to your nature, and should you lose faith in yourself or in life, or be afraid to stand up for your ideals, you could be very unhappy. Being naturally generous and forgiving, and desirous of doing good in the world, you may impulsively enter into associations and undertakings which you do not fully understand, and find yourself imposed upon. Just be wiser next time and temper your love of service with reason. At heart you are romantic and you are capable of great intensity in love. But romance can quickly fade if your mate is not of the same esthetic nature, for you abhor the unlovely, discordant, and inharmonious. Don't kill out the drama and glamor of your soul. Live up to your ideals.

Wear a lot of color, especially the pastel shades, if you want to attract friends.

LET'S TALK IT OVER

You will like people who have your Heart's Desire number. A friendship between two similar Heart's Desires is always remembered. This pleasant tie does not necessarily hold people together, but its memory always lingers.

History tells us of many deep and moving love affairs that have been intense and beautiful, but many times separation has been the fate of the lovers. There are other sides to our characters, and these, in close companionship, are as positive as the Heart's Desire. I knew two people, madly in love but unable to live together without quarreling. They would not accept their differences in temperament, Destiny, Birth Force, and Ultimate goal, and they eventually separated.

It is necessary for everyone to accomplish his or her Destiny. We are all named for a definite purpose and task in life. We have talents, natural abilities and fixed states of mind

(Birth Number) which give us our place in life. At the same time the Heart number is there, demanding expression and outlet in love affairs, business and worldly activity also. The conflict comes when the ideals are hidden or kept separate from the work we do out in the world.

For example, the ideals of honesty and true service may seem hard to carry out in the world of business competition, but so strange is the law of our lives, that unless we live up to the ideals of our soul's urge, we can fail suddenly and unexpectedly, or slowly and surely. The world is full of people who have never been themselves or dared to express that deep inner urge waiting within.

Whatever the nature of your inner urge is, it should not be denied. It should be wisely recognized and developed. For example—you may have the timid, sensitive inner nature of the Number *Two*, making it hard for you to compete with others, causing you much unhappiness, misunderstanding, even criticism from others. It is YOUR inner urge, and you should follow it. Recognize and appreciate your natural desire for peace, refinement, and the more cultural things of life. Accept your desire to get on with others peacefully and without quarreling as a good trait and then, through inspiration from books, meditation, religion, or spiritual principles, go forth, quietly, until others fully recognize your power. Use your gift of persuasion to help others find harmony and agreement even in your business world. Gradually you will find your whole life broadening, opportunity opening up along the lines of your Destiny, and a new glow and greater happiness will touch your whole life.

Whatever *your* Heart's Desire number may be—study it, recognize its strength. Make it the lovely part of your nature and use it for success and happiness. Then you will be true to yourself and the best and finest in your nature.

Here are a few suggestions to help you understand the Romance in your life and to guide you in your love affairs and long-time close associations.

LOVE AFFAIRS

Number *One* Heart loves deeply. Romance remains when the love is fully returned and the loved one lives up to the standards of charm, cleverness, and individuality so important to the Number *One*. However, pride, dignity, and reserve may not allow the Number *One* to act or admit to being romantic. Self-restraint is strong, and the Number *One* may appear cold and distant. Even though it loves deeply it expects to be the head of the family.

The Number *Two* Heart is a sweet, gentle, and considerate lover, sometimes giving too much for fear of offending or not pleasing the loved one. It is very dependent upon the encouragement and appreciation of its loved one and is easily hurt by criticism, sometimes showing temper—speaking bluntly when hurt or not happy. It is companionable and never happy alone. It needs love.

The Number *Three* Heart is always romantic, always in love, giving of its love deeply and completely. It is a charming companion, but may turn away when admiration and affection become commonplace. Self-confidence is built upon the approval of the opposite sex and admiring friends. It remembers a sorrow or broken love affair a long time.

The Number *Four* Heart is the serious lover, sincere and dependable. Home and family give it the sense of security it desires. It does not have a flare for romance in love-making but takes care of its own. It wants its loved one to share in its daily interests. It is embarrassed by too much sentiment.

The Number *Five* Heart admires the opposite sex and wants love and companionship but is not too domestic in nature. It will grow restless and seek change, freedom, and variety in companionship and social life if held and bound too closely, even by a loved one. It is mostly a better companion than serious lover, even in marriage and domestic relationships.

The Number *Six* Heart is the idealist in love and romance. Very protective, even possessive, almost smothering the loved one with attention, gifts, and expressions of love, it seeks to give the best life has to offer to the loved one, but demands the expression of love and approval in return. It must feel loved and appreciated. It enjoys sentiment and demands appreciation and admiration.

The Number *Seven* Heart is something of the stoic—can live without love. It is very selective in friendship and romance and has a high sense of perfection. When it finds its mate and gives its love, it is deeper and stronger and more lasting than its calm, reserved, and even cold manner allows.

The Number *Eight* Heart belongs to the world of important endeavor. It seeks a strong and capable mate and wants its loved one to be equal to its ambitions. It does not like weakness and lack of strength of character in others. It has a warm love-nature, but is often too busy to be romantic long.

The Number *Nine* Heart has the compassionate heart. It is romantic and impressionable, influenced by the good will of others and appreciation of its good works. It enjoys the praise of its loved one and its fellow man—sometimes trying to be the hale-fellow-well-met, neglecting its personal love until it is about to lose it. When it, too, finds its true love, it is the dream lover and companion.

Your Heart's Desire is the lovely thing about you. Recognize the full force of its influence in your life and live up to it, regardless of what your Destiny or your talents may be.

Sit down in quiet meditation and listen to what your inner urge or Heart's Desire is telling you about yourself. Add its spiritual purpose to everything you are doing.

CHAPTER VI

YOUR PERSONALITY
How Others See You

A harmonious and well-expressed personality is an asset and credit to anyone seeking success in this day of competitive effort and struggle for attainment. When it is understood and made part of the character and talents, it opens many doors leading to opportunity. The personality should, at all times, be the channel or avenue through which the true character is expressed. A man's or woman's personality is not the true self, nor does it represent the inner nature. Instead it is the outer self, the presentation card when meeting others in social or business activities.

It is human nature to judge a person from the personality. This can lead to misunderstandings and even business failure. A pleasing personality may cover up weakness and lack of talent, even honesty and sincerity. Or again, a man or woman of fine character and ability may be passed by because of an unattractive or dull personality. Now and then a person, discovering the power of a pleasing personality and the influence it can have over others, may overplay this characteristic, failing in the end when a test of character and ability is presented.

Personality is like an identification card. It is the way others see us and think of us on first acquaintance. First impressions are gained from the personality; and the way one's personality is expressed is the basis for future progress and growth. Thought should be given to making the best of the personality, for everyone born, rich or poor, good-looking or otherwise, has a compelling personality when it is cultivated and made a pleasant part of the character and daily activities.

Many personal traits are revealed by the personality. Often the individual is not aware of these mannerisms, habits, and personal ways of doing things which may unconsciously be carried to a point of eccentricity. As a person grows older these traits may become habits, very fixed and difficult to change, making the individual self-centered and inclined to give too much time to little things rather than to that of cultivating the character, talents, and true personality.

Nevertheless, in true character building, it is well to add the characteristics, charm, interesting ways, according to the number of the Personality, to the talents of the Birth Force, and the more powerful urge of the soul or Heart's Desire, when endeavoring to get ahead in the world.

The habit of accepting people for what they seem to be is the root of much of the confusion and conflict in business, in politics, and worldly affairs. It often takes long periods of bitter experience, even war, to learn that behind a pleasing personality and fine promises, other traits of character may be hidden, to be revealed later at unexpected moments. In love affairs—look behind the Personality to the Inner Nature before you take the step.

RULE FOR FIGURING

Personality—Sum of all the consonants in the name at birth.

It is read "You will *appear* to be." The impression you make upon others. Your outer self and the way you like to do personal things.

Example:

$$
\begin{array}{cc}
\underline{\quad\quad 3 \quad\quad} + \underline{\quad 6 \quad} & = 9 \text{ Heart's Desire} \\
1 \quad 1 \quad 1 \quad\quad 9 \quad 6 & \\
\end{array}
$$

```
        3         +     6        = 9 Heart's Desire
    1   1   1           9   6
    A b r a h a m     L i n c o l n
    1 2 9 1 8 1 4     3 9 5 3 6 3 5
          26                34
          8       +         7      = (15) 6 Destiny
      2 9   8   4     3   5 3   3 5
          23                19
          5       +         1      = 6 Personality
```

Mr. Lincoln was liked by everyone. He had the kindly outer-self, the helpful *Six* as his Personality number. His personality, as far as dress was concerned, was not all that might be expected of a President of the United States. But he was true to his Destiny and inner nature at all times. His *Nine* Heart, being the number of compassion, gave him a tolerance, higher even than the service and humanitarian spirit of the *Six* of his Destiny.

The deeper the study of names and numbers, the more revealing they will be found to be and the more astonishing it will be that the true facts of character and purpose in life are revealed by these names right from the time of birth.

(Special note: A mathematical shortcut to the Personality number—add 9 to the Destiny number digit and subtract the Heart number digit. This will be the Personality number.)

LET'S TALK IT OVER

From the Personality number it is possible to know your type and style of wearing apparel. Naturally the Heart's Desire and the vocational talents affect the selection in individual cases. However, as the personality is the way we express ourselves under ordinary circumstances, it is well to be true to one's own personality and to cultivate it for our best advantage in all social relationships.

The following descriptions give a few suggestions as to style and manner of each number.

NUMBER ONE PERSONALITY

The *One* should always be outstanding—not forceful or aggressive, but dignified and correct in lines and detail. Even a short person with a number *One* Personality should never be overweight. Straight lines, loose, but well-fitted are right. Number *One Personality* is a likeable personality and often very persuasive in manner. The number *One* should wear and also furnish the home in bright and cheerful colors.

NUMBER TWO PERSONALITY

The *Two* should always be neat and make cleanliness important—and generally does. The number *Two* may even be fussy about having everything exact in detail. A pleasing personality with gentle manner is the number *Two*. A knack of wearing clothes can be cultivated, but loud or showy apparel should be put aside for soft, flowing, easy-to-wear, neat, and shining clothing. The number *Two* Personality should study styles and adapt them to its own personality and not be plain or colorless.

NUMBER THREE PERSONALITY

The *Three* is generally friendly and easy to talk to. Being of artistic nature, the Three likes to wear jewelry and more fancy clothing with ribbons and bows. The number *Three* should not overdress or wear extreme styles, but should be attractively dressed—prettily and in good materials.

NUMBER FOUR PERSONALITY

The *Four* looks well in tailor-made styles, combining the straight lines of the number *One* and the neatness of the number *Two*. Good material of durable wearing qualities should be chosen, for the practical qualities of the number *Four* show in personality as well as in the other sides of the character. The number *Four* should never be overdressed.

NUMBER FIVE PERSONALITY

The *Five* is inclined to be up-to-date at all times, versatile in selection but may go to extremes, just to be daring and in the limelight. The *Five* Personality should not deliberately be flashy and needs to realize the value of a good personality, stylishly expressed, modern, and fitting the occasion.

NUMBER SIX PERSONALITY

The *Six* often fails to give importance to looks or clothing. The bearing is generally sympathetic and inspires confidence—the motherly and fatherly type. The number *Six* is not style-conscious as a rule but enjoys good clothes of good material. *Six* likes to be comfortable in easy-to-wear clothing. The number *Six* should always be well dressed and give thought to the way it looks and is dressed but cannot afford to be overweight.

NUMBER SEVEN PERSONALITY

The *Seven* gains through a well-dressed and well-groomed personality. Likeable, friendly, and a good talker when well acquainted, it may be somewhat aloof in manner and appear hard to know or meet. Good style is important—straight lines, with touches of sparkle and dash. A colorful, although correct, personality means much to the *Seven*. Confidence comes to the *Seven* through being well dressed and in good clothing, even expensive materials.

NUMBER EIGHT PERSONALITY

The *Eight* should always be well dressed and present a successful-appearing personality. It likes good materials—plaids, tweeds, and heavier types of clothing (sports clothes). There is a touch of showman in the *Eight* and it is generally not overlooked in business association or social gatherings. The *Eight* Personality is friendly, persuasive, and positive in manner and speech.

NUMBER NINE PERSONALITY

The *Nine* should never wear black, but often does, feeling well dressed according to fashion in black. The number *Nine* is all-inclusive and gains through the use of color in business and as the expression of the personality. A "good-fellow" manner is characteristic of the *Nine* Personality and it gains many friends through a warm and generous manner. It can look young a long time if care is taken of skin and attention given to the posture. It may cultivate careless dress, for it, too, like the *Six*, wants to be comfortable. It can influence others because of its pleasing manner, but it can be distant and abstract when not interested. It sometimes appears to lack in forcefulness and attraction, although as a rule the number *Nine* has a magnetic Personality.

CHAPTER VII

THE REALITY NUMBER
Your Final Attainment

Security and protection for the latter days of life are a much-desired and hoped-for way of living. Farseeing men and women plan and prepare for this period during their lifetimes. Others, fearing loss, loneliness, and lack, even doubting their ability to prepare for old age, avoid even thinking about it.

The latter days of life can be as secure, interesting, enjoyable, and successful as any other time in life if the signs and numbers directing this period are studied and taken into consideration early in life. Even later in life the "sign" of how to succeed is there showing the right way.

Your interest in these "latter days" will depend somewhat on how old you are. If you are young, your interest lies more in what is going to happen right *now* or very soon. If you are in the late thirties or early forties, you are apt to wonder from time to time if you can keep up the pace of earning a living many years more. You may feel also that unless something very much to your advantage happens soon, you may not make it. If you are in your fifties or sixties and life has not been all that you had hoped for, the promise of opportunity, usefulness, and satisfaction for these latter days is still present if you direct your affairs according to the "way" for the latter days of your life.

The plan of life, to which you were dedicated from the day you were born, already has been outlined by your figuring, up to the present time. There is one more signpost and number waiting to guide you. This is called your "Reality Number" or "Ultimate Goal" and is the key to a useful, happy, and protected latter days of life. It is found by adding your Destiny number to your Birth number, thus summing up all forces of your being.

The influence of the Reality Number is very subtle. Most people are entirely unaware of its persuasive presence. Strangely enough, it is very noticeable in young children in the way they act and their personal interests. Gradually, however, the demands of the Destiny, the need to earn a living and the personal ambitions take over and the slowly moving influence of the Reality number is ignored or forced into the background. But it is there and comes to the fore very definitely as the years pass by, forming the banks of the river of experience, gaining in power, until all experience is channeled into the activities of your Ultimate Goal.

A useless and wasted latter days of life is impossible and old age no longer something to fear when the Reality number and its potentialities are made part of everyday living. A whole new vista of living, acting, and dreaming is written in the essence of the Reality number.

If its requirements seem strange to you, or not possible at the present time, begin to build it into your interests and affairs and prepare for the future by thinking about it, reading and studying its principles and methods. Take up hobbies or "do-it-yourself" endeavors until you are at least familiar with what it represents and stands for, in this way preparing yourself for the time when it becomes your way of life.

RULE FOR FIGURING

Add together your Destiny Number and your Birth Number. This sum is your Reality Number.

Example:

Refer to the figuring of Henry Ford's name and birth (p. 111). His Destiny number was *Five*. His Birth number *One*. Therefore the number *Six* was the ruling number for his latter days of life. Service to humanity crowned all his undertakings.

The following descriptions are brief outlines of the meaning of the Reality Numbers. Refer to the Meaning of Numbers for a fuller description of experiences and vocation.

NUMBER ONE REALITY

The talents, abilities, interests, and individuality of the number *One* will support the latter days of life. The individual will be very independent, very clever, and find originality of thought giving opportunity for leadership. The possibility of becoming very set and fixed in opinions may cause problems in association.

NUMBER TWO REALITY

The field of diplomacy is open to the number *Two*. The talent for getting on with others and bringing many together for a common good in public works and friendly association means success. The arts, music, museums, libraries give pleasure and opportunity. The *Two* is inclined to turn to religion, spiritual work, and teachings. A beautiful humility, born of the awareness of "that something" called God, attracts people and opportunity to touch the minds and hearts of mankind.

NUMBER THREE REALITY

The opportunity for a rich, full life is present, the privilege of true self-expression, perhaps greater than at any time during the life. Even the character who has not previously been able to express the thoughts and feelings in words, music, gaiety or along any line of creative interest will be surprised at the growth and development which come in this respect. To scatter the forces and talents in self-indulgence at this time of life is to waste the opportunity for a wonderful use of the coveted power of imagination.

NUMBER FOUR REALITY

The opportunity to actually accomplish and put into form many of the ideas not before possible is present. There will be work to do and many practical circumstances to meet in order that a foundation may be placed to build upon. Religious, scientific, and educational interests can support and build a useful life. System, order, and organization are important and must be added to the activities. There is a work to be done in the latter days of life.

NUMBER FIVE REALITY

This does not promise retirement and indicates an active latter days of life. It is not a dull period, gives opportunity for travel, a variety of experiences, and a great deal of freedom of action and thought. All progressive, forward-moving activities for the advancement and improvement of civic living give opportunity. Too many irons in the fire can lead to uncertainty and scattered forces. Seek a worthwhile work along lines of public administration.

NUMBER SIX REALITY

The latter days for the number *Six* should be filled with useful endeavor having to do with humanitarian service.

Through this service, love and protection will be the reward for the latter days of life. The best things in life, comfort and financial support, will be present when the thoughts are for the good of others in a broad and impersonal manner. Duty and responsibility will be there also, but the means to do and the accomplishment can be easily attained.

NUMBER SEVEN REALITY

The right to retire and to follow the mental interests is present. Because the *Seven* has specialized knowledge, gained through the years, others will seek this knowledge, wisdom, and understanding. Opportunity lies in the field of education, science, occult thinking or study; and time may be given to writing, invention, and to the unusual, even odd, lines of endeavor. The desire may be to withdraw from the crowd and to become absorbed in some introvert line of activity.

NUMBER EIGHT REALITY

The promise of recognition, position, and authority for the latter days of life is present. Life will demand good character, self-discipline, courage, and executive ability. Through this, opportunity to supervise, regulate, and direct the affairs of others will be present. The care of property and land may be part of the task of supervision. Research, investigation, counseling, advisory positions give usefulness and personal satisfaction. Philosophical thought and interest add strength to the character and undertakings.

NUMBER NINE REALITY

The world of philanthropy is the reward of the number *Nine* Reality for the latter days of life. Service to mankind and the realization of the brotherhood of man is part of the reward. To be able to live above the jealousies, fears, and greed of mankind is part of the victory of the latter days. The world of drama, art, literature, beauty in all its forms gives personal and financial reward. To live personally and to desire only personal love is to miss the goal of love and companionship which will come through work done for all people, regardless of race, creed, or culture.

You have now studied the five basic positions for reading the character and destiny shown in all names given at birth. The next chapters will go deeper into the analysis of your character and delve into the moods, feelings, interests and attitudes of mind which make you *different* from others and show "why" you feel and act as you do.

LET'S TALK IT OVER

Your skill in reading names lies in your ability to make "relationships." There are only nine numbers. These are combined in as many arrangements as there are words in the English language. So wherever a number appears or wherever it is found, as you go out into the world of affairs and human relationships, it means something to *you*. It is a *clue* to experience. It is a *signboard* to guide you. It is there to prepare you for what is coming up or is likely to happen.

The next step is to discover if it has any *special* meaning for you. Use the same rule, repeated many times in the lessons. If it is your Heart Number—there is something there to call forth the inner qualities of your nature, to awaken them or to test them. It may be that only by depending on this strength can you win or will you win. It tries to help you. Also there will be something sweet and lovely there to reward you.

If it is your Destiny Number, there is an opportunity for advancement, but *you* must search it out and find the advantage there. The opportunity may even fall into your lap if you can adjust to its requirements.

If the number is your Birth Number, you will need to put

your best foot forward, give more consideration to what you can do and try to do it better; and, in this way, place a foundation to stand upon for security and certainty. Others may challenge you, but you can do it, although it may not be easy.

If it is your Reality Number, train the talents indicated by the number of your Ultimate Goal. These rules are never out of my mind, and, along with the divisions of the charts which follow, help me solve the problems and the sorrows of human relationships in marriage, regarding children, domestic, and business affairs. They are my means of psychoanalysis and psychiatry.

PART TWO

PLANES OF EXPRESSION

SPECIALIZED TRAITS AND POINTS
OF INTENSIFICATION

YOUR HIDDEN CHALLENGE

CHAPTER VIII

PLANES OF EXPRESSION I
Type and Temperament

A well-balanced temperament—self-control under trying conditions, mental and emotional stability—are assets highly valued in these days of keen competition, scientific endeavor, and challenging conditions.

From your name at birth you have found your Field of Opportunity, discovered your Destiny and why you were born, your mission in life, your outstanding talents and learned to listen to the deep inner urge of your soul.

From the Planes of Expression, described in this lesson, you will discover the degree of balance between your mental and emotional qualities and the level of action and living from which you do your best work. Your Planes of Expression will add so much more information about your character that it may astonish you. They will tell you in what way you are different from others or if you perhaps have genius, or are just an average individual doing good work in your way, but not outstanding.

We are fourfold. We have a body, a mind, a heart, and a spirit. These qualities combine to make us what we are and they are the avenues of communication through which we think, work, love, plan, dream, design our life, and express our feelings. According to the degree of balance among these four qualities or the intensity with which we express one or more of the four planes, are our temperament, disposition, our reactions to people, circumstances, and to ourself.

HOW TO FIGURE THE PLANES

These four levels of consciousness are called the *Planes of Expression* and are found from the numbers in the makeup of the name at birth, from which the total numbers or digits have been previously figured.

The four Planes are called:

Physical—Representing the *body*
Mental—Representing the *mind*
Emotional—Representing the *emotions*
Intuitive—Representing the *spirit* and *inner knowing*.

All fours and fives are assigned to the Physical and Practical planes.

All ones and eights are assigned to the Mental plane.

All twos, threes, and sixes are assigned to the Emotional plane.

All sevens and nines are assigned to the Intuitive plane.

The numbers *Four* and *Five* are placed on the Physical plane. *Four* is a worker, builder, has a good sense of form, is economical and practical. The number *Five*, not as practical, though curious about life and many things, chooses the support of the material world for security and permanent interest.

The numbers *One* and *Eight* are placed on the Mental plane. *One* has strong will and determination, even touches of imagination, based on mental facts. The number *Eight* represents the power of the mind, logical deduction, efficiency, and control of both the practical and the emotional. Reason predominates.

The numbers *Two, Three*, and *Six* are placed on the Emotional plane, for they represent the heart of mankind. Feeling, imagination, and sensitive response to human emotion direct their affairs.

The numbers *Seven* and *Nine* are intuitive numbers. The *Seven* deals with analysis and technical facts, but delves into the hidden and unknown and uses inner guidance to gain its goal. The number *Nine* is not influenced by reason or sentiment; it is abstract, impressionable, deeply sensitive, and imaginative, but from a higher plane than simple emotion. It is capable of touching the heart of the universe.

Examples:

Figure the name of this famous inventor without summing up the final digits at this time:

```
G u g l i e l m o   M a r c o n i
7 3 7 3 9 5 3 4 6   4 1 9 3 6 5 9
```

Born April   25th   1874
      4 + 7 + (20) 2 = (13) 4

Physical	4	(two 4's, two 5's)
Mental	1	(one 1)
Emotional	6	(four 3's, two 6's)
Intuitive	5	(two 7's, three 9's)

His type is emotional, imaginative, having six emotional numbers and five intuitive numbers. He could not be stopped by cold hard facts. He *knew* above all reason, and, no doubt, he seemed to be a very temperamental man to the Mental and Practical type of thinker. His *four* Birth Force helped him, however, put his ideas into form.

Not all names show such outstanding emphasis on the higher planes. Most people are average and have a general balance, varying one degree or two on the different planes. This gives a good balance for work and attainment. It may not show outstanding temperament, but it indicates an individual capable of meeting life with talent, ability, and understanding on any level of living.

The Planes of Expression mean: Place of power in the world; levels of living and working; attitudes toward life and others; balance of temperament; manner of going about work and undertakings; the level from which judgments of life are made; type and individuality; talents and skills.

For example: Two men may have the same destiny, say a

Seven, placing each in an educational, professional, or scientific field of work and opportunity. One may carry this out in a practical way, having many practical and physical numbers in his name. The other may live on a more abstract plane of thought and action, be interested in invention, research, even spiritual purposes, having many intuitive numbers and few practical or mental numbers. The differences in temperament, type, and talent are clearly indicated by the Planes of Expression.

It is important, even when describing the Destiny, the Heart's Desire, the Personality, the Birth Force, or the Reality, to know from what level of living the individual will carry out the main requirements of character and Destiny designated by the name at birth.

Type and temperament are so varied in people that it is impossible to illustrate them all. But as another example, figure the name of an outstanding general of the American army:

$$6 \quad + \quad 2 \quad + \quad 5 \qquad = (13)\ 4 \text{ Heart's Desire}$$

```
John  Joseph   Pershing
1685  161578   75918957
```

$$2 \quad + \quad 1 \quad + \quad 6 \qquad = 9 \text{ Destiny}$$

Sept.   13th   1860

$$9 \quad + \quad 4 \quad + \quad 6 \qquad = (19)\ 1 \text{ Birth Force}$$

Physical	4	(four 5's)
Mental	7	(four 1's, three 8's)
Emotional	2	(two 6's)
Intuitive	5	(three 7's, two 9's)

The mental numbers rule over emotion but are supported by good intuition and practical talent, sense of form and order. Reason rules emotions. Notice the practical *Four* of his Heart's Desire—the broad universal number *Nine* as his Destiny—the executive and mental number *One* on his Birth Force—with a (13) *Four* birth day. He was well qualified to work out his destiny and was quite a different type of man than Guglielmo Marconi.

MEANING OF THE PLANES

The Physical Plane represents the body and form of man. It is governed by instinct and deals with that which can be touched, seen, and is real. It is not much given to imagination or the fanciful and prefers that which is known, pointing to facts, but often going no further than common sense. This is the foundation of life, for here the form and pattern of existence are maintained.

The Mental Plane embodies man's mind and reason. It is the level of mental relationship and analysis, gathering facts, weighing one against the other, not accepting even the apparent, unless it can be proved and analyzed. It represents will, determination, positive states of mind and can be cool and cold in its calculation when imagination tries to color facts. Fine mind, brilliant thought, and executive ability give leadership and position.

The Emotional Plane represents emotion, feeling, and makes life warm and sympathetic. Facts give way to imagination, inspiration, the vision and creative thought without practical foundation. Sentiment, rather than reason, rules the actions, the responses to life and to people, influenced by the affections and love. It dreams of the beautiful and fanciful. Logic is not too important for the plans of the emotional character.

The Intuitive Plane represents the spiritual level of inner knowing—higher than facts, higher even than imagination, guided by revelation and abstract impressions. Through intuition, man expresses this divine wisdom and revelation on the mental, emotional and physical planes of action and awareness. The intuitional plane gives mankind reverence, worship, compassion, tolerance, invention, prophecy, and that "inner guidance" which touches up and quickens all other levels of living. It is what is meant to "be saved by Grace."

The Planes of Expression will enable you to truly understand people and to place them in their right places in business and happy domestic relationships. A man and woman may have much in common, having several major numbers alike, but later fail to find happiness together because of differences in temperament and ways of thinking and acting, shown on the Planes of Expression. Through understanding of this, discord and unhappiness can be smoothed out and a happy life result with romance remaining. To be exactly alike in all phases of character would mean dullness and boredom. To be different and to understand this difference in each other adds fun, progress, and more impulse to accomplish worthwhile things together.

LET'S TALK IT OVER

This lesson on Planes of Expression—to me—is one of the most important lessons of the course. It tells so many things about a man's or woman's character and personal feeling that it is like reading a novel or autobiography. My clients have said to me "How do you know that?" I know because of what the Planes of Expression stated so plainly.

You will find every chart you figure is different and you will be astonished now and then to find a cipher (0) on someone's Plane of Expression. This is as accurate a description of character as many numbers on a plane. It does not mean what it suggests—a blank, a lack, or some sort of deformity or limitation of expression—it simply means that *the individual's response on that plane is not outstanding;* that some other plane is the key to the individual's type and talent.

Never condemn anyone for a low point on any plane. Instead let it be a guide to vocational placement in business and a means of understanding the temperament of the people around you, especially your children and loved ones.

When a chart shows a low degree on the physical plane, it means the practical side of the character is not the dependable quality; or perhaps, there is a lack of caution and sense of values. Long periods of endurance or hard physical work will break down the body. *No* Physical Numbers indicates the physical plane is not the place of power for the individual. Also, if physical work and application are shunned or avoided, this can be well understood; and while the character will profit by cultivating and developing a better sense of practical values, the talents shown by the other planes should be cultivated for success and self-satisfaction.

Many physical numbers give fine endurance, ability to stand hard conditions, and, even though the individual may be ill from time to time, the endurance to "pull through" again and again is there. There will be strong positive opinions and a cautious practical nature, a demand for the things of the world including the substantial and comfortable. Ability to maintain and keep system and order and the gift of application and concentration are talents. If the physical level is made up of more *Fives* than *Fours*, there will be more inspiration, more impatience and impulse with less power of concentration, but a practical demand for the things of life rather than dreams.

(Note: In reading the Planes of Expression, the general meaning of the numbers applies as in every other division of the name.)

When there are *no* Mental Numbers, the individual does not necessarily lack in brains or mentality. (Many brilliant men and women show no Mental Numbers.) *Do not make the mistake of thinking so.* It simply means the character is not a mental type—even with a high I.Q. "The reason why" is not important to this individual—like the little lady who could never explain why she did certain things, causing family problems, but who in her own way was kind and helpful. She had a cipher on the mental plane and was high on the emotional plane.

Many Mental Numbers give fine reasoning powers, strong will, determination and executive ability, but, in dealing with a character strongly mental, it is necessary to supply the facts. Reason may rule over the heart, even though love and sentiment are in the nature. Mental Numbers give ability to push things through to a logical conclusion. Too many Mental Numbers give headstrong qualities and an unreasonable nature; sometimes the health is not good.

If there are *few* Emotional Numbers or they are lacking in the name, the ability to express the feelings may be limited or not seem important to the individual, like the businessman who gives his wife everything but does not think it important to tell her he loves her. If there are *more* Emotional Numbers in the name than on the other planes, the heart and affections rule over logic and reason. The emotions tend to give a happy disposition and love of beauty, a sympathetic nature and artistic feeling and talent.

Too many Emotional Numbers may give wasted energy and lack of self-direction, too much imagination, and a high-strung disposition, but if the emotions are recognized as a talent and trained for usefulness, beauty and warmth are added to the world to soften the hearts of young and old.

In the majority of names, the Intuitive Plane is not the outstanding one, for intuition is a dynamic quality, and for general well-being and normal living only a touch of it is necessary. An absence of Intuitive Numbers is seldom found, however. Most names have one at least, for to live wisely, everyone needs an "aerial to the sky" for guidance and protection.

If you find a name low in intuition or without Intuitive Numbers, look to the major positions and numbers. You may find the Intuitive Numbers there. More intuition on that plane might, in this case, be an overbalance and give a confused or erratic expression of temperament.

Life is a wonderful thing; years of reading names have taught me that no one is without all the strength, courage, guidance, talent, and ability needed to make a success of life. If the talents and abilities are not found at one point of analysis, they will be found, to some degree, in another. Even with retarded natures, the Planes of Expression can be a guide to understanding the character.

Too many Intuitive Numbers make for a spiritual sensitiveness. This may give great dramatic talent—in literature, religion, prophecy, invention, but not in accordance with the normal ways of thinking and acting. Health can become a problem.

When the intuition is *average*, it gives depth of feeling and ability to understand mankind and humanity without too much personal feeling. The Intuitive Numbers, especially the letter "r" *(Nine)*, give the feeling of the brotherhood of man that brings all people to the aid of those experiencing great calamity.

The ability to think, work, love, and to succeed in any line of endeavor does not belong to one plane alone. However, we often live more in one side of our natures than another. This makes the difference in type and shows the reason why people, like two blades of grass, are never exactly alike. In the home and family, children may differ to such a marked degree that it takes a wise parent to understand and train each one in the right way. This is the same in the business world and gives many opportunities for the vocation.

On the whole, most men and women are well-balanced individuals, capable of meeting life from *all* levels of living and thinking, having some degree of each of the qualities of the Planes of Expression in their natures. They make solid citizens.

It is the *extremes* of temperament or intensification which make for unusual reactions to life's opportunities and help to make life interesting and not humdrum. These also cause some of the strange happenings in the world of crime and fill the divorce courts.

Examples:

Four Politicians (running for high office)

1		2		3		4	
Physical	4	Physical	8	Physical	4	Physical	7
Mental	4	Mental	4	Mental	2	Mental	5
Emotional	6	Emotional	5	Emotional	6	Emotional	5
Intuitive	5	Intuitive	4	Intuitive	3	Intuitive	2

The second and fourth made it into office. They were high on determination and tenacity. The other two, emotional and intuitive, had more imagination than mental determination.

A Famous Actor   Two Painters

1		2		3	
Physical	5	Physical	5	Physical	8
Mental	4	Mental	2	Mental	2
Emotional	7	Emotional	6	Emotional	8
Intuitive	7	Intuitive	6	Intuitive	4

Notice the feeling and intuition in all three examples and the lack of force on the mental plane in examples 2 and 3. All three, however, were successful in their fields.

A Clever Criminal and Confidence Man

Physical	9	Emotional	5
Mental	2	Intuitive	6

Not a mental type, but with unusual ability to influence others, due to the strength on the physical plane, with unusual skill in a practical way. His intuitions and emotions gave him insight into the feelings of others. He could have been a fine architect.

A Great Statesman (an unusual chart)

Physical	10	Emotional	10
Mental	5	Intuitive	5

Ten physical numbers always give prominence in any name. Great imagination and depth of feeling added to his ability to inspire others.

From these charts you can understand, when there is a problem or question to be discussed in a family, community, or even the United Nations, why it is difficult to gain agreement without argument and why there are so many differences of opinion.

The Meanings of the Totals on the Planes of Expression in the next chapter will give you added insight into character and why a perfectly normal individual—friend, husband, or wife— will suddenly show temperament and disposition unrecognized before.

CHAPTER IX

PLANES OF EXPRESSION II
Peculiarities of Temperament and Aptitudes

In the past, educators and reformers presented set patterns of behavior to which people were expected to conform regardless of personal inclinations.

Educators and teachers of the modern day endeavor to discover and develop the natural skills and aptitudes of the individual. This gives more personal satisfaction and greater accomplishment and promotes the welfare of the community.

From the Planes of Expression, man's fourfold nature has been previously described, showing the balance of temperament on the four levels of consciousness. The "way" the talents of each plane will be expressed, just "how" the individual will accept responsibility and portray character and aptitude, is shown by the digit or "total" number on each Plane. This total number will typify the peculiarities of the nature, show the way the feelings will be expressed and the response to circumstances in all social, business, and domestic relationships.

READING THE TOTALS

1		2		3	
	Totals		Totals		Totals
Physical	4	Physical	3	Physical	7
Mental	1	Mental	2	Mental	3
Emotional	4	Emotional	6	Emotional	5
Intuitive	3	Intuitive	4	Intuitive	1

In example No. 1, the total on the physical plane is four, a *physical* number. All work will be done in a practical way, and the ability to establish order, system, and organization will be strengthened because of the 4 Total.

Example No. 2 shows an *emotional* number on the *physical* plane, indicating a less serious nature, inclined to be careless at times and inclined to add the artistic and inspirational to the practical work and interest.

In example No. 3, the seven *intuitional* number on the *physical* plane adds technical skill, mathematical interests, and clever hands, with flashes of intuition to add knowledge and understanding.

The striking thing about example No. 2 is the emphasis on the *Emotional* Plane with another emotional number as the Total (6), showing a very emotional nature requiring love and approval at all times, also a strong desire to serve humanity.

The *Mental* number one on the *Intuitive* Plane in chart No. 3 shows strong opinions about spiritual matters, one who makes his opinions known, who has a mental approach to religion and worship and who desires facts, not fancies.

In reading the Totals, the numbers there do not change the nature of the Planes. They are more like direction finders to show how the consciousness of the Plane will be worked out. They are like a dash of seasoning added to the ingredients of a recipe to give more flavor and taste.

Read the Plane first—then the Total.

The information you will receive about the character—the

temperament, the skills, talents, peculiarities of nature and disposition—will be very revealing and surprising. It will help you solve many of your problems in human relationships. The attraction between people of seemingly different nature and levels of living may be found in the Totals of the Planes of Expression. Many problems of domestic association may be resolved when the Totals are carefully studied.

Surprisingly, a similarity of Totals on one or more planes will often give a closer tie in romance and friendship than the Major Numbers. There will be so *much in common* in the way the character is expressed that even the stronger requirements of the Destiny and Ultimate Goal may be neglected.

* * * * *

The following instructions were presented to the California Institute of Numerical Research, Inc. by one of its outstanding members, Mrs. Ruth Lester of Glendale, California. They were tested and proved through the years of study and research by the qualified and trained members of the organization.

TOTAL ON THE PLANES OF EXPRESSION

NUMBER ONE

A MENTAL NUMBER ON ALL PLANES

PLANE

Physical—Very active and enthusiastic. Outgoing. Not apt to finish what is begun. Soon tiring of the plan or work. Leaders. Work hard to get what is desired. Original. Outstanding, expecially if 10 numbers are shown.

Mental—Original in thought and deductions. Quick responses to ideas or conditions, good or bad. Witty.

Emotional—Changeable, original, capable of meeting all kinds of people. Can touch all levels of living. Nervous and high-strung. Can demand much in love and marriage.

Intuitive—Great inspiration. Ideas come quickly like a flash.

SUMMARY

The number *One* Total on *any* plane gives inspiration and success through work which fires the enthusiasm and a feeling of daring. Otherwise the manner can be dull and disinterested. It is challenged by obstacles. The number *One* is independent and individualized in work and undertakings. It may act in a different manner—however, if not happy or pleased, causing many difficulties in business and domestic association. The number *One* Total on any plane gives strong likes and dislikes and a desire to live according to its personal feelings and beliefs. Charm and wit characterize the number *One*. There is a tendency to live things up quickly, to be easily bored, and soon tire of an association or activity. A strong desire to be at the head of any undertaking generally opens the way to leadership and important positions. The number *One* Total on any plane gives good financial attractions. At times the number *One* may cling to a personal plan or idea with bulldog determination, as it does not accept subordination easily.

NUMBER TWO

AN EMOTIONAL NUMBER ON ALL PLANES

PLANE

Physical—Sensitive, very apt to lack self-confidence. Needs to be with people. Gives attention to details. Charm and cleverness in gathering information. Often inwardly afraid of big things without help or assistance or approval. Uncertain, and can worry if things are not just right. Collects, takes up hobbies.

Mental—Accumulates, collects knowledge, things, and information. Strong and firm in convictions although naturally cooperative and agreeable. Afraid to undertake too much without assistance. Feels it knows a lot, but too sensitive to meet opposition alone.

Emotional—Sensitive to music, rhythm, timing. Receives ideas and impressions through sensitivity. Always needs love and understanding and right environment. Will share with others. Negative if left alone too much.

Intuitive—Ultra-sensitive to spiritual facts. Feels so much it wonders why others do not understand. Can be radical and extremist.

SUMMARY

The number *Two* Total on any plane colors even the most practical task with spiritual feeling and esthetic qualities. Its emotional qualities show forth as a love of beauty, fine sense of rhythm and timing. The desire to have things done well and with detailed perfection gives business and vocational opportunity. At times, personal and business problems may result because of too much attention to detail or going to extremes which lead to loss of time, delays, and missed opportunity. As the number *Two* is the Number of association and partnership, right relationships and helpful association are important; otherwise self-consciousness can lead to subordination, negative expression, worry, fear, and subordinate positions. Courtesy and good nature mark the character. However, at times, outspoken reproach and disapproval may be expressed in contrast to the expected gentleness generally shown. Strong opinions along some particular line are part of the nature, even to the point of becoming the "escapist" when the *Two* does not find others agreeing with its ideas. Musical talent is present. Illustration and painting may be a vocation or a hobby. Right environment and helpful companionship may correct many personal problems. Ability to bring others together for a common purpose is a business asset.

NUMBER THREE

AN EMOTIONAL NUMBER ON ALL PLANES

PLANE

Physical—Demonstrates and expresses in an artistic manner on the material plane. Functions in a *Three* manner even in practical matters. Does not like to face realities. Uses imagination to make things go. Talented and artistic in work and endeavor. Careless about order and system.

Mental—Creative on the Mental Plane, uses knowledge and facts in a creative manner and colors them with imagination and vision. Thinks things out for self and uses imagination to get results. Talks boastfully about self, personal interests, and plans. Colors all activity with a touch of fancy. Not too serious. Can be a grand person and interesting talker.

Emotional—Very imaginative and personal where emotions are concerned, both in work and in love affairs. Wants admiration and to be popular. Ponders over things and then acts impulsively. Artistic and talented. Often scatters possessions and money and can talk too much. Needs artistic outlet.

Intuitive—Colors ideas from on High with imagination and much personal feeling. Capable of inspiring others to higher interests and faith. Fine speaker. Much artistic talent. May be reticent and not put self over without help from others. Psychic responses.

SUMMARY

Three—on any plane indicates an emotional response to circumstance, work, and happenings. Hard physical work of long duration is not natural for the sensitive, high-strung, creative number *Three* on any plane of expression. This should be understood in judging the temperament of this happy, inspirational, and loving number. A fine tenacity will be shown and endless application when the field of endeavor gives an outlet for the artistic and imaginative feeling and thinking. Otherwise, the *Three* can be judged as careless or indolent. The gift of words is an asset, even though at times too much talk scatters the strength and sidetracks opportunity. However, this talent should be cultivated for added opportunity. Love affairs bring many experiences, now and then a jolt, because of too strong a desire for appreciation and admiration. The number *Three* does not like to be alone or live alone because of a companionable nature, but can learn to do so if deeply hurt or unhappy. The ability to make others happy and to express joy and goodwill are a part of the *Three's* stock in trade. A love of pleasure and fun characterizes the nature, but this should not be the real aim of life. The creative talent should be used to strengthen the Plane of Expression upon which it is found. *Threes* on any Plane may have presentiments or natural psychic prophecy.

NUMBER FOUR

A PRACTICAL NUMBER ON ALL PLANES

PLANE

Physical—Hard worker, organizer, manager. Carries out ideas for others easily. Not an originator. Steady, sure, deep concentration. Serious-minded, very capable. Tenacious. May be stubborn against opposition.

Mental—Planner, executive in charge of affairs, large or small. Gets results. Determined, but can become tied down by caution or held back by being too serious. Responsibility. Many experiences through in-laws and relatives. Sometimes has to give up just as things are going right. Manager in large concerns and big businesses, but may work for self or in own shop or undertaking.

Emotional—Has good evaluation, sense of form and practical values, colored by artistic feeling. Stubborn, if held down or restricted over too long a period. Likes to have work properly appreciated. Can accomplish in spite of opposition. May be suddenly explosive if not pleased. May resent authority. Tenacious in love affairs and regarding possessions. Sometimes gives up or accepts unfavorable situations in spite of ability and caution.

Intuitive—Not truly creative. Cannot be depended upon for imagination. Does not care too much for the vague or abstract. Receives ideas of impressionable nature and does something practical about them or calls the ideas impossible. Likes form and ceremony in religion.

SUMMARY

The number *Four* on all planes seeks to establish order, system, and the practical in work and living conditions. *Four* expects faith and loyalty to be respected and laws to be fulfilled. The ability to debate well is one of the assets, if there is sure knowledge, but *Four* can also be argumentative or go from point to point to prove or disprove the question under discussion until the mind is satisfied. This may appear to be stubbornness and opposition to others. The number *Four* does not like sudden changes so should be given time to plan, build, and construct according to pattern and the established order of things on the plane on which it appears. *Four* loves the family and the well-established home and traditions but finds many family and in-law problems to work out. A dominant member may bring a degree of repression. However, the *Four* needs to guard against being dominant itself in opinions and ideas. The *Four* is not happy unless occupied or putting something into form or order. It is warmhearted, generous to loved ones, likes to stand well in the community and get things done. Protocol is important to the number *Four*.

NUMBER FIVE

A PRACTICAL NUMBER ON ALL PLANES

PLANE

Physical—Contacts people, likes to travel. Succeeds through work having to do with the public, giving an active life. Adapts to change. Good salesman when interested. Versatile and resourceful, but restless under routine. Likes to regulate people and affairs.

Mental—Quick in thought and action. Curious. Wants to know what is going on. Impatient if compelled to do the same thing over and over, or if not good at it. Likes to have more than one iron in the fire. Keeps things moving. Promoters, agents, public service.

Emotional—Searcher and investigator. Wants to know and find out what others feel. Emotionally colorful and interesting, but likes variety and turns away from dullness. Sees everything and does not miss much. May not meet a crisis well and needs to avoid temper and criticism. May change emotional interest easily or without regret.

Intuitive—Can get anything from the intuitive plane. Understands Higher law. Knows things without education and wonders why. May not fully believe what it receives, but can make use of knowledge—teach and instruct.

SUMMARY

The number *Five* Total on all planes seeks knowledge and information according to the plane on which it is found. The perceptions are quick and it likes to know what is going on, for curiosity is an outstanding characteristic. It is attracted by the new, the odd, the unusual, even the mysterious. It likes to be in the midst of exciting conditions and to be there if something is happening. It does not walk the beaten path long and may change its interests, plans, ideas, and intentions quickly and suddenly if the grass seems greener elsewhere or if bound too long by the same old condition or routine. Its power of observation, its progressive nature, its love of public activity represent talents that repay it financially. It should, however, avoid too many irons in the fire. It has the intelligence to do brilliant work and to promote business and public affairs. A natural salesman, it is able to talk well on any subject, even if not especially trained as a speaker. It desires to do useful work, seeks to help others in a friendly way, but can be possessive, taking over without question the affairs of others, feeling it knows what is best for them or the situation, thus making it difficult, in the long run, for others and causing many problems. Versatile in thought and action, it meets many experiences, keeps young and alert if not too impatient, critical, or contentious. The number *Five* can promote civilization if it works from established undertakings, even though promoting new and untried lines of business. It can be a rolling stone, however, gathering no moss, if restlessness and constant change govern the activities.

It often ventures in where "angels fear to tread," both to its advantage and sorrow.

NUMBER SIX

AN EMOTIONAL NUMBER ON ALL PLANES

PLANE

Physical—Works with things of beauty. Practical artists, dieticians, professional service in practical manner. Helps others and takes responsibility. Artistic talent. Kindergarten teachers, contractors, architects, mining engineers.

Mental—Carries responsibility. Can be depended upon to do what it has been asked to do or has promised to do. May feel burdened, unappreciated, but carries the burden to the end. Worries, carries responsibility of others on its shoulders, yet conscious of the fact it is doing so. Takes care of children or family, promotes welfare of humanity. Through mental powers, succeeds in big business. Many emotional affairs—possibly unusual and unsought. Needs education in the arts and sciences.

Emotional—Expresses beauty, harmony, music, and helpful service. Feels things deeply and tears itself to pieces through worry over someone who does not do the right thing. Honest and true. Can make others unhappy by too much discipline, or by demanding that others live up to its ideals. Responds to admiration and appreciation.

Intuitive—Apt to be quite personal about faith and religion. May put people on a pedestal and then experience disappointment because others do not live up to its ideals. Does big things in mind and often lives in visions of grandeur rather than actions. Can be ministers and artists.

SUMMARY

The number *Six* Total on any plane is a natural teacher, nurse, physician and humanitarian, and has an artistic nature with deep appreciation of beauty, harmony, music, color and the luxurious. Service to mankind is its keynote, in a personal way or in the world of welfare and human rights. It is always called upon to serve in some capacity, which it does willingly, but it will be aware of the service it is giving, expecting appreciation, compensation, and recognition for the service rendered. It is capable of sacrificing itself for a cause or ideal and can be greatly imposed upon because of a warmhearted, high sense of justice, honesty and willingness to fight for the rights of others.

Having high ideals, the number *Six* can be very demanding, even dominant, exacting, and a firm disciplinarian, but often fails to get the love, approval and appreciation it so deeply desires because of its insistence that others live up to its demands and ways of thinking and believing.

There is a love of the home, family, garden, animals, and comfortable living. The number *Six* never outgrows its desire for love, affection and approval, even in the latter days of life. It has the talent and business ability to attain the best in the world for itself through its desire to add beauty and loveliness to all endeavor. The *Six* maintains, supports, and upholds high standards and seeks to represent these at all times. When a *Six* lacks the feeling of usefulness and appreciation, it can scatter its forces and live in confusion and resentment. Many problems come through the affairs of children. Family inheritance influences the life of the number *Six* on all planes.

NUMBER SEVEN

AN INTUITIVE NUMBER ON ALL PLANES

PLANE

Physical—Mathematician, broker, analyst, technical worker, doing excellent work in any field of scientific endeavor. Delves into things. Should not be placed where there are crowds and confusion. Not at its best in public positions. An innate sense of refinement, self-control, dignity, and reserve. Many peculiarities of temperament. May be close with money. Can be rude and demanding. Not socially inclined, not too friendly. Selective in work and friendship.

Mental—Very introspective, can be a recluse. Wants to be alone and work alone. Likes to think things out, prove and test, and can live too much within its own realm of thought and action. Silent or secretive, shrewd and observing. Successful through knowledge, technical or mathematical skills. Talkative, at times, when on familiar ground or well acquainted.

Emotional—Thoughtful, selective, reserved, sometimes repressed in emotions. This could lead to frustration and inhibition of the emotions. Creates beauty from the depth of meditation and appreciation of perfection. Needs to ferret out the inhibition and to express its feelings through beauty and more creativity.

Intuitive—Can be great adepts—teachers. Can probe deeply into the abstract and gain occult knowledge and understanding. Should not repress its feelings for health's sake. Wants everything to be in correct relationship. Unhappy if this cannot be attained. May write, compose, or invent. Should watch out for false concepts or ideas. Sometimes attempts to mold others to its will.

SUMMARY

A number *Seven* Total on any plane gives specialized skills, intuitive knowledge. Colors its work with precision and mathematical endeavor, probing into the reason behind any idea or concept. It does not take anything at its face value and demands perfection in work and from others. The number *Seven* is reserved, has a silent side to its nature, keeps things to itself; yet asks questions and demands answers to its questions. The number *Seven* is charming in personality, witty, and warmhearted, but being very selective and strong in its likes and dislikes it can seem cold, hard, and distant, seldom enjoying a crowd, noise, or confusion. It can live alone and needs time to be alone—meditate, study, and to think, for in this way it receives some of its best ideas. It is sometimes the recluse. The *Seven* has strong self-control until very annoyed and then may show temper, criticism, and sarcasm. There is artistic appreciation in the nature and a right place for every *Seven* when its fine skills are developed.

It can be thoughtless towards others—impulsively generous at one time, or, again, demanding and with tight purse strings at other times. The number *Seven* on any plane should overcome the sense of separateness and personal complexes and learn to meet life and the world as they are, for health and well-being.

NUMBER EIGHT

A MENTAL NUMBER ON ALL PLANES

PLANE

Physical—Ambitious for power, position and authority. Gains recognition. Has executive ability. Able to handle big things. More dependent upon others than realized. Makes money for others. Uses other people's money. Does not like to spend its own money. Needs group work and organizations and then can be very powerful and outstanding and well-known for its accomplishments.

Mental—Natural executive, very ambitious mentally for power and position. Likes to accomplish big things and to be recognized for what has been done. Hidden pride. Good businessman and woman. Making big money is not easy. Many expenses to be met. Can be very philosophical and belong to societies and groups.

Emotional—Strong feelings. Strength of emotion. Dominant and businesslike in love affairs. Strong desire to appear at its very best or just a little better than others, not so much for the sake of competition, but to show accomplishment, and for self-satisfaction. The grand lady. Likes the big house even without money. Interested in psychology. Love affairs associated with business.

Intuitive—Enters into the higher realms with a perfect sense of power. Can be organizer of religious activities and philosophical societies or groups. Makes use of intuitive knowledge. Uses Spiritual knowledge in a business manner. Does research and historical investigation.

SUMMARY

The number *Eight* Total on any plane gives executive ability, talent for organization, and supervision of large undertakings. The number *Eight* has fine character, excellent mental qualities, good judgment. The ability to weigh and balance for right action and performance rewards the *Eight* on any plane with recognition, authority, leadership, and association with the important people of the world. A natural ability to judge, to estimate the strength or weakness of character in others, to command obedience and respect adds to its position and usefulness. The number *Eight* is an efficiency expert, a firm disciplinarian, and inwardly demands the same strength from itself.

The number *Eight* is always active, strenuous, never satisfied, and constantly reaching out for better results and greater attainment. It may seem forceful, overwhelming, and dominant to others. Life is never easy for the number *Eight*, who is always on the wheel of attainment. As a companion or sweetheart it has little time for dreaming, sentimentality or romance, even when deeply in love, as there is always some task or plan which demands its attention. The *Eight* attracts money and deals with finances; since the *Eight* has many expenses, it does not always gain the full reward for its efforts, more especially so if it makes money its goal in life. Money is the reward when the *Eight* works for a cause or purpose that represents the good of many people. As a counselor along the lines of the plane on which it is found, it can be very successful. It expects to be the authority and does not take orders unless it respects the source of the authority.

NUMBER NINE

AN INTUITIVE NUMBER ON ALL PLANES

PLANE

Physical—Publisher, importer, writer, dramatic actor, instructor, director where the spectacular is required. In positions where broad and universal contacts are important. Colors all activity with dramatic feeling and acts with intuition and impressions in practical situations.

Mental—Capable of meeting and working with people of all races and nations. Sometimes finds it difficult to pin mind down to "right now." May be thinking and planning for big things while the things at hand need attention. Needs to be placed where it does not have too much personal concern over details.

Emotional—Very dramatic. Great sense of importance. Always acts in a dramatic manner. Likes the attention of admiring groups or crowds. Can become very negative without love or approval, forming habits hard to break, which it may not understand in itself or know how to handle otherwise. May be impersonal and distant in love and emotional relationships. Adds color and feeling to all undertakings. Capable of outstanding creative work in any field of endeavor.

Intuitive—Brings down unusual ideas from on High. This inspiration can influence many people. Inclined to dwell in the abstract, even be vague and indefinite. Not practical. Can go around in a daze, dreaming and not doing. Extremely impressionable and idealistic.

SUMMARY

The number *Nine* Total expresses compassion, tolerance, good will, and generosity. It unconsciously adds color and drama to the undertaking on the plane on which it is found. The manner is independent although charitable. It likes to take part in philanthropic activities for the general public welfare.

It may react in a cold and indifferent manner if appealed to by others for personal reasons. The abstract side of its nature makes it a dreamer and a great actor on the stage of life, but difficult to understand, as it does not listen to reason, may promise and then forget. It has great talent and can accomplish fine work in any field of endeavor, although it is fundamentally the dramatist, guided and influenced by an intuitive relationship to the Universal mind.

The *Nine* needs others to direct it, for, being impressionable and dreaming of big, broad accomplishments, it can be led away by others, although it has excellent business ability when its talents are directed and put to good use. The *Nine* may express very negatively, get caught in habits hard to break if it allows egotism—the desire to be the "hale-fellow-well-met"—and too much interest in the opposite sex to mar its finer character. The number *Nine* on any plane has an inner need for love and companionship and needs a sympathetic and understanding mate, but also is of dramatic and artistic or philanthropic nature. Repeated opportunity with splendid financial attraction supports the endeavors of the number *Nine*. Its success is maintained when its efforts are appreciated and its broad concepts of beauty and grandeur understood and worked out for the good of many on a wide scope of attainment. Foreign travel broadens the scope of success.

CIPHER ON THE PLANES OF EXPRESSION

PLANE

Physical—Lack of physical endurance or practical application.

Mental—Finds it difficult to meet the cold, hard mental facts of life and does not explain the "what" or "why" with logic or mental relationships. May lack will power and force of decision.

Emotional—Emotion is not easily expressed. Does not express its ideas well in words or fancy. May even lack sentiment and sympathy.

Intuitive—Not apt to be interested in the impressions and abstract ideas of the intuitive nature. May be lacking in real philanthropic interests and the forgiveness natural to the higher planes.

SUMMARY

A Cipher on any plane describes character as definitely as a digit. It indicates a character who does not work or live on that level of consciousness. A lack of numbers may, in reality, be a balancing force, due to that particular type of number being emphasized on the major positions. Many numbers on the plane would then be an overintensification, resulting in extremes of feeling and action, making life difficult for the individual.

At times, a missing number or numbers on a plane of expression may be found as a pinnacle experience (Chapter 12) or on the Table of Events (Chapter 16) when life takes a hand and forces that type of development for some future purpose.

When a "0" appears, this should not be considered a weakness—"to thine own self be true." However, it is helpful in understanding personal problems if this quality of the missing plane is recognized and quietly developed, through reading, observation, and self-analysis.

Life would be dull if all people were alike. Read I Corinthians, 12th Chapter, 4 to 12: "Now there are diversities of gifts, but the same Spirit."

Each individual has the task of living up to the pattern of Destiny and talent shown by his particular name in this lifetime. There have been many lives in ages past. There are many still ahead in the great Eternal Plan to be lived and enjoyed.

LET'S TALK IT OVER

One time I analyzed the name of a well-known doctor. He had little faith in Numerology but had consented to the analysis to please a friend.

He had a *Six* Total on the Emotional Plane. From this, I knew he was a very conscientious physician and was doing fine service and humanitarian work. The *Six* Total told me, also, that he worried a lot over lack of appreciation on the part of others and what he considered irresponsibility in associates, and that he was a very strict parent and husband. He was startled by the truth of my statements and finally, with reluctance, acknowledged my characterization. Later, his friend told me he had a beautiful home, wealth, two nice children, but was not happy, as his wife and children were resentful of his dominant manner.

The Planes of Expression give marvelous insight into the states of mind which make people so different from each other and unable to agree, even if the effort is made to do so, resulting in sorrow, loss, divorce, and misunderstanding. This is why understanding the Planes is so important in analyzing a name, for, otherwise, many human complexes would not be revealed.

The talents, shown by the totals, add to the ability to get on in the world and indicate why some become unusually successful and outstanding. The higher or larger the total, the more talent is present on that plane, giving more force and impulse to do and accomplish.

Examples

Ten numbers on any plane are a dominant and powerful force. They are mostly found on the Physical Plane. An outstanding president, a religious leader, and a foreign statesman each had names with 10 Physical numbers.

Nine numbers on any plane, very often found on the Emotional Plane, are a big test of character, as there is so much talent but so much intensity of feeling. From youth, this individual needs wise training, and even with business or scientific tendencies an effort should be made to direct the talents along dramatic lines. Travel and broad contact with people of importance and worthwhile accomplishment are important. The 9 Total is very impressionable, and, on any plane, should, by all means, avoid the habit of drugs and liquor.

One of America's best-loved comedians passed on from the habit of heavy drinking. He had a recognized and popular public life, but had not found a faith or inner awareness of the Spiritual laws of Being.

The number *Eight*, as a digit on any plane, also gives power and important positions. All *Eights* should study philosophy, character analysis, psychology, as well as business methods.

The number *Seven* gives deep feeling, very often hidden or repressed. Good education, college training, intellectual association, good books to read help overcome an inner repression or sense of frustration which may fill the mind about the self or others. The *Seven* may become a stoic or priest and a person of great refinement. If a useful life is not found, sex complexes can lead to an unhappy life.

The number *Six* should not be too hard on others or too demanding in love affairs, hurting those it loves.

Eleven numbers on any plane (found very often on the Physical plane) may give the power of spiritual healing or the qualities of a great physicist.

Trust the numbers and their meanings, even if at first they may not seem to apply to the one for whom you are reading. It may be you do not know what is deep in the nature, or you may be unaware there is hidden talent. Or you may be using your personal judgment or prejudice, instead of depending on the numbers and their meaning and positions. All these have a way of digging in and uncovering what is really there in character, vocation, habits, and experiences.

CHAPTER X

SPECIALIZED TRAITS AND POINTS
OF INTENSIFICATION
How You Differ From Others

The name given a new-born babe, in any language or any nationality, is a declaration of character and individual rights. Why, then, is there so much suffering and unhappiness in the world, sometimes throughout a lifetime? Because so few people understand how to use the talents with which they were born or how to turn extremes of feeling and desire into constructive living—even into genius.

There are three easily recognizable arrangements in names which may forecast disagreement and negative reaction to circumstance and experience.

FIRST—THE RELATIONSHIP OF ONE NUMBER
TO ANOTHER

You have heard of things being at *sixes* and *sevens*. You can easily understand why, from your study of the meaning of numbers. The number *Six* represents the home, the family, the children and the welfare of others. It is a friendly number. The number *Seven* is reserved, reticent, dignified, not overly interested in the responsibilities of domestic life, and not too friendly towards people. It likes to read, needs to be alone from time to time, and can be very disturbed by noise and confusion. When two people living together have these two numbers outstanding in their names, these differences of thought, action and feeling can easily mar their happiness. Each one is right, but vastly different fundamentally and, unless an effort is made to understand each other and to give and take in their daily affairs, discord can result. Sometimes after many years of unhappiness, an adjustment will be made, but had they known *before* marriage from their numbers, much delay and unhappiness could have been avoided.

As another example, take the numbers *three* and *four*. The number *Three* is naturally happy, enthusiastic, romantic, imaginative, and needs inspiration, admiration, artistic expression, and romance to be truly happy. The number *Four*, always practical, is serious, cautious, careful—inclined to be slow and methodical, and finds its satisfaction in living under order, system, and routine. These two patterns are perfect in their way, but in close relationship resentment may develop. The serious *Four* is likely to repress the enthusiastic *Three,* and the *Three* can likewise confuse and unsettle the steady-going *Four*.

SECOND—INTENSIFICATION

Intensification is found from repetition of the same number in the body of the name at birth rather than from the main position. If a number is repeated many times, that quality of thought and feeling is a marked trait of character and a possible talent. At the same time it may become a negative phase of character due to an overintensification or an overemphasis on that quality.

Very few names have a perfect balance of human traits, but the design for successful living is there in every name when discovered and wisely cultivated.

Example:

```
K e n n e t h        J e s s i c a
2 5 5 5 5 2 8        1 5 1 1 9 3 1
```

There are four *Fives* in the makeup of the name Kenneth. The characteristics of the number *Five* are very marked and will influence everything he does. There is a love of change, variety and a demand for personal freedom which, without direction and understanding, could lead to lack of application and a tendency to make impulsive changes. If the versatility of the number *Five* is well-directed, the quick perceptions and the progressive thought and feeling give business opportunity and an interesting public life.

In the name of Jessica, the intensification of the number *One* gives strong character, self-determination, will power, and executive ability. Jessica will like to think for herself and to plan for others. On the negative side, she may be dominant, very insistent, and resentful of orders, refusing to take part in what others plan or want to do. Her fine talents then become negative and limiting. Rightfully used, however, her originality of thought and firm convictions will place her in a position of leadership and authority.

Many times a number is not found in a name. This is also an intensification or trait. It is not necessarily a fault, but it describes character as definitely as any overintensification.

To help you understand this, study the names of flowers.

```
R o s e          P a n s y
9 6 1 5          7 1 5 1 7
─────            ─────
(21) 3           (21) 3
```

There are no twos, no threes, no fours, no sevens, and no eights in the name Rose. It would not be a Rose or "smell as sweet" with other letters or numbers in its makeup.

In the name Pansy there are no nines, no eights, no fours, no twos, no sixes. Notice, however, the repeated sevens in the Pansy's name—not at all like a Rose. Both are beautiful flowers.

To say to the Rose, in condemnation, "You have no sevens in your name," or to a Pansy, "Why can't you be like a Rose with a nine in your name?" would be a mistake and lead to confusion. It is the same with human nature. It is wisdom to be true to ourselves at all times, to live our lives as they were destined to be and to carry out our Destiny gracefully and with self-respect.

Names vary in length, but there is an average arrangement in the repetition of numbers in the majority of names. Names show such striking differences it is only by knowing the average chart that you will be able to analyze the specialized traits and outstanding characteristics shown by the Points of Intensification in any name. The average name has 14 to 18 letters; many are longer and some are very short.

1—A–J–S	generally occurs three or four times.
2—B–K–T	generally occurs once.
3—C–L–U	generally occurs once.
4—D–M–V	generally occurs once.
5—E–N–W	generally occurs three or four times.
6—F–O–X	generally occurs once.
7—G–P–Y	may be missing.
8—H–Q–Z	generally occurs once, may be missing.
9—I–R	generally occurs three times or more.

Examine the chart—notice the *One, Five,* and *Nine* are repeated more often than the other numbers. This is because all people have the will and initiative to get on in the world (1). Love of freedom, curiosity in anything new is a common human trait (5). The spirit of the brotherhood of man (9) restores itself in the hearts of people, no matter how often trampled in the dust. If a name of average length shows any of these numbers low or not present, it will be apparent, at once, that peculiarities of disposition and talent are indicated.

As a general rule, the numbers *Two, Three,* and *Four* are

found only once in an average name. Therefore, if these numbers are repeated, these qualities are doubled in force.

The number *Three* is apt to be repeated more often than the *Two* or *Four*, for personal self-expression is a strong urge in human nature. The number *Six* is found mostly once, and if it is repeated, it is a very strong characteristic. Any repetition of the higher numbers is a marked characteristic.

The number *Seven* may be missing in many names. Discrimination, analysis, and high sense of perfection are not outstanding human traits. One *Seven* in a name gives a desire to prove things, to know the reason "why" and to get at the motives behind any happening.

The number *Eight* may, surprisingly, be missing, even in the names of very successful people. But occurring even once, it is an indication of ability to meet difficult conditions and to work under pressure. Occurring several times, it indicates a life of many tests and long periods of mental endurance, but outstanding ability.

The number *Nine* occurs many times in most names. When it is a low quality, compassion and forgiveness may be lacking. The Points of Intensification are deep in the nature. Their qualities may not always show on the surface.

Reading the Points of Intensification

The meanings of the numbers are repeated simply to help you recognize your talents, for, as has been said many times, a number never changes its meaning—just its position.

Average *Ones*—An average number of ones (3 to 4) gives the necessary initiative, will power, executive ability, qualities of leadership, determination, and individuality necessary to get on in the world.

Many *Ones*—Five or six or more will show very strong opinions and fixed ideas. The individual will stand for his rights with strong determination, sometimes in an aggressive manner, or again, winning by silence. Ability to get things done, original ideas give leadership. Many ones, above the average in names, give a tendency to rule and a determination to have its own way. Many ones may bring a health problem, affecting the head and lungs. Wit and humor can be a talent.

No *Ones*—(or few ones) indicates less self-determination and inability to stand up for the personal rights or to put over personal plans against the will of others. But the individual will be easier in association. The character may be charming and lovely, more interested in others than the self. Before judging a character as lacking in ones, follow the rule—look to the major number. There may be a one in the Birth number or Heart's Desire.

Average *Twos*—Tact, diplomacy, and cooperation are not too high in the makeup of human nature. The average person has a natural desire to associate with others, so at least one degree of the courtesy of good manners and general helpfulness of the two is necessary for all and is generally found in a name of average length.

Many *Twos*—Give a fine degree of consideration for others, especially in little things. It has a very sensitive nature and a desire for companionship. The ability to bring others together in harmony and agreement is a talent and often a business asset. Being sensitive to environment, to people and to lack of beauty or culture, it may appear shy and retiring. The ability to do things well, to gather information with patience and skill is characteristic of its nature. Many twos give a sense of timing and rhythm and may give a talent for dancing or music. The number two is a feminine number, and many twos in a man's name may give an effeminate nature, but a great appreciation of the arts. An interest in history and activities having to do with the past and the cultural development of people and races may mean success. Very adaptable, even too much so. An inner fear of people, even though liking them. Can work with the detailed arrangements of lovely and delicate things. Very unhappy when spiritual faith is denied.

No *Twos*—No twos gives a lack of consideration for others and an impatience with the sensitiveness of others and their attention to details. True cooperation is not present, with carelessness regarding the fine points of accomplishment. The individual may be kind and helpful due to ones, threes, and sixes, but mostly in their own way, not as others would desire. A mother or father may do everything to protect the family and children but still not give true consideration to the real interest and needs of the loved ones. Look for the missing two in the major numbers. It may be present in other ways and not be entirely missing.

Average *Threes*—The number *Three* represents imagination, enthusiasm, and creative talent. It gives the ability to express the ideas, feelings, and fancies in words written or spoken. It likes to do big things and has the ability to visualize the end from the beginning. It is a happy number and, at the same time, gives a great deal of self-importance and personal feeling. Two threes are not uncommon, although one three is the average.

Many *Threes*—Four or five threes are an outstanding indication of talent. The imagination is very positive, and there is artistic talent which may be expressed through music, painting, acting, designing, writing of novels, and the creation of artistic clothing, jewelry, and articles which appeal to the love of luxury in human nature. Too many threes give a strong self-interest, even selfishness, scattered energies, and lack of orderly direction. A tendency to talk too much because of too much emotion may lead to a wasted endeavor. Admiration, romance, and popularity are very important for happiness and continued success. Does not like hard, physical work, but, if inspired, will work long and patiently to get results.

No *Threes*—The gift of creative imagination does not belong to the three alone, nor the gift of words. The ones are good talkers and have a degree of imagination. The fives are good salesmen, and the sevens also talk interestingly and colorfully if interested or acquainted with a subject or idea. All numbers, in fact, have some degree of imagination and the ability to talk about what interests them, but, with the three, the "gift of gab" and fancy is a natural talent and business asset. When there are no threes in the name, not even on the major positions, fanciful ideas, sentimental speech, romance, and flights into imagination are not natural tendencies.

Average *Fours*—The strong points of the *Four* are concentration, application, a good sense of practical values, and ability to stick to things. One four gives the ability to put work and plans into form and to maintain and sustain needed order and system.

Many *Fours*—Two or more fours intensify the practical tendency in the nature and add to the ability to appraise, estimate, and to know values and the worth of material and concrete plans. The concentration is very good, the ability to understand details and to build and put ideas into form is very high. There will be work and effort required. The in-laws are the pleasure and the problem, as with all fours. Three or four or five fours on the Points of Intensification will indicate ability to build, construct, and to establish practices of supporting and lasting nature.

No *Fours*—The natural application and concentration of the number *Four* are not strong traits when there are no fours on the Points of Intensification. It is important to look to the major numbers in such a chart; other talents may be outstanding. When there are no fours, assistance and help will come through others, but lack of application may be the weakness of the nature. Few people lack in the quality of the number Four. It is the foundation number of all endeavor. This number will generally be found somewhere in the name or as a future experience.

Average *Fives*—It is human nature to enjoy the excitement of public contact. Change and variety stand for progress and growth. Most names have an average number of fives, the reason why people move, travel, make changes, enjoy excitement, feel the need of fun and entertainment and something doing. They easily move forward into the new. Change means progress and keeps the world moving forward.

Many *Fives*—Five or six fives, unless there is a balancing force of fours or sixes in the name or on the Points of Intensification, are apt to give a restless nature, lack of application, interest in too many things, or a turning from one line of work or interest suddenly, without completing either task or work. May be unconventional, Bohemian in interest, and seem to break many laws. However, opportunity is present through legal and civic activities and all types of salesmanship. Not domestically inclined unless the home life is filled with interesting people and variety. Needs a line of business which promotes travel and contact with the public and many people. Being critical of others may become a fault.

No *Fives*—This is very seldom found, for all people have a love of freedom, curiosity, and response to life and experience and like to be part of worldly affairs; otherwise there would be no progress in the world. With no fives or one five there will be a dislike of crowds and a desire to be left alone. Often one is afraid to face the world in an aggressive manner, so it is very important to study the major numbers and positions in order to discover the real talents shown by the other Points of Intensification. Fixed—not easily adaptable.

Average *Sixes*—Six is the humanitarian, the idealist, the teacher, often the physician, the nurse or the one who is interested in children or welfare work; loves the home and the beautiful, luxuries and comfortable things of life, and seeks to give these to others. One six in a name gives these qualities. The Six has a keen sense of right and wrong, and willingness to take responsibility.

Many *Sixes*—Three or four or more sixes give strong opinions and fixed ideals which are not easily given up. The individual with many sixes in the name may become confused or broken in spirit if the ideals are taken away or destroyed. However, the personal tendency is to try to persuade others to adopt its ideals and concepts about right and wrong. Many sixes give generosity and a fine humanitarian spirit. But the nature is strict, dominant and demanding. Loyalty is expected and many hurts are experienced when this is not given. Traditions are strong; sometimes radical ideals mark the nature and the position in life.

No *Sixes*—In many names the number is missing. The true sense of duty is not overly strong in the majority of the people of the world. This lack is generally made up by other qualities and talents needed to promote the progress of mankind. Do not condemn the individual without this feeling of duty and responsibility, and do not expect it of a husband, wife or child if it is not expressed. A certain luck supports the endeavors. Others help and take care of things undone. No sixes in a name often indicates interesting situations and happenings. In the home and marriage, both for men and women, the domestic problems are apt to be taken lightly.

Average *Sevens*—This is the number of analysis, technique, accuracy, observation, investigation, and demanding to know the reason why. Therefore, one seven in the name will give this quality and a questioning attitude of mind. It gives a keen mind, a tendency to analyze and to question; also discrimination and ability to look under the surface with intuitive perceptions and a sense of perfection. This quality is frequently missing in the makeup of most people.

Many *Sevens*—Two sevens intensify the gift of discernment and the desire for proof, indicating a scientific, technical turn of mind and one who likes mathematics or works with figures, charts, and laboratory research. Many sevens are skillfull in work and clever mentally, do specialized work, no matter what line is taken up. Faith, alone, is not enough. They are not good mixers, being selective and difficult to know or understand. Many sevens may give odd and unusual ideas, and, if there is a lack of good education, the talents may turn to schemes and hidden undertakings. All sevens want the best and desire to be paid for what is undertaken and can, at times, be very close about money. They are thinkers but solve problems through intuition. They dislike to show emotions.

No *Sevens*—The caution and analysis of the seven is not

present. Often there is more inner happiness. Not inclined to look under the surface for motives and reasons for the things that happen, but is more open-minded.

Average *Eights*—The number eight is a strong number, self-sufficient and businesslike. It has the ability to direct, supervise, and control others, and is generally at the head of groups or organizations and in positions of authority. Being so strong in will, mental qualities, and efficiency, it appears dominant; and the ambition to attain, so characteristic of the number eight, leads to independent action and thought, often colored with a philosophical attitude of mind. The ability to see both sides of a question, to weigh and balance, gives the ability to direct and control others, resulting in recognition and positions of authority. It is not an easy number, though having business ability. Strain about money or finances affects the life. There is natural ability to rise to emergencies and to keep control of situations. Business training and money evaluation should be cultivated.

Many *Eights*—Too many eights, even two eights, gives an intense nature with too much drive to accomplish work or plans and for money and position. They are capable of executive supervision and generally are an authority on some subject. They are good judges of character and often counselors to people in all walks of life. They may have literary ability, especially along lines of correspondence, magazine printing, and publishing; interest in research work, organizing and coordinating the works of others. Many eights in a name make life hard, even for the talented individual, with many frustrations and personal tests. The mental energies should be expressed with more inner poise and less discontent. The reward is public recognition and standing in the community.

No *Eights*—There is not so much self-control when there are no eights in the name. There is more dependence upon others, and often less strain about money in the long run, and more help or luck from others. The individual with eights has a more intense life to live and, even though very capable, may have more problems than when there are no eights in the name.

Average *Nines*—This is the number of the brotherhood of man and is found three or four times in most names. Without this influence, mankind would have destroyed itself long ago. The number nine gives compassion, tolerance, benevolence, and goodwill towards mankind, and it is because of this number that all races, religions, and all peoples live in the world together, even with difference of opinions and traditions. Number nine gives the color and drama to life and the ability to understand all levels of living. It is impressionable, intuitive, has deep feeling with appreciation of the grandeur of life—qualities belonging to all people.

Many *Nines*—Give impressionability, imagination, and generosity, often to an extreme, and lack of direction and balance of feeling, thought, and action; a tendency to follow dreams and impressions without practical direction or without emotional balance, with little actual accomplishment, but adding beauty, warmth, and inspiration to others. The individual with many nines will not be easy to reason with, but is often forgiven because of the generosity that is in the nature. Six or seven nines can give so much feeling that the character may be overly sensitive, moody, and not too well physically, but have flashes of intuition and wisdom to accomplish, without reason or so-called common sense. Great religionists, noted dramatists sometimes have many nines in their names. One should avoid habits of food and drink under periods of disappointment.

No *Nines*—This is sometimes found in names, but is not common. Nine is an outstanding characteristic, and, if this is not made up or balanced by nines somewhere on the major positions, it can be an indication of lack of broadness, tolerance, and compassion in the nature, even though sixes may be present. The number six is the humanitarian number and renders service to others. On the other hand, the number nine is the philanthropist, giving without thought of return. No nines indicates a nature that is helpful, kind, and capable, but without the feeling of universal forgiveness or giving which characterizes the number nine. A lack of nines may limit the extent of the accomplishments. Studies of comparative religions and character analysis will be helpful.

VOCATIONAL POINTERS

Many ones and eights give business interest, not carried away by emotion.

Many twos and threes and sixes give artistic ability, opportunity along professional lines, inspirational service, and instruction.

Many fours and sevens give scientific, mechanical, and mathematical tendencies.

Many fives give versatility, also sales promotion and public administration.

Many sevens and nines give literary ability.

Many eights give philosophical feeling expressed through printing and publishing, correspondence, and newspapers.

LET'S TALK IT OVER

As you become expert in reading the indications on the Points of Intensification you will read names and counsel others more expertly than the average student of Numerology. Many years of study, research, and experience have proved the outstanding value of this knowledge. Remember, too, not to condemn anyone for any characteristic lacking in the name. There is a tendency, at first, to feel that the individual with one or more ciphers on any Plane of Expression or on the Points of Intensification is not a balanced person. Not infrequently the person is accused of having karma with little success being possible until this cipher is made up. Many successful people have had one or more ciphers on the Points and have attained greatness.

Also, qualities of thought and action, which seem to be lacking on the Points, may be very outstanding on the major numbers, and it would be an overintensification to have more of the same qualities on the Points of Intensification, which would certainly indicate lack of balance. It is necessary to observe constantly every division of the name and to synchronize one division with all the others. Look over Henry Ford's name again. He has missing numbers on the Points of Intensification, but they are all to be found on the major numbers and the Planes of Expression, showing him to have had all the tools necessary to accomplish his life's work, to serve and help the public *in his own way.*

Or, again, life itself may have a period of experience, prepared for the individual sometime in the future, as shown by the Table of Events, to be developed in a natural way when it is needed and can be put to the best use.

But at present, do not try to look into the future. This is to be given in a later lesson. When I read a name for anyone, I follow the steps for analysis I have given you very carefully, covering each point, weighing it against the other characteristics, watching, with interest, the character develop before me from the name and numbers.

It is my firm belief, after reading so many names, that being true to our type and to ourselves is life's greatest lesson and eventual happiness.

THIRD—SPIRITUAL DEVELOPMENT

The third situation under which negative experiences will take place results from several general indications—race consciousness, religious beliefs, and family traditions. Mankind, according to the Divine Plan, is developing and growing in spiritual consciousness and understanding. Not all people are on the same level of mental, emotional, and spiritual development. Experience and mistakes then become the school of life and a push towards inner growth and self-realization. Due to religious beliefs, and also family traditions, some souls linger longer in pain and suffering than is necessary. At all times, however, and under all circumstance, the names at birth point the way to right action and the road to happier living and greater success.

For example—If you live in a house with the number nine, symbolizing the experiences there, and you do not understand the instructions it is giving, disappointment, emotional experiences, and upheavals may test your character. The number nine is the number of the brotherhood of man, compassion, tolerance, and philanthropy. Under this number, desire for personal love, personal popularity, and for money alone is to court the possibility of disappointment and loss of personal love. When the soul realization is gained that love is giving and, through understanding, that all people are God's people, then true, personal love, usefulness, and abundance will begin to build up for protection and personal satisfaction.

When the number eight describes the character, ulcers are a possibility until the realization is gained that rest is as important as action. All reward is not through ambition, recognition, and money. It is sometimes wise to take time out to realize that God's abundance is everywhere and is to be attained through prayer and inner poise, as well as through constant activity and effort.

Chapters 9 and 10 are a source of endless satisfaction in analyzing character; business opportunity and the qualities of character that make people so entirely different from each other are described.

Note:

Even when a father and son have the same names—the numbers on the birth force (the month, day, and year of birth) and the reality number will point out many differences in character and ultimate success.

CHAPTER XI

YOUR HIDDEN CHALLENGE
Your Hidden and Undeveloped Talents

How dull life would be without its incentives, its challenges, and its victories!

A few people find "getting on in the world" easy. The majority of men and women, however, learn from experience that what they want must be earned and worked for.

No one is really perfect in character or action, and there are many problems to be met to reach any goal. After all, the thrill in living is to rise above the obstacles and frustrations by one's own talents and determinations.

When repeated failure and the lack of good things in life are constantly experienced, the clue to this often lies, unrecognized, deep in the individual's own nature.

There is a challenge in everyone's life, to be discovered, ferreted out, and brought to the surface for a better balance of the life's forces and as an asset for financial success. This challenge may show itself in several ways—as a personal feeling which is like a bad habit, or as an antagonistic trait, causing lack of friends and popularity, or, again, as a spasmodic cleverness, untrained and of little value in the long run.

The Challenge may be compared to a weak link in a chain; once it is discovered and corrected it can bring the whole chain of circumstances in the life and environment into a useful and constructive expression and be the added impetus for success.

191

A man or woman may be very talented, have fine qualities for leadership and be headed for lasting success, then suddenly fail or lose out, due to a small fault or personal habit of seemingly no consequence, at least to the one having the habit or Challenge.

In some cases, lack of understanding of the fault may lead to rebellion against others and life itself and continue to mar the progress and happiness which would be there if the Challenge were met and understood.

YOUR CHALLENGE

Dig deep. Discover your Challenge.

Do not attempt to overcome it—BECOME IT.

Accept its support in meeting life's requirements.

Work with it. Bring it into harmony with the skills and talents you were born with.

Handle it with grace and charm. It will add romance to your life through its own natural channels.

The Challenge is found within the birth force. The rule of subtraction is used. Subtract the smaller number from the larger on any position.

There are three types of Challenges: The outstanding Challenge, the mixed Challenge, and the cipher Challenge. The cipher Challenge also has three divisions: The single cipher, the double cipher, and the complete cipher.

The Challenge varies in every name. However, there are certain numbers found more often than others. The numbers *one, two, three,* and the *cipher* are most commonly found on the Challenge. The numbers *four* and *five* are next in repeated appearance. The number *six* often stands alone and is a positive Challenge. The numbers *seven* and *eight* are found more often in association with a cipher or as a *final* Challenge. The number *nine* is never found as a Challenge for it is the highest number and all other numbers are subtracted from it. The *cipher* can take over the qualities of the number *nine*.

First—Subtract the digits of the *month* and the *day* from each other.

Second—Subtract the digits of the *day* and the *year* from each other.

Third—Subtract these two remainders from each other.

Fourth—Subtract the digit of the *month* from the digit of the *year*. (Always subtract the smaller number from the larger on any position.)

OUTSTANDING CHALLENGE

Example:

August		9th		1949		
8	+	9	+	(23) 5	=	(22) 4 Birth Force
1		4				
		3				
		3				(Outstanding 3 Challenge)

Subtract the digit of the month and the digit of the day from each other:

$9 - 8 = 1$ *The 1st period Challenge*

Subtract the digit of the day and the digit of the year from each other:

$9 - 5 = 4$ *The 2nd period Challenge*

Subtract these two remainders from each other:

$4 - 1 = 3$ *The 3rd period Challenge*

Subtract the digit of the month and the digit of the year from each other:

$8 - 5 = 3$ *The 4th period Challenge*

In this example the number 3 will be the main Challenge throughout the life, as well as an asset when it is recognized as a talent to be developed.

MIXED CHALLENGE

Example:

```
    July        13th        1947
     7     +     4     +    (21) 3    = (14) 5 Birth Force
           3                 1
                   2
                   4           (Mixed Challenge)
```

1st period Challenge.
    Subtract the month and day (7 minus 4) = 3

2nd period Challenge.
    Subtract the day and year (4 minus 3) = 1

3rd period Challenge.
    Subtract these two remainders (3 minus 1) = 2

4th period Challenge.
    Subtract the month and year (7 minus 3) = 4

The mixed Challenge is not commonly found and does not show special talents. A different Challenge will be experienced during each period; the final 4 indicates that, later in life, there may be a Challenge to hold life on an even keel. Order, system, and organization will be supporting qualities, if cultivated.

(The timing for each division will be given under the Pinnacle instructions. The Challenge and the Pinnacles work together.)

CIPHER CHALLENGES

Examples:

(Use the same rules of subtraction.):

```
May    5th    1956              Jan.   2nd    1918
 5  +  5  + (21) 3 =(13)4        1  +  2  + (19) 1 =4
   0      2                        1      1
      2                              0
      2                              0
```
(Single Cipher)   (Double Cipher)

```
         Mar.    3rd    1956
          3  +  3  + (21) 3 =9
            0      0
               0
               0
```
(Complete Cipher)

Example 1 shows a Cipher for the 1st period; the number 2, appearing three times, becomes the true Challenge.

In Example 2, the 1 is the Challenge for two periods; for the 3rd and 4th period, the Cipher, which has a subjective influence at all times.

In the 3rd Example, the Cipher is the main Challenge. This is not easy. The choice is left open to the individual and may cause confusion and misdirection at times until the qualities and characteristics of the Major positions, the Planes of Expression, and the Points of Intensification are allowed to fill in the Cipher.

READING THE CHALLENGE

The number appearing on the Challenge may also be found on other positions of the name. It may even be intensified on the Points of Intensification. That it appears again on the Challenge, indicates there is still something required of the individual, in the nature of the Challenge, to round out the character and to be made an asset in meeting the requirements for success and happiness. If the number on the Challenge is not found in the name, it is even more important that this special talent, way of thinking and acting be made a constructive part of the character.

As you observe your Challenge, you will be surprised at how often it appears in your affairs. Friends, family, and business associates will face you, bearing in their natures your Challenge number.

NUMBER ONE CHALLENGE

When a One appears on the Challenge, the feeling of opposition, of being held down, often by relatives or those with stronger wills, will be experienced. When the Challenge is a One, a steadier will must be cultivated, a finer determination expressed with dignity and self-respect.

Resentment should be avoided. Little is gained by placing the blame on others. Fighting against the hurts or headstrong action leads to mistakes and to unreasonableness. The quick wit, originality, and personal ideas should be valued and trained.

Even though there may be many ones in the name at birth and the character very positive and dominant, a broader expression of purpose must still be cultivated.

NUMBER TWO CHALLENGE

The number Two Challenge is one of the most commonly found, for the quality of sensitiveness is natural to the human race. It is a very fine characteristic. Without it, response to the fitness of things would be lacking and the coarse and rude phases of life would predominate. When hypersensitiveness is allowed to take over, it can represent fear, timidity, or lack of self-confidence and be a source of deep suffering. A feeling of subordination often prevents success and gives a tendency to be unduly influenced by what others think or say. Sensitiveness represents intelligence and understanding of the finer relationships of life. It is only when it is allowed to become hurt feelings, jealousies, and fear of people that it is negative. The number Two Challenge should value its natural talent for relating facts, perfecting details, and for knowing what is correct and right. The cultivation of harmony and decorum gives self-confidence and the feeling of usefulness.

NUMBER THREE CHALLENGE

The number Three Challenge indicates that deep in the nature there is a fine imagination, the gift of words, speech, and an artistic talent, but a barrier against the full expression of these qualities is also present. This may be due to a repression through others or to the fear of appearing too forward, but just as often may be a repression within the self. Many artists and professional people have the Three Challenge, and sometimes it is late in life before the full measure of the talent is brought out. A better use of the creative imagination can result in the writing of a book, or a painting, or even a design for a lovely creation. In seeking romance and popularity, hurtful words, spoken impulsively, may bring loss of friends and the admiration so greatly desired. Sometimes this is due to a strong dislike of personal criticism and because there is, even though not always recognized, a deep feeling of personal importance. Do not bury the talents. Bring them out and learn the value of constructive speaking. Learn to be a real friend, interested in others as much as in the self.

NUMBER FOUR CHALLENGE

The number Four Challenge is an outstanding Challenge and not so frequently found as the first three numbers. The number Four is the practical number, serious, and gifted with a sense of values, so these qualities lie deep in the nature of the number Four Challenge. Regardless of what other indications are found in the name, there is still a work to do, a task to accomplish based on patient, steady, repeated effort, slow and sure building up of the success and material possessions. Too many changes, restlessness, and going from one thing to another do not bring the permanent accomplishment possible with the Four Challenge. The Four Challenge likes security and should work for it. The Four is capable of putting things into form and is also capable of thrift, integrity, and facing life squarely. When combativeness is in the nature, more education is a great help. Too strong opinions can be a problem. A deep-seated desire to put some idea or concept into form should be brought to the surface and worked for.

NUMBER FIVE CHALLENGE

The number Five Challenge indicates all that the number five stands for; but, at the same time, versatility, curiosity, love of change and variety can be a problem. A deep feeling for personal freedom is present, and many times, resentment and impatience may be expressed when the desire to be elsewhere is thwarted. Sometimes this desire for "freedom" to escape responsibility causes mistakes in selection of place and association. The number Five Challenge becomes a fine asset when a place in the public is found and a work that allows for promotion, travel, publicity, and contact with crowds or large groups. When the restlessness of the Five is allowed to become dominant, real satisfaction in accomplishment is never reached, especially if criticism and strong dislikes are allowed to grow. When the roots of an accomplishment are constantly torn up, restlessness defeats the life. Make use of the quick perceptions, the resourcefulness, and interest in life's many phases for success. A Five Challenge does not like to be confined. It desires and needs new contacts and new places from time to time, but also clings to old traditions.

NUMBER SIX CHALLENGE

The number Six Challenge is a domestic one. It shows a challenge in the affairs of the home, concerning children, family, and love affairs. The Challenge may be in the dominance and possessiveness deep in the nature. There is a high ideality, love of art, the beautiful, and the home; but mixed ideals of loyalty, obedience, and a determination to be the boss or head of the family often cause unhappiness in marriage.

A good sense of duty and feeling of responsibility is in the nature, even though the analysis of the name, up to this point, shows no sixes on Points of Intensification or Major Numbers. There is an ability to give service to humanity and to teach and heal. There is musical ability and appreciation of nature in its grandeur and loveliness. Sometimes the Six Challenge finds life hard because of a feeling of lack of appreciation. Learn to give more appreciation; then the problems in home and marriage will not be so marked.

NUMBER SEVEN CHALLENGE

In the Seven Challenge, the feeling of aloneness and separation must be overcome. The Seven must dig down and bring its knowledge, understanding, and gift of knowing in a specialized way to the surface for the good of the world. There is generally a big test or repression in the life and affairs; this is sometimes too much pride and a reserve which holds the feeling hidden and underneath the surface. The Challenge may be something that has happened in the family life or in its own life, which is kept hidden or which is considered an embarrassment. The Seven Challenge should forgive and forget and meet the barriers by being more real and natural, but also through cultivating the keen powers of analysis and discrimination so particular to the nature. The ability to know the real from the false in business, work, or in association is an asset and source of power. The Seven Challenge wants so much. It can attract the best in life when it takes the time to study, learn, and perfect its skills along the technical, educational, and specialized fields of endeavor.

NUMBER EIGHT CHALLENGE

The number Eight Challenge is not an easy one. It is necessary to make careful relationships with the rest of the name and the Reality when it appears as a total Challenge. When an Eight Challenge appears, there is often a cipher for one of the earlier periods. The Eight Challenge has a fine opportunity for position in the world, if the motives are good and the ambitions worthy. To bluff or pretend only results in delay and uncertain success. A philosophical attitude of mind should be cultivated so as to be able to see both sides of a question, especially about life and its meaning. The ability to become a wise counselor lies deep in the nature.

The Eight can meet opposition and long, slow frustration by its own efforts if it stands on its own feet and seeks to understand life's realities. A musical talent may be surprisingly latent.

THE CIPHER CHALLENGE

The Cipher Challenge is a very common Challenge—part-time, or for the entire life. It stands for naught or *all*. The universe is symbolized by the circle. It contains all things, but still can be emptiness, depending on the mentality or desire of the individual. Anyone having the Cipher Challenge has the right of *choice*: just to drift along in life; or to rise above the seeming problems to become truly great. Although big tests come, many wonderful and understanding people have the complete Cipher Challenge. The individual with the Cipher Challenge has the right to create his own world, and if he fills his Challenge with love and compassion and true helpfulness to mankind, his work and his undertakings will succeed surprisingly well. When a period Cipher is present at any age or time of life, it should not be taken lightly, for during that time a selection must be made which should be according to the Destiny and outstanding talents. A Cipher is similar to the number Nine. With a Cipher Challenge, cultivate a desire to make the world a better place.

LET'S TALK IT OVER

You will find it very interesting to watch for your Challenge number in your friendships.

I have many close and very-much-liked friends with the number Three prominent in their names. The number Three is my Challenge number. I enjoy their inspiration, creative imagination, and ability to enthuse over what they are interested in. However, being of rather serious and practical mind, I am often annoyed at their bubbling over and what seems to me to be exaggeration. I have had to learn that enthusiasm is one of life's greatest gifts, and to cultivate some degree of it myself.

Do not be discouraged because you have a Cipher Challenge. In many ways it is a special privilege. A given number on the Challenge holds you to that specific effort. A Cipher gives you broad opportunity in any direction you may choose. The Cipher takes the place of the number Nine Challenge. It indicates there is a warm soul and a universal consciousness back of it. There may be big experiences to take, but the latent force to meet it is there.

Make the same comparisons with your Challenge number to the other positions in your name as you have been doing. For example, when the Challenge is the same as the Heart's Desire there will be a Challenge in the nature of the number, which may try to defeat the attainment of the Heart's Desire until the Challenge is developed and made constructive (the same with every position, according to what the position means). This is simply following the rule that has been given so many times before. It is only through this method of procedure that you get to the real problems and many experiences that come into your life.

THE HABIT CHALLENGE

The *Habit* Challenge is quite different. It represents a talent that is natural, but becomes a Challenge when it is overintensified and may even become an annoying personal characteristic.

It is called the *Point of Security* and is found from the number of letters in the name at birth. It represents a dexterity and skill so much a part of the nature that it is hardly recognized as a natural ability. It is a part of hustle and bustle of everyday living, a method of action that is thought of as just a personal characteristic or "It's just my way." It represents both the constructive and negative side of the number. When an individual is not inclined to self-analysis, far too often the negative side predominates, becoming a negative trait or annoying manner to others.

RULE

Count the number of letters in your name at birth and reduce to a single digit. Give yourself credit for the talents the number represents. Then check your thoughts and actions to see how many times you slip into the annoying side of the number's characteristic.

HABIT CHALLENGES ONE THROUGH NINE

The number *One* Total—Your ideas are good, but do not become dominant because of a single-track mind.

Two—You do things properly and well, but do not become fuss-budgety over little things.

Three—You are talented, but do not be vacillating, dreaming instead of doing.

Four—You are careful, serious, and a good worker, but do not be on the opposite side too often, or run away if you are a 22.

Five—The whole world gives you opportunity if you are not constantly critical or changeable.

Six—You can create beauty at home and in business, but you can be dominating, also too possessive.

Seven—Your fine sense of perfection gives you specialized skills, but watch out for that inner resentment which separates you from others.

Eight—Your ability to see both sides of a question is a business asset, but do not complain about conditions at the wrong time or tactlessly.

Nine—Your ability to add color and drama to your undertakings can warm the hearts of everyone, but watch out for those moods—up today, down tomorrow.

Note: Some of the big and sudden happenings in your life will be in the nature of your *Point of Security*.

Lesson number Twelve will begin Part Three of the course, *Reading Personal Experiences*, taking you into the advanced studies of the letters of your name, which describe the past, the present, and the future.

There will be many questions in your mind. You will be asking about signatures, changing names, naming the baby, marriage, locations, music, color, and many other things.

From what you have previously learned you should already be able to read vocations and talents. However, all these will be explained later after you have learned to read the experiences you or your client are taking.

PART THREE

To every thing there is a season, and a time for every purpose underneath the heaven.—Eccles.

THE PINNACLES: TIMING THE FUTURE

YOUR PERSONAL YEAR NUMBER

PERSONAL MONTHS—PERSONAL DAYS

THE RACE CONSCIOUSNESS

THE TABLE OF EVENTS

MEANING OF THE ESSENCE

VOCATIONS AND TALENTS

CHAPTER XII

THE PINNACLES:
TIMING THE FUTURE
The Road Ahead

It is often hard for people to account for the changes which take place unexpectedly in their affairs, or to understand the sudden ups and downs which occur when everything seems to be going smoothly.

Why will someone suddenly grow tired of the work being done successfully, and for no sane or apparent reason, give it up to follow an entirely different career? Why may a successful man suddenly fail or, on the other hand, someone who has had a long period of failure come into authority and recognition?

"Change is the watchword of progress." Were this not so, men and women would become so self-satisfied, or so discouraged, there would be no true mental or spiritual growth for anyone and little progress for the world, resulting in ultimate stagnation and tragedy.

Changing conditions give all a chance to succeed. The man who is down today has a right to expect to succeed; and the man who is in power has the prospect of losing that power unless he is adaptable to change, alert to the future, and understands that experiences, even ups and downs, are tests of sincerity and spiritual awareness.

It is possible to prophesy through numbers, for prophecy is *TIMING*—looking forward to events yet to take place.

A number, being a definite symbol of the nature of things, can, when applied to events, reveal the nature of that event, specifically and definitely—not to forecast ill or evil, but as a means of preparedness for the road ahead and for broader attainment, materially and spiritually.

The *Pinnacles* (like the *Challenge*) are found written on the Birth Force. They are well-defined road maps and indicate the highway of life the individual is to travel during the *four* main periods of experience of the lifetime. They show the nature of the thought and effort to be put forth, any given period of time, to work out satisfactorily the Destiny as shown by the name at birth. They give an outlet for the successful use of the talents and personal capabilities from the day of birth to the end of the life.

The Pinnacles are protective and instructive. No one escapes the experiences of the Pinnacles. From the illumined mystic to the most ordinary individual, the signposts hold true. The mystic, however, welcomes the steps to be taken into the future and makes them part of the glory of accomplishment. The ordinary man calls them fate and does not sense the purpose behind the experiences.

A cycle of nine years is the keynote to reading and timing the Pinnacles. Nine months is the natural period of time for the full growth and birth of a human life. Seven is often spoken of in the Bible as a cycle. It is not a cycle of fulfillment. A seven-month birth is premature. Cycles of nine outline the duration of each Pinnacle. Seven represents the occult, that which is hidden and to be discovered. Nine represents revelation, the interpretation of Love and Service.

The First Pinnacle—Represents the spring of life and is very personal.

The Second Pinnacle—Covers the summer of life, the period of responsibility and the family.

The Third Pinnacle—Covers middle age and the more mature attitudes of mind. It is the reaping and the extension of consciousness into the national and international phases of activity. It is the autumn of human endeavor.

The Fourth Pinnacle—Represents the winter of life, so-called old age, and has to do with the human and spiritual welfare of mankind. It gives much opportunity for a successful use of the experiences of the past.

There should never be an unhappy or wasted old age. Growth from youth to the latter days of life is promised through constructive expression and eager consent to the duties of each Pinnacle.

Each Pinnacle is a period of development. Each period is *accurately timed*.

FIGURING THE PINNACLES

The rule of *addition* is used—in contrast to the rule of subtraction for the Challenge.

First Pinnacle—The sum of the digits of the month and day of birth.

Second Pinnacle—The sum of the digits of the day and year of birth.

Third Pinnacle—The addition of these two numbers (first and second Pinnacles).

Fourth Pinnacle—The sum of the digits of the month and year.

Example:

```
              (16) 7
              (10) 1
         (14) 5    5 (14)
     August   6th    1934
        8   +  6  +  (17)8  = (22) 4 Birth Force
            2      2
                 0
     Challenge  0
```

In this Example:

The first Pinnacle is a five—(the sum of the digits of the month and day).

The second Pinnacle is a five—(the sum of the digits of the day and year).

The third Pinnacle is a one—(the sum of the first two digits).

The fourth Pinnacle is a seven—(the sum of the digits of the month and year).

TIMING THE PINNACLES

Figure *slowly* and *carefully*. *Start* with the given number *36* (4 times 9).

Next—Subtract the number of the digit of the *Birth Force* from this number *36*. This gives the period of time the *first Pinnacle* is active—and the *age* its influence ends.

(It is always the Birth Force number that is subtracted from the number 36.)

Now—Add nine years to this age—the time the first Pinnacle ended. This is the period of time the *Second Pinnacle* will influence the life.

Again—Add nine years to the age the second Pinnacle ended. These nine years cover the period of time the *Third Pinnacle* is directing the affairs.

From this age—The ending of the third Pinnacle, the *Fourth Pinnacle* will govern the affairs to the end of the life.

This is the rule for timing the Pinnacles—for everyone.
(The Challenge is timed with the Pinnacles.)

Example:

Study Henry Ford's Pinnacle experiences (July 30th, 1863).

$$\frac{7}{}$$

Pinnacles 4

$$\frac{1 \qquad 3}{}$$

July   30th   1863

$$\frac{7 \ + \ 3 \ + \ 9}{} \ = (19) \ 1 \ \text{Birth Force}$$

$$\frac{4 \qquad 6}{}$$

$$\frac{2}{}$$

Challenge 2

During the first part of his life, until he was *35* (36 minus 1—his Birth Force), he was under the number *one* Pinnacle. Being the same number as his Birth Force, it gave him a start along the lines of his talents, encouraging the development of ideas, executive ability and self-determination. Many tests of will and initiative had to be met, as a "one" Pinnacle is not an easy period. Being naturally a sensitive man (twos on Challenge and the (11) 2 at Heart), he did not find it easy to dare to do what he felt he could do. A *four* Challenge running with the *one* Pinnacle indicates a lot of hard work and many practical requirements. He must have made many mistakes and, at times, must have been difficult to direct and reason with, but he had to move forward, urged on by his creative ideas.

Later, between the ages of *35* and *44* (his second Pinnacle and the next nine years) he was directed by the number *Three*. Observe the *three* of the 30 of his birthday. During this time a desire for personal expression, to follow his own personal ideas, was strong. A *three* period is always good for promoting the career if the talents and energies are not scattered through too much time given to personal pleasure or to romance and the opposite sex. Since he had a *six* Challenge underneath the *three* Pinnacle, there was a duty to be met and understood, acting as a challenge but also a humanitarian feeling, urging him on. He made good use of imagination and deep emotional feeling, and the whole world has benefited by his creative genius.

His third Pinnacle, from *44* to *53* (the next nine years of his life), was under the four. A lot of hard work, management, application, and attention to practical matters enabled him to put his ideas into definite form and to establish a concrete foundation for future work. At the same time his sensitive feeling was growing (two Challenge), and he did branch out into other fields of endeavor.

His final Pinnacle, lasting from *53* to the end of his life, was a seven. This is the number of study, analysis, writing, and scientific undertakings. He did all of these things and became more and more retiring, although recognized and brought to the foreground by his skill and cleverness in his business affairs and his personal interests in maintaining old and interesting historical relics of the past. (The number 2 likes to collect and gather old and valued possessions.) To be happy under any seven Pinnacle, one needs to know something well and make use of this knowledge.

A More Difficult Chart:

$$
\begin{array}{ccccl}
 & & \underline{4} & & \\
\text{Pinnacles} & & \underline{8} & & \\
 & 4 & & 4 & \\
\text{Feb.} & \underline{2} & & 1847 & \\
 & 2 & + \ 2 \ + & 2 & = 6 \text{ Birth Force} \\
 & \underline{0} & & 0 & \\
 & & \underline{0} & & \\
\text{Challenge} & 0 & & &
\end{array}
$$

A famous scientist. Notice the practical Pinnacles and the tremendous Challenge. He worked all the time, experimenting and building, daring, until in the end he gave the world beauty and light, living up to the humanitarian purpose of his Birth Force.

A Great Artist:

For comparison, let us study another interesting Birth Force. The birthdate of a musician and composer and well-known orchestra leader.

$$
\begin{array}{c}
\underline{3} \\
6 \\
\quad\;\, 9 \qquad 6 \\
\text{Mar.} \quad 15 \quad 1881 \\
\underline{3 \;+\; 6 \;+\; 9} \qquad = (18)\; 9 \;\text{Birth Force} \\
\underline{3 \qquad 3} \\
\underline{0} \\
6
\end{array}
$$

At one glance the artistic talent and vocation of the life is apparent. There was no other way to go. Even though he frequently met a challenge to his expression and work and may have been highly emotional at times, he created music and was known as a true musician and great artist.

Not all people have such definite and outstanding Pinnacles as we have seen here. With most people each Pinnacle is different. But each Pinnacle number is a signpost, a road map for the best attainment and method of procedure at that *given time.*

MEANING OF THE PINNACLES

Number One Pinnacle

As this is the number of individuality, executive ability, and leadership, when it appears as any Pinnacle, it forces the individual to stand on his or her feet and to forge ahead. As a first Pinnacle, it is often a hard period, for the younger person may not be prepared to meet life with force and initiative and may be rebuffed by the hard experiences which must be met to

bring out the powers of leadership and executive ability. Sometimes, in trying to understand the forces operating in the life,
the young man or woman may be headstrong and have too
much self-importance, resisting direction, showing a great deal
of egotism, and be hard to direct or understand until the right
direction for the use of the talents is found from a careful
study of the name. For the second and third Pinnacle it gives
the opportunity to do and dare and to make use of personal
ideas. On any Pinnacles, the number *one* forces the individual
to stand up to life, to think and act for himself or herself; and
with women, this is frequently sudden or unexpected. At the
same time, the opportunity is there to move forward and to develop the personal and often unsuspected talents. As a final
Pinnacle it is also a forceful period and may be a release—a
chance to do a broader work along the lines of the personal
ideas developed during the other Pinnacle periods, or to carry
out unexpressed desires. There is an opportunity present to be
outstanding and at the head of a work or undertaking. It is not
an easy period of life, for it demands courage, will, and determination to take a useful place in the affairs of the world.

NUMBER TWO PINNACLE

This is the number of partnerships, associations, and
unions. It brings many people into the work or undertaking,
and involvement in the affairs of others at home or in business.
It is not a period of independence, for the best results are
through harmonious relationship with others. The test of the
period is in the ability to get on with others and to work with
them without getting involved beyond the need brought about
through the necessary associations. Sometimes the individual,
moving into a *two* Pinnacle, has to learn patience, cooperation, sharing, and consideration of others. During a first Pinnacle, a young person may seem unduly sensitive and unable to
take hold of things. Nothing is gained by running away from
any situation; and parents may need to establish right associa-

tions, give a good education, make a careful study of the talents and abilities, and help the young person understand life, people, and himself. To force a child, or to fail to understand the sensitive forces operating at the time, is to bring about complexes, extreme sensitiveness, or just the opposite—foolhardy aggressiveness. All *twos* on the Pinnacles work best in association with many people, the moving public and cultural considerations. There is often statistical ability, a feeling for details and finished fine work, patient, careful accuracy and precision. This holds true throughout the *two* Pinnacles, for the best results are by friendly and interested cooperation in work. Difficulties in partnerships, associations, and friendships may come about. Personal hurts through others, divorce and separations are the tests to be taken unless the true spirit of cooperation is cultivated. The individual under the *two* Pinnacle must also be careful not to hurt others and to be fair in all dealings. When the (11) 2 Pinnacle is the indication for any period, there can be a breaking of an association in a surprising way and a lesson to be learned in spiritual thinking and faith. Even men, through the hurts received in partnerships or in love and marriage, turn to religion, philosophical and spiritual thinking and study. What seems to be a big change in the life is almost always good in the end, for it brings the character to deeper understanding of the self and of the rights of others. Rewards come through fine technical or unusual lines of activity or production.

NUMBER THREE PINNACLE

This is the number of inspiration, creative ability, and artistic feeling and opens the door for more personal expression on any Pinnacle. It is an easy Pinnacle in that the work or undertakings are not physical, but deal with imagination and feeling. It gives opportunity through writing, speaking, the theater, designing, illustration, or for origination of ideas of a creative nature. This may be in business as well as the artistic fields. It is a time of pouring out the feelings and allows for general enjoyment of the pleasures of life, as it carries a natural attraction for money and the easier phases of living. When it is found on the first Pinnacle there is always an artistic opportunity present, but, very often, a young person shows little tendency for hard work and seeks to enjoy life without too much practical effort. The first Pinnacle can be wasted, causing regret later on, if an effort is not made to direct the talents while the time is at hand. Education along creative lines should be given even if not ultimately chosen as a career. Under the second or third Pinnacle it can be a blessing, giving more personal opportunity to develop the talents and personal ideas than at any other time. However, extravagant and careless expression of the emotions and feelings can lead to so many unhappy experiences that others may be called on to help the individual out of trouble. The eternal triangle often appears, and friends, while helpful, can be misleading; money can be lost through the influence of good talkers and those who appeal to the emotional nature. Even on the last Pinnacle, control over the emotions is necessary to keep the reward of love, friendship, and money. Women, especially, often make mistakes and lose money through being carried away by affairs of the heart. Under a three final Pinnacle the individual has the right to the joys and pleasures of life, but should also make a special effort to find usefulness in an inspirational and creative manner.

NUMBER FOUR PINNACLE

This is the number of order, system, application, practical thought, and endeavor. *Four* is the builder, serious and desirous of gaining results of a concrete nature. It is always a manager and builder through placing facts and ideas in their proper order for definite results. When it is found as a first Pinnacle, the young person will respond to serious and practical ideas and often goes to work early in life, due to a practical need to find occupation early. But, generally, the work of the *four* Pinnacle lays a good foundation for the future, even if there are many economic problems and much hard work. The family and in-laws are very often a responsibility and also an accepted duty on any Pinnacle. The individual must get down to work, manage and organize for definite results. Many times, however, it is a welcome period and a chance to put into form the ideas and plans dreamed of for many years. Under a *four* Pinnacle, any person not willing to face the practical facts of life will find that economic management cannot be escaped. For a fourth Pinnacle, it may be the first time during the life that the opportunity to organize, build, work, and get results in a serious and worthwhile manner is experienced. However, anyone who has not grown in maturity and attitude of mind during the previous Pinnacles may find this four Pinnacle difficult or a period of economic endeavor. Many fine works have been accomplished by men and women during the latter days of life, even if just a hobby is developed. When a *four* appears on any Pinnacle it is not a leisure time. The reward is through application and the effort to get tangible results and to keep on the job until it is accomplished, even if practical problems arise.

NUMBER FIVE PINNACLE

The number *five* on any Pinnacle represents activity, public life, and the unexpected. It is never a settled condition, but gives an interesting and eventful period of life with freedom to come and go, make changes, and to be part of what is going on in the world. On the other hand, the *five* Pinnacle may be a period of restlessness, uncertainty, and constant change, depending upon the type of individual taking a *five* Pinnacle experience. Living a first *five* Pinnacle, a young person is apt to be restless, lack in application, and make changes suddenly before the reward of an effort or work is attained. Much experience is gained, however, which frequently becomes an asset later in life, for it gives the ability to meet the public and the changing and progressive interest of mankind. The number *five* stands for progress and advancement on any Pinnacle if taken in the right spirit; but it is somewhat uncertain regarding finances—steady income at one time, uncertain income at another, yet money always comes at the right time and when really needed. It gives opportunity on any Pinnacle for civic interest, legal pursuits, advertising, and administrative advancement. It does not represent the home or domestic life, since a woman may find she is led into some kind of public life from desire or necessity. On a second or third Pinnacle it can represent a period of great freedom, especially if it follows a six or four, and can be a very happy, interesting time of life. It requires the ability to adapt to new friends, new lines of work, and new contacts. Quarrels and legal affairs can cause problems and annoyance; it is important to be sure that all legal undertakings under any *five* Pinnacle are carefully understood and not entered into hastily. For a final Pinnacle it again represents freedom and an active life. It does not prophesy retirement, however. It calls for an effort to take part in progressive undertakings and to help others understand their experiences. Try to keep a few roots down, even though living an active life. When sudden changes occur or when restlessness builds up, avoid hasty, impulsive actions.

NUMBER SIX PINNACLE

The number *six* on any Pinnacle indicates duty and responsibility to the family. It also gives an opportunity to do useful, humanitarian works, to help those in need, to teach, heal, and to bring comfort to many people, young and old. During any *six* Pinnacle the time is given to useful work, for there is money to be made and a happy, useful life to be experienced. It is not a time for personal thought or self-interest, or personal plans only. The affairs of the home, children, love affairs, trust funds, and inheritances enter in many cases, and the opportunity is present to settle down to making money and building up the finances. Health problems may enter in through family or loved ones, and money will be spent in this regard; but through giving and helping at home and out in the world, much can be gained and a useful life realized. For a first Pinnacle it indicates duty at home and often early marriage, or responsibility to a parent or brothers and sisters. It brings love and protection through the family with good enough financial conditions. Sometimes it is wise in advising a young person under the *six* first Pinnacle *not* to marry too early, for the duty of the first Pinnacle may last a whole lifetime, unless a five or seven Pinnacle is ahead. On any Pinnacle it represents duty and responsibility which, if accepted, can bring a rich reward and add satisfaction and financial success. For a final Pinnacle, the duty can be really worthwhile, crowning the life and giving recognition for the fine work done in the past. If a man or woman has not married during the lifetime, the opportunity for love and marriage is possible under the final *six* Pinnacle. It does not indicate a lonely or useless old age. If an individual has not gained wisdom and a true sense of service during the lifetime, the latter days can be given over to the family, baby-sitting, and care of loved ones without personal freedom. The problems of children, family, money, marriage, divorce, and home life color all *six* Pinnacles and are met through love and loyalty and humanitarian service.

NUMBER SEVEN PINNACLE

The number *seven* on any Pinnacle is a period of soul development. The number *seven* is a strongly individualized force. It represents knowledge and understanding of the deeper forces of life—that which is not on the surface. Under a *seven* Pinnacle, educational studies, scientific interests, specialization of the talents for outstanding use and recognition should be cultivated. It is the number of perfection and demands the best, but is also proud, exclusive, and something of the separatist. When any *seven* Pinnacle begins to operate, the individual under its influence seems to care less for worldly activities, likes to study or investigate things in a specialized way, desires to be alone, and outgrows old associations. When the *seven* Pinnacle is misunderstood, its introvert nature may bring about a withdrawal within the self and a feeling of repression, causing problems in family and personal relationships. Negative states of mind may develop—moods and complexes which defeat understanding of what life is all about. Even though money, at times, may seem limited and not all desired, knowledge and skill will bring success and big money. Often, under a *seven* Pinnacle the individual is restless and the grass seems greener on the other side of the fence. These changes result in lack of accomplishment. Seek knowledge and education instead. For a first Pinnacle it very often brings a repression in some way. This repression may be lack of money for education, very strict parents, or poor health. Wise parents will see that the child has a special education, that careful diet and health matters are taken care of with more understanding in training than restrictive measures of discipline. There is a quiet attraction for money through the *seven*, so poise and faith should never be lost if finances seem difficult. Patience, care, and study help attract what is needed. A *seven* on any Pinnacle demands *truth* and right living. There can be no bluffing or subterfuge while working through a *seven* experience. The *seven* has a way of finding things out about the self and others. It is not an easy marriage vibration and often partnerships are difficult, with problems, for the *seven* can be cold, separate, and more interested in studies and work than in ordinary worldly activities. When knowledge, understanding, and training of the mind have been attained, a *seven* Pinnacle brings a fine reward and a power to attract all things, even love. Under the *seven* Pinnacle make contact with those who are interested in the educational, scientific, and cultural phases of living.

NUMBER EIGHT PINNACLE

The number *eight* is a number of strength, courage, ambition, authority, and enterprise. It stands for attainment through endeavor, requiring intelligence, ability to judge, understanding of people, and establishment of efficiency and good management. The opportunity for recognition is there, and for broad activity of a progressive nature. During an *eight* Pinnacle, both men and women find themselves in charge of business, property, or professional activities which depend upon a steady and repeated effort for success. An *eight* Pinnacle is not an easy one, for it does not tolerate weakness in the individual or efforts to escape from facing the issue, but demands full measure of intelligence and application. During an *eight* Pinnacle, recognition and authority are promised, many possessions and property are gained, and a fine success is possible. However, expenses are high, so careful management of the affairs and budgeting is necessary. Often there is a big expense necessary to maintain the undertaking during an *eight* Pinnacle. As a first Pinnacle the young man or woman, as under the four, goes early into business or professional work and can get a fine start in life, but is often forced to be the means of support for the family or relatives. During any *eight* Pinnacle it is not a time to trust to luck. Good judgment and understanding of people are necessary. Many problems and disappointments may be experienced through misplaced trust in others. An interest in societies and organizations brings support and friendship. Philosophical studies bring important contacts. Any *eight* Pinnacle gives an opportunity to become a V.I.P. if a repeated effort is made. Work intelligently rather than with emotional feeling.

NUMBER NINE PINNACLE

The number *nine* represents the drama and color of life. It represents beauty, art, and the philanthropic. It expects, from the person working under the *nine* Pinnacle, a great deal of tolerance, compassion, and that warm force of love that inspires and uplifts but which is greater than personal love. A number *nine* Pinnacle is not easy to live up to, as a rule, unless the character has these qualities of thought and feeling well developed in the make-up. It is not easy to express love and tolerance at all times in this modern world of stress and strain. By the time the *nine* Pinnacle has been completed, the lessons of tolerance and compassion will have been learned or great disappointment will be realized. *Nine* is not a personal number. It represents civilization, all people, and all religions. The lines of work, under a *nine* Pinnacle, which are business, artistic, or philanthropic, have a fine chance for success and to attract money and fortune. Travel and a full life reward the individual if the principles of the *nine* are expressed. Otherwise, if the desires are personal, self-interested, and resentful of others, the *nine* Pinnacle can be a very unhappy one. It should not be. Aim high, for the best and most useful for all mankind. When the *nine* is the first Pinnacle, a love affair, a marriage, or a line of work may be completed and left behind, with some sorrow or regret. On the other hand, this completion can be a blessing, for it takes out of the life, or brings to a head and to a completion, things no longer needed for the progress of the individual. If losses seem to occur, they should be forgotten, for the *nine* Pinnacle will always bring something else better and rewarding if the individual's thought and feeling reach out to the philanthropic and the brotherhood of man. Money can be made and lost and, just as easily, be made again. The number *nine*, while it tests the character for the amount of compassion, tolerance, and warm appreciation of the higher forces of life, also rewards and assists in every way possible. For a latter Pinnacle, it gives wonderful opportunity to do great work in the world along the lines of the chosen talents. The number *nine* Pinnacle is not a phase of life that can be evaded if the reward of better things is to be attained and disappointments overcome. During a second and third period, many experiences of emotional nature appear to develop warmth and ideality. Narrowmindedness is not rewarded. Self-seeking and desire for personal love alone are not enough. Forget the self and grow. Bring tolerance to all undertakings, and true love will come.

LET'S TALK IT OVER

When I read a name, my first study of the Pinnacles is to get a sort of bird's-eye view of their pattern. What is the nature of the *first* Pinnacle—and the *last?* In some cases, the easier experiences come early in life; in others, during the latter part of life. I like to know this, for it helps me to understand my client's experiences and how to correctly advise him or her with the future in mind. Many clients, returning for advice, have told me that I said such and such a thing would happen when they were older.

After I get the pattern in mind, I immediately relate it to the major numbers. Are these numbers present on the Pinnacles, or are the Pinnacles something entirely different? Is a number missing in the name, but found on the Pinnacles; or, perhaps, is a number already intensified in the name, again present on the Pinnacles, yielding a fine opportunity to succeed in that manner—? All these relationships prepare me for the problems my client will relate to me.

There seems to be something of fate written in the Pinnacle numbers for everyone's life, and it is surprising how they sometimes deliberately force the individual into a line of work not indicated by the talents and natural inclinations shown in the name. Many times an artistic, sensitive, and impressionable man will have fours and eights on the Pinnacles, forcing him into a practical line of endeavor. Starting life under a four, he may go to work early because of practical needs and never get back to the work of his heart's desire. Or, again, a practical man, according to his name and Destiny, may have three, six, and nine on the Pinnacles and find himself in a creative work, or in the field of art, never even planned or considered.

Now and then you may find all four periods influenced by the number nine, as it was for a person born on September 9th, 1908. (Figure this.) It is all nine Pinnacles and a complete cipher Challenge. Only an old soul could take this experience. It is because of the many strange combinations of numbers and forces that I believe we have lived before and have had many lives developing the soul and training the heart. Otherwise, there would be no progress in life, and all would be dull routine of living.

Nine on all Pinnacles may bring a disappointing life and a health problem if the thoughts, motives and ways of thinking are entirely personal. On the other hand, any line of work or undertaking can succeed under the nine Pinnacle, as the whole world becomes the field of action and gives the opportunity for prominence and success.

The majority of lives have different numbers for each Pinnacle. Each Pinnacle, in itself, is a period of experience, combining reward and tests of character.

It is a great help to observe when a Pinnacle is changing and how long it will last. If you learn to correctly interpret the Pinnacles, you will be able to plan and prepare for your future, know when to make changes, and to recognize and take advantage of your opportunities as they come up on the wheel of life.

Events and experiences move through the Pinnacles, sometimes slowly, sometimes quickly, year by year. These are interpreted by the *Personal Years*, your next lesson.

CHAPTER XIII

YOUR PERSONAL YEAR NUMBER
How to Direct Your Affairs

After the Pinnacle has been found and the general trend of affairs interpreted, the next step, and an important one, is to place the individual in that pinnacle.

This is shown by the *Personal Year* number. The Personal Year number is one of the most useful points of analysis in Numerology. When you learn to figure it, you will use it constantly for yourself and for others; and it can be figured in your head in a few minutes.

Every year has its own number. This number is the symbol for the trend of events to be unfolded during the current year. The Personal Year shows how to avoid trouble, how to direct the personal affairs and how to get the best from the experiences scheduled to be lived through during the twelve months of the year. It is a prophecy and a forewarning, and in association with the Pinnacle, it is possible to know in advance what to expect, what is likely to occur, and more especially, how to prepare for the experiences and the obligations of the longer period of the Pinnacle.

While the Personal Year may be read apart from a Pinnacle, it does not stand alone. It is a directing and supporting force, year by year, to the main requirement of the Pinnacle.

However, the Personal Year has its own identity for each year of life and makes its demands on its own account.

There is a time for everything under the sun, and wise businessmen or women succeed when others fail, for they read the signs of the times. The Three Wise Men were present at the birth of the Christ, for they read the signs of a new birth, while others slept in darkness and superstition.

RULE FOR FINDING THE PERSONAL YEAR

Add the *digit* of your *month* and the *digit* of your *day* of *birth* to the *digit* of the *current year*. (*Always omit your year of birth*.) This rule is always the same for all people.

For Example:

Take the current year, 1961. 1961 added together is 17 or 8. The influence for the world all during 1961 is an 8.

Find the Personal Year for a man born March 7th, 1912. First figure it in its entirety.

$$\begin{array}{llll} & \underline{7} & & \text{Pinnacle} \\ & 3 & & \\ 1 & (11)\ 2 & & \\ \text{March} & \text{7th} & 1912 & \\ \underline{3} & +\ 7\ + & \underline{4} & = (14)\ 5\ \text{Birth Force} \\ 4 & & 3 & \\ & \underline{1} & & \\ & 1 & & \text{Challenge} \end{array}$$

Now find his Personal Year for 1961, an 8 current year.

$$\begin{array}{lll} \text{March} & \text{7th} & 1961 \\ 3 & +\ 7\ + & 8 \quad = (18)\ 9\ \text{Personal Year} \end{array}$$

(Add his month and day of birth to the current year.)

During 1961 this man is working through a nine Personal Year and is ending his third Pinnacle, a three. In 1962, he begins a new cycle under the influence of his last Pinnacle, the seven. Use the rule of 36, as given for the Pinnacles. He finished his first Pinnacle when he was 31 (his birth force, 5, subtracted from 36). He was 40 when he finished his second Pinnacle, the (11) 2, and was 49 as he ended the third Pinnacle, the three. In 1962 he entered his final Pinnacle.

The above is the rule for finding ANY Personal Year.

The study of the cycles, as they influence life, gives an answer to many human problems. At the beginning of a new cycle there is an impulse to be up and doing, to get ahead. A new inspiration is felt, and there is a strong desire to get things done. It is like planting a seed in the garden for new life and growth. As a cycle closes there is a desire to be done with things, some situation or some individual—a wish to get free from the old, but little urge to force any issue.

These beginnings and endings confront every one throughout a lifetime. It is only when people, from fear of change, fail to move forward with the "times" that trials and tribulations continue. Life is more fun when one takes advantage of the interesting things the Personal Years have to tell.

"There is a time to plant, and a time to pluck up that which has been planted";

"A time to reap, and a time to sow; a time to keep silent, and a time to speak."—Ecclesiastes

NUMBER ONE PERSONAL YEAR

Between January this year and January next year, your affairs are making a new start. You are now entering upon a "new" cycle of experiences, and the next nine years of your life depend a great deal upon what you do *now*. This year is a time to have courage, to make plans, and to avoid inertia or indecision. You must look to the future and be willing to change and advance for the sake of progress and happiness. It may be necessary for you to let go of things having to do with the past in order to take advantage of new opportunities, so be determined. Do not drift or have fear of the future, for if you do you may lose out during a "beginning" time, such as you are experiencing, because in standing still or looking back you are caught in the ebb tide of opportunity, missing the opportunity which is present but which must be seized.

This is not an easy year and you will need to use a great deal of system and organization to get the desired results. This year calls for strength of purpose and clear thinking, but it has an opportunity hidden in its movement if you are alert enough to recognize it. Try to broaden your activities and in meeting conditions or circumstances which come up unexpectedly, call upon your executive ability and originality of thought. Life is now testing your character and your courage. You must show what you have and what you can do.

Study your plans and your surroundings and do not be afraid to take a chance with a new idea or plan, but avoid being impulsive or headstrong in making changes or moving forward. You are at the crossroads and wisdom is needed to get on the right track. It is up to *you* to do the thinking and planning for yourself and others. You may not fully realize this until the Fall of the year, even though several times during the Spring and Summer you will be called upon to make vital decisions concerning your future and what you want out of life.

During the Spring and Summer take care of your health and that of loved ones. In fact, make an effort to direct all conditions of your life towards a more constructive expression. In April there is a break and a chance to move ahead. Take some action now for improvement. In May, rest and have poise; say very little. August and September, according to your Year Number, bring many things to a head, and the Fall can open the way to new opportunities and decisions you may not have counted upon. Keep moving forward all during the year for you may be able to work out your plans earlier than anticipated. December is a practical month—carries a practical number. Be very wise now and get down to work in a concrete manner, upon your former plans.

The colors this year to help you "win" are Flame, Copper, Lilac, and Crimson.

NUMBER TWO PERSONAL YEAR

Between January this year and January next year, your success and happiness depend to a great extent upon how much tact, diplomacy, and cooperation you use in dealing with others, especially when things are not running smoothly. Last year you were required to be determined and to take the initiative. This year results are gained through "sharing" and willingness to wait for development. There is advancement and progress in the year; but many plans of last year cannot come to a fulfillment without further time to mature. Time is the keynote to the years' experiences. Because of this you may experience periods of delay, for results cannot come to the surface all at once. You should try to understand this and be content to grow quietly; for any attempt to force conditions in a dominant and aggressive way is apt to bring even more delay or to result in disharmony and broken partnerships. If you try "too hard" you may become confused and cause trouble in associations, both at home and in business. Instead, cooperate with circumstances and try for that arrangement which will bring more "peace" for yourself and others. In this way you can *win* what you could not force, bringing about results beyond your expectation.

During the early part of the year there is a tendency for agreements or associations to break up unless you are more than patient and considerate, especially during February and March. According to your numbers—*May* could find you deeply disturbed about what others have said or done. But "snap out of it" for your own good, and forget your self-importance for the time being. Even if you seem to be subordinated and held down, try to cooperate. Next year is *your* year, so this year you can afford to share and to do more than your part to bring about agreements of a harmonious nature. Quarrels and separation and unhappiness result from being mean, cold, and selfish now. This year should bring you new partnerships, new friends, and the opportunity to cement a tie of love and friendship, if you are tactful, diplomatic, and not afraid to give of what you have—time, love, or patience.

In July your numbers indicate a closing of conditions and you may finish up some association or arrangement by natural growth, or because of necessity. Show compassion, tolerance, and understanding in your partnerships now. From August on, your Year Number indicates the opening up of new arrangements, new living conditions and new agreements, which if properly directed should bring more peace of mind and satisfaction. Do not talk too much but keep things to yourself during the year, especially during the Fall. Look underneath the surface to make sure your roots are growing and that all arrangements are accurate and carefully understood. This is very important during the early part of the year.

The colors for the year to help you "win" are Gold, Salmon, Garnet, Prune, and Cinnamon.

NUMBER THREE PERSONAL YEAR

This year you must put your best foot forward and do everything possible to improve *yourself*. Between January this year and January next year there is a "quickening" force operating in your affairs and now is the time to make use of the creative, inspirational, and imaginative ideas and ideals which flood your heart. It is important to fasten on to the dreams and visions which flash through your mind from time to time. In business, as well as friendship, inspiration and imagination can mean improved finances and happier associations. If you just drift along, want everything without effort, and allow yourself to be disturbed emotionally about what others do, this can be a wasted year and an unhappy one; but on the other hand, if you will make a *real* effort to express and carry out some of these ideas in a constructive manner, this can be one of the happiest years of your life. Friends will be of importance and value. They will help you and you will be able to help them if you act in the friendly manner the year requires. You should try to make new friends and to join with the old ones, especially those who are attempting to do creative and worthwhile things in the world. Practical results may not be apparent at first; they come more definitely later in the year and especially next year. Now, you should be busy developing the dream or inspiration, especially that part of it which gives you a fuller self-expression.

Pleasure, travel, active social life, and entertainment keep you busy. Love affairs show a tendency to take on color and interest, your own or those of friends and family. During the early Winter and the Spring, friends may cause you some annoyance or emotional disturbances, but do not allow this to get under your skin; try to understand your emotions and the things others do. You should make a definite effort to avoid worry or fretting about little things. This is your optimistic and cheerful year, and you can gain far better results through being joyful and happy than through moods or worry. Money, opportunity, love, travel, pleasure, happiness, and popularity should be yours this year, but dependent upon your own inspiration and good cheer. Do not be extravagant or waste emotion, energy, or money, but do try to scatter a little sunshine and faith wherever you go. Don't talk out of turn, however, for through talk, gossip, and careless speech, unhappy problems could develop. At the same time there is a personal opportunity through words, lectures, and writings expressed in a constructive manner.

During the early part of the year, make sure of all of your relationships and associations so as not to get on a detour. Even this creative year calls for good common sense. Talk your ideas over with others to help you find the way, but do not be talked out of them. Your numbers indicate a quickening of events in February. June brings many things to a head. July shows a new direction of plans, and September can bring the quick opportunity to do what you want to do, with some friends helping. December carries pleasure, but duty too.

The colors for this year to help you "win" are Rose, Ruby, Amber, and Russet.

NUMBER FOUR PERSONAL YEAR

This is a very practical year for you. Between January of this year and January of next year, you have work to do. The plans and inspiration of last year must now be put into more concrete form. You are not likely to have much time for personal pleasure; circumstances from time to time will force you to look at things from a material point of view and to "stay on the job" whether you want to or not. But do not mind this, for by the time the year is over you will feel considerable satisfaction in what you have accomplished, even though you have had to keep "digging" and put your shoulder to the wheel. If you manage well, face the facts and get down to business as the year requires, you can lay a foundation for security and lasting conditions in the future. Order, system, organization, management and application are important, and in all matters pertaining to business, property, agreements, contracts, papers, or legal matters, details should be attended to with patience and honesty.

The practical side of the year may bring health and financial matters of your own or family, placing the responsibility upon your shoulders. You must attend to these things lovingly, and attempt to get orderly results this year that you may have the freedom and fuller life which next year promises. This practical year is indicated as a time for buying, selling, trading, and for all activities concerned with building homes, lives, and property, and doing things which give a practical foundation for the future. This is a splendid time for you to make the effort to put your ideas into concrete form; but you have need of being thrifty, careful, economical, and efficient in doing this, for there is little to be gained through trusting to luck.

At times finances may seem practical and slow, or expenses high, but through good common sense, you can meet all requirements and come out ahead. Should you allow yourself to be careless, finding it too much trouble to manage properly, or attempt to evade the responsibility and work, you may regret it later, for you could find the burden still present when next year comes. Each year brings its own peculiar requirement and opportunity, and next year is your freedom year.

During the early Spring, strike a goal of work and routine and stick to it. Consider health matters in March. June shows a new trend of events in a practical way, with the possibility of decisions to be made. As this is a practical year, August shows the best influence for a vacation and pleasure. September brings many practical problems, but should show you results. October and its number bring the first showing of the change, activity, and new conditions of next year. December carries a quiet force. Keep poised and have faith, for Christmas will bring reward for the work done during the year.

Colors to help you "win" this year are Blue, Green, Emerald, Silver, and Coffee.

NUMBER FIVE PERSONAL YEAR

Between January this year and January next year, changing conditions and eventful happenings will add new life and color to your undertakings, forcing you into step with progress.

After the work, application, and practical conditions of last year, the change, freedom from routine, and unexpectedness should be very agreeable to you. However, there is an element of uncertainty running through the year and you may experience a feeling of being unsettled from time to time. But on the whole the year affords you a splendid opportunity for advancement and progress. If you keep alert to what is going on in the world, and an open mind, you will find you are able to renew all your affairs, clearing up old conditions for more personal freedom and personal advancement. Change and the "new" are keynotes to the year, and you have a right to a fuller life than during the past few years. Without change there is no growth, but to "live" does not mean to sow wild oats. Instead it means to plan a definite goal for advancement and to be resourceful enough to make the adjustments which are necessary for improvement.

You may feel restless, impatient with things which move along slowly; or experience resentment towards those who hold you down or bind you. You should watch this, for haste makes waste and could lead to deep regret later on in the cycle of life you are now passing through. It seems to be necessary to make every effort to open a channel for progress, but this is not gained through quarreling or through burning your bridges behind you. If you feel that progress can come only through breaking up old conditions, be sure you do this in a constructive way and do not jump impulsively from the frying pan into the fire. All changes should be to the advantage of others as well as yourself, if you wish to get the best out of the year. Break up some of the old routine and turn many of the details over to others, but with wisdom and discretion, for the eventfulness, excitable conditions, and your own inner unrest can make the year very active. The changes, new contacts, and new opportunities may confuse you, but accept them all in the spirit of progress and advancement. Live up to the "push" which life is exerting upon you. Get fun out of meeting conditions and show versatility of thought and resourcefulness in action. Travel, move, at least do something to freshen up the home, social, and business activities.

During February keep poised and think things out quietly. April brings conclusions and a decision about new things. During the summer be careful of what you say, but push ahead. August brings practical problems to think about for future actions. September should show thrilling change or freedom. Your numbers say take care of your health in November.

The colors you should wear this year to help you "win" are Pink, Cherry, Wisteria, and Claret.

NUMBER SIX PERSONAL YEAR

Between January this year and January next year, you have responsibilities to meet, obligations to pay up, and duty to accept, for Service is the keynote to success and happiness this year. In fact, this is your "duty" year, for unselfishness, truth, justice, charity, and humanity should be your motives in everything you do; it is not likely you can get satisfactory results any other way. There is much you must harmonize too, as this is a peculiar year, for love, money, health, and friendship can depart suddenly if disharmony is allowed to persist. If there is difficulty between you and your loved ones, try to erase it, for love can come to you if you are generous and loving enough to receive it. Through expressing love and sympathy you can even gain financially during the year.

A strong desire to get settled may be in your mind, both in business and domestic affairs, and the end of the year should bring considerable satisfaction in this respect. There is something to be "talked over," and it may be necessary for you to take advice from friends, relatives, or those in authority; but if you are willing to make the adjustment and to consider the good of others as well as yourself, you should realize improvement in all the affairs of your life. Keep your ideals high too, and try to avoid any feeling of resentment because of unfairness; you must give even more generously than you receive to bring about the improvement and more settled conditions which the year holds out to you. You may even have the opportunity to instill ideals into the hearts and minds of others, especially younger people, if you live true to them yourself this year. There is a "care" of some sort present. This may be due to family, relatives, business responsibility, or through matters of health, but money should come to meet these obligations if you accept them as a privilege and do not make them a burden. Others may impose upon you or try to take advantage of your good nature; but even so, with effort and good business judgment, you can make fine progress. Get settled in your business affairs for future improvements and bring about more satisfactory living conditions and domestic relationships. Love affairs may bring interest.

The action of the year is slow but it is only in this way that the ultimate good can be attained. This may seem to be more noticeable during the Spring and up to about June. But from then on, your plans and adjustments can be pushed forward.

The Fall of the year may still bring much responsibility and need of helping others, but by October or November you should realize you have worked things out to a more definite conclusion; pointing towards more time to yourself next year. March, according to your numbers, brings deep conclusions and decisions. June is a good holiday month, for July brings practical matters, which you, yourself, must manage. September brings home affairs to be lovingly handled, and December is again a sort of wind-up.

Colors for this year to help you "win" are Orange, Heliotrope, Henna, and Scarlet.

NUMBER SEVEN PERSONAL YEAR

This is a very important year for you as so much depends upon a right state of mind. It is a sort of sabbatical year and you should spend more time than usual in quiet pursuits and be interested in the more intellectual phases of living. Quality should be your standard so you should reach out for more understanding of life and try to gain a more intuitive insight into your affairs. Between January this year and January next year, you are likely to be conscious of a desire to know more and to specialize your knowledge and talents. You may have a desire to be more alone; to get away from the hustle and bustle of everyday life. If you can do this it will be to your advantage for you should rest, build up your health, and improve your mind. What you *think* is of great importance, for there is much to think out, and it is much better for you to say very little and to think clearly, than to fight for your rights, argue, or attempt to explain. This is a mental house-cleaning year and you should set your mental and spiritual house in order. During the year you will have many interesting and unusual experiences through being left alone and through conditions over which you seem to have no control. But you are laying a foundation for inner strength and power and for soul realization which will make big changes in your life. Out of the year will come a goal and plan of great importance which can hardly be realized until later, when you will move forward in life to a new level of expansion and living.

Your desire to understand yourself, your more quiet and more studious attitude, may be misunderstood, and you may be criticized or condemned because you seem so determined to think for yourself and to make a better use of your mental faculties. People in your home, business associations, and social life may be hard to understand, and you may experience unreasonableness in others. Just make sure you are not unreasonable yourself, for this could cause misunderstandings and disappointments in your associations. Reason things out with fairness, understanding, and poise, and you will find unexpected reward. It will be better, too, to allow others to work out their affairs without interference from you. You see, you are in the school of life this year and are under higher discipline; if you seem to be out of things, it is only to awaken in you a better understanding of yourself and of life's finer relationships.

Avoid any feeling of confusion, humiliation, or repression. This is a waiting year for you, but there is no real limitation which you cannot overcome through poise, faith, and inner attraction. In fact, in spite of the seeming problems, this can be one of the most wonderful years of your life; if you use the right method, the year will bring you recognition and carry you to the front in your sphere of life. Do not try too hard, or force issues, for this is a transition period, bringing release of some sort as a reward, when the year is done.

Colors to "win" with this year are Purple, Brick, and Pearl.

NUMBER EIGHT PERSONAL YEAR

This year you will feel ambition stirring and a deep desire to better your financial conditions, so it is necessary to be very businesslike, efficient, and practical all through the year. There is a big opportunity in the year for advancement and improvement of your standing and credit; but conditions are not going to be easy, for you will be called upon to exercise good judgment and business efficiency. Between January this year and

January next year, you must put on a fighting spirit and go after things, but you must also take great care to direct your energies properly. Brains count, and right from the start it is advisable to strike an aim and a goal, and to pick up all loose ends in business, home, and property affairs. Organization and reorganization are the keynotes to success and advancement. You are likely to feel a great deal of mental strain in making ends meet and in accomplishing what you have in mind; but this is a business year, and if you are efficient, turn over the details to others, and use your head, the year will end with an improvement in position and finances.

It is very important that you do not overestimate your ability or the value of anything you are dealing with, especially in investments or in buying and selling property and in making exchanges. Avoid sentiment and emotion and be businesslike in your undertakings. Do not "drive" too hard for in this way you can overdo and upset your health. Even in love affairs, do not be too dominant. You must face the facts of what you are doing all year, and quietly and determinedly try to elevate and improve your position. If you are cooperative and helpful to others, you should find those in authority recognizing your ability.

About September, after you have made your business attempt, buying, selling, and adjusting or exchanging, you will begin to get a whole new idea about the reorganization of your affairs. You will probably decide to be done with something for your own good, freedom, and peace of mind. Do not be too materially minded now, for while money is power, you may find more power in being free of something than in trying to hang on. There is a living condition to be met and worked out behind the mental unrest, so you must carry it through for the sake of your character and your future. Others may be against you during the year, so be sure your judgment is good. You may move or change your living conditions if you desire in the Spring, but there are a lot of little things to take care of before you plan ahead in April. July may bring, according to your numbers, an adjustment between members of the family and in business partnerships. August brings a feeling of being alone, but accept this to take time to rest and tone up your digestive system. September is the high point, and the Fall will be given over to working out the idea which comes about this time. November tends to give a new start from an old standpoint.

The colors to help you "win" this year are Canary, Buff, Tan, Opal, and Ivory.

Number Nine Personal Year

This year brings many of your affairs to a head. Between January of this year and January of next year you will realize a completion and also the fulfillment of some of your dreams. You are now closing a cycle of experience, one that you began nine years ago, leading to a beginning and new start with next year. The completion is not a failure or sorrow. It is in reality a reward, for through it you open the way to new opportunities and new interests in life. During the year you must be ready and willing to let go of the old and undesirable in your life to make way for the real and worthwhile. It is important to make a definite effort to be through with things which have no further value. If something you are trying to hold on to asks for freedom, or desires to get away, be understanding; for if you try to hold it, it may get away anyway, especially if Life sees fit to make this change. Be tolerant, compassionate and forgiving, for then you will find this one of the most wonderful years of your life; a reward of love, sympathy, understanding, and fulfillment of your plans can result and bring financial assistance as well as loving appreciation.

During the early Winter and Spring, affairs should improve and bring you an opportunity to do what you feel is necessary, but during the summer you may feel alone, held back, and unable to keep things moving forward in a steady manner. Do not try to do so. Give life a chance to help you out, and keep your mind open to broader interests and larger activities which can be born now, even though not carried out fully until the new cycle opens with next year. During the year you may find your interests growing away from some of your former associations and activities and unconsciously turn your thought and attention to interests which have not been a part of your life before. Make these interests of universal nature and avoid being small, personal, and selfish, for this could lead to disappointment in the end. Love affairs will hold your attention— others if not your own—and you may find you are involved in these without your desire. But there is something for you to do to help others straighten out their affairs, as this is a year of impersonal thought and feeling. Through what you do for others your reward is given.

This is not a good time to start new issues. The tide of life is out rather than in. Keep busy and accept opportunity if it comes to you, but until September you may not see the way clearly and will need to make changes and adjustments on account of the closing force of the year. Do not overwork. Take a vacation in July. Your health must be kept up to par, for you have much to do next year. The Fall of the year finds you marking time, going slowly, but with mutual assistance if you are cooperative and generous in your thought and feeling. If something goes out of your life, let it go, for it is clearing the way to your future happiness and good.

Wear colorful garments this year. Avoid black.

LET'S TALK IT OVER

For many years, at the beginning of each new year, I have been asked to give a lecture on "The Meaning of the Coming Year" according to Numerology. "What's in store for me next year?" everyone wants to know.

Even the trend of events for the general public can be viewed for the current year, giving a clue for business direction and general management of affairs.

Many personal problems can be solved through intelligent use of the instructions given by the Personal Year. *In family affairs*—a man and wife, very fond of each other and having much in common through the major number of their names, may sttill disagree on ways and means. One may be opening a cycle beginning a number *one* Personal Year, and be eager to be up and doing, while the other, perhaps under the number *seven* Personal Year, wishes to study, rest, and take time out for a while. When each understands the "why" of the other's feelings and attitudes *for the time being*, there can be real harmony, happiness, and mutual understanding.

With children—knowing each child's Personal Year is a guide for right training, year by year. It helps to understand the child's needs and why obedience need not be demanded. Parents make mistakes by insisting on the same methods and training, year after year, not understanding when certain rules are good and when they are not. The trend of the Personal Year holds true for young and old. They are especially valuable for right rules and regulations for young people.

For example, during a *one* Year, a child should be encouraged to use his own ideas, to have courage, and to express some degree of aggressiveness. In the *two* Year, the lesson of sharing and cooperating with others is important, very different from the number *one* Personal Year. During the *three* Personal Year, the child should be introduced to art and beauty and, at the same time, be allowed to have fun and pleasure, meet the opposite sex, with some personal spending money and with cultivation of the trait of imagination.

The *four* Personal Year calls for real discipline—for order, care of the possessions, and respect for the routine and regulations of the family. Practical values should be cultivated; therefore reasonable economy is sometimes necessary. During the *five* Personal Year a child will not respond to rules and regulations as under the *four* influence. Impatience with routine and regulations will be present. More freedom should be allowed, with public interests cultivated, and encouragement should be given to take part in community activities. Restlessness, impatience, and a tendency to disregard rules and regulations are the desire to find out what life is all about.

As the *six* Personal Year is a duty year and one for family responsibility, tasks of real importance affecting the home and loved ones should be given the young person. Traditions of the home, family, and nation should be presented, based on love and emotional nature. Charity, helping others and giving are part of the lessons of the year. Animals and pets, flowers and gardens, and the beauty of nature help to cultivate a warm and loving nature. Under the *seven* Personal Year, the child should be encouraged to take an interest in books, reading, science, philosophy. Opportunity should be provided for the child to be alone at times. Doubts about the self should be removed by encouragement to experiment, build, investigate. Pleasant association with intelligent people is a good influence.

Under the *eight* Personal Year—banking, buying, and selling should be taught the child, and the use of money for worthwhile endeavor rather than for pleasure. If the child is old enough to understand, the rules of organization may be given through care of personal money and a personal business undertaking.

Under the *nine* Personal Year the qualities of mercy, tolerance, compassion, and the brotherhood of man should be taught. This is a very important year for a growing child. Selfish interests may mar the progress for the coming cycle. As this is a very impressionable year, the child will be easily influenced by outside interests of a dramatic nature, good or bad. Guide the impressions and emotional impulses to experiences in giving through charity, hospitals, art galleries. Direct an interest toward famous people.

When the individual Personal Year is the same as the digit of the *Current Year*, the opportunity to move on with the times is there and is an assistance towards accomplishment.

Romance walks hand in hand with the Personal Year. It is there for you and your beloved to hold and keep and enjoy. When the new year comes, find *your* Personal Year and *his*, and help each other to live up to requirements, month by month.

CHAPTER XIV

PERSONAL MONTHS—PERSONAL DAYS

Everything in its good time. The events to be experienced during any Personal Year are unfolded month by month during the twelve months of the year—under the requirements of the Pinnacle.

These three forces, acting in the affairs of an individual, describe a pattern:

> First—The Pinnacle
> Second—The Personal Year
> Third—The Personal Months

Each part, in its own way and working together, outlines the events, happenings, personal obligations, and the opportunities set down for that period of time for the individual's best growth and attainment.

PERSONAL MONTHS

The Personal Year, as already explained, is found by adding the month and day of birth to the current year. The Personal Month is then found by adding the number of the Personal Year to the calendar month.

Numerical Value of the Calendar Months

January	1	July		7
February	2	August		8
March	3	September		9
April	4	October	(10)	1
May	5	November	(11)	2
June	6	December	(12)	3

The months of a year are numbered according to their calendar sequence.

For Example:

Suppose you are in the sixth year of your present Pinnacle or, in other words, working through a *six* Personal Year—your duty year—and are thinking of taking a vacation in June or July. To find out which month would be the better month to get away for a while:

Add your Personal Year number (six) to the number for the calendar month of June.

June—The *sixth* month of the year plus the *six* of your Personal Year equals *three* (6 + 6 = (12) 3). This is your Personal Month number for June.

July—The *seventh* month of the year plus the *six* of your Personal Year equals *four*. This is your Personal Month number for July (6 + 7 = (13) 4).

June, a *three* Personal Month, would be a happier month to take a vacation and to do what you personally desire to do for the time being.

July, a *four* Personal Month in your *six* duty year, would be too serious a time for a vacation. Economic conditions might prevent or relatives demand care. You are not likely to get away this month for a personal vacation.

Using the same rule, your Personal Months for your *six* Personal Year would be:

January	(1 + 6)	a 7 Month	July	(7 + 6)	a 4 Month
February	(2 + 6)	an 8 Month	August	(8 + 6)	a 5 Month
March	(3 + 6)	a 9 Month	September	(9 + 6)	a 6 Month
April	(4 + 6)	a 1 Month	October	(1 + 6)	a 7 Month
May	(5 + 6)	a 2 Month	November	(2 + 6)	an 8 Month
June	(6 + 6)	a 3 Month	December	(3 + 6)	a 9 Month

Therefore, to interpret the trend of events, month by month, for any Personal Year, add the number of your Personal Year to the calendar number of each month.

Observe the following chart. Study it carefully, for it gives a bird's-eye view to the trend of events during a nine-year cycle and points out what to do, when and how, month by month, year after year.

A Nine-Year Cycle

		YEARS								
MONTHS		1	2	3	4	5	6	7	8	9
January	(1)	(2)	(3)	(4)	(5)	(6)	(7)	(8)	(9)	(1)
February	(2)	(3)	(4)	(5)	(6)	(7)	(8)	(9)	(1)	(2)
March	(3)	4	5	6	7	8	9	1	2	3
April	(4)	5	6	7	8	9	1	2	3	4
May	(5)	6	7	8	9	1	2	3	4	5
June	(6)	7	8	9	1	2	3	4	5	6
July	(7)	8	9	1	2	3	4	5	6	7
August	(8)	9	1	2	3	4	5	6	7	8
September	(9)	1	2	3	4	5	6	7	8	9
October	(1)	2	3	4	5	6	7	8	9	1
November	(2)	(3)	(4)	(5)	(6)	(7)	(8)	(9)	(1)	(2)
December	(3)	(4)	(5)	(6)	(7)	(8)	(9)	(1)	(2)	(3)

The Personal Months also proceed in cycles of nines except for breaks during the transition of one year to the next. These breaks are very important in planning for future activities—to make sure to do the right thing at the right time.

Observe that September, each year, brings the full force of the Personal Years to bear upon the affairs in every year; that October, each year, has the same number as the oncoming year, but only as a signpost and advance notice for making plans ahead. However, these plans cannot get fully under way until the requirements of the present year have been completed.

Notice that the *first two* months of each year are the same number as the *last two* months of the year before. Events do not begin and end all at once.

Notice there are more *six* duty months in the third, fourth, and fifth year. There are more sevens in the fifth and sixth years.

The nature of the events and happenings of the *months* are the same as the *meaning of the numbers and events* given for the Personal Years; only the period of time is shorter—thirty days instead of twelve months. They must always be read in connection with the trend of events of that Personal Year.

A *four* Month in a *four* Personal Year will relate to practical and economic matters—while the *four* Month in a *six* Personal Year will relate to duties and family matters.

It is interesting to observe the vibration for the Christmas month each year.

In a *one* Personal Year December is very practical, so be economical and meet the practical circumstance with good grace and good management. It is your fault if you feel economic pressure—you have been warned.

In a *two* Personal Year December is a *five* month, a good time to take a trip and to plan for variety in the Christmas activities including a few surprises, breaking up the routine to a pleasant degree. It is not a time to go overboard in seeking excitement, however.

Christmas time in a *three* Personal Year is your time to serve, have the family in, do nice and lovely things for others and to give to those in need. You are ending your *three* Personal Year.

The practical *four* Personal Year brings the quiet *seven* at

Christmas time. Take a trip for a rest. This is not your duty Christmas. Join with a few selected friends for talk and educational interests. If you find yourself alone, take time to rest—you may need all your energies next year.

A *five* Personal Year brings the number *eight* for the Christmas month. This hectic *five* year of changes and unexpected happenings gives you a business opportunity in December, help through others, and the possibility of a trip, perhaps short, combining business and pleasure.

The *six* Personal Year, after all its duty, brings the number *nine* for Christmas. This is often a different Christmas from the usual custom. A family duty may be about completed, perhaps with a slight disappointment, but it can be an opportunity to do many things that mean progress, growth, and advancement for your own inner satisfaction. Let go of things or people no longer part of your future. You are getting ready to leave much of the year's responsibility behind you.

In December of your somewhat restricting *seven* Personal Year, you will be anxious to get under way with your new plans in this *one* month. But take a look ahead to January of your next Personal Year, under the *eight*. This is a *nine* month, so do not force things now; just plan and spend the Christmas month with people interested in what you are doing without being extravagant or over-confident. It may be February of the next year before things begin to move forward, after a few rearrangements in January of the *eight* Personal Year. *So many people make mistakes right here* and upset the plans for the whole *eight* year.

As a busy *eight* Personal Year ends you will realize you have had to put your shoulder to the wheel during the year. December, as an eleven-*two* month, brings many little things to attend to, still in association with others. The signs of several things coming to a head (as next year is a *nine* Personal Year) may cause some worry. But wait; cooperate; do not hurry results; use tact and diplomacy and go to church for spiritual refreshment. Prayer and faith are valuable now.

Christmas in the number *nine* Personal Year is a *three*. Now is a good time to take a trip for pleasure and to join with friends in social activities and for plans which will give you time for relaxation and fun. Next year you begin a new cycle of experience and need a little pleasant relaxation now. Express friendship and make new friends. Bring joy and happiness to others by your own efforts.

As you can now realize, the Personal Years and the Personal Months are invaluable as a year-by-year and month-by-month guide to personal accomplishment, success, and personal happiness, always under the direction of the Pinnacles. This is important to remember; otherwise everyone would be taking the same experiences.

As you guide and direct your life by these signs you will gradually realize that you do not have the troubles and problems others have, that you are more poised, less disturbed by general conditions and are keeping yourself and your affairs under control.

PERSONAL DAYS

Each day of the year also has its vibrations, as well as each year and month, and carries a personal message for consideration in making plans.

Clients often say, "I am going on a trip next month. What is a good day to go?" Or, "When is a good time to move?"

Before answering the above questions, it is necessary to know what *kind* of a trip: business, pleasure, scientific, or concerning family affairs? Trips are taken each year for different reasons. Moves and changes of residence are made, as a rule, for the reason indicated by the Pinnacle. They are then directed and worked out by the requirements of the Personal Year. Having these in mind, the Current Day and the Personal Day can be considered, to give the best immediate opportunity.

The *Personal Day* is found by adding your *Personal Year*, (already explained) to the month and day under consideration. You wish to know what kind of day February 10, 1963, will be:

February   10   1963
    2   + 1 +   1   =4, the Current Day number for everyone

To find *your* Personal Day, discard 1963 and substitute your Personal Year number. Perhaps you are in an *eight* Personal Year.

February   10   8 P.Y.
    2   + 1 +   8   =(11) 2, an eleven-two day for you

Your Personal Day does not stand alone, however. It is part of the Current Day. The Current Day should be carefully considered before acting on the indications of any Personal Day.

Business men and women will profit greatly by observing the general trend of events day by day during any calendar month of the year. Many mistakes can be avoided and opportunity be taken advantage of at the right time by keeping a Numerology calendar of the days of the month. This will reveal why certain things take place, why events are delayed, or why the unexpected happens on certain days in spite of plans and arrangements.

It is necessary to figure only the first *nine* days of the month, for the indications are the same for the month after the first nine days, except for the *intensity* of the double numbers. (The first of the month, the tenth of the month, the nineteenth of the month, and the twenty-eighth of the month have the same general chart of events.)

Take for example, the month of February, 1958. February is the 2nd month of the year. 1958 is a *five* Current Year. The final Pinnacle is always the same number, for every day of the month. The Pinnacles are given above the dates; the Challenges are given below the dates.

$\frac{7}{9}$	$\frac{7}{(11)2}$	$\frac{7}{4}$
$\underline{3+6}$	$\underline{4+7}$	$\underline{5+8}$
Feb. 1st $2+1+5=8$	Feb. 2nd $2+2+5=9$	Feb. 3rd $2+3+5=(10)1$
$\underline{1-4}$	$\underline{0-3}$	$\underline{1-2}$
$\underline{3}$	$\underline{3}$	$\underline{1}$
3	3	3

$\frac{7}{6}$	$\frac{7}{8}$	$\frac{7}{1}$
$\underline{6+9}$ (11)	$\underline{7+1}$ (12)	$\underline{8+(11)2}$
Feb. 4th $2+4+5=2$	Feb. 5th $2+5+5=3$	Feb. 6th $2+6+5=(13)4$
$\underline{2-1}$	$\underline{3-0}$	$\underline{4-1}$
$\underline{1}$	$\underline{3}$	$\underline{3}$
3	3	3

$\frac{7}{3}$	$\frac{7}{5}$	$\frac{7}{7}$
$\underline{9+3}$ (14)	$\underline{1+4}$ (15)	$\underline{(11)2+5}$
Feb. 7th $2+7+5=5$	Feb. 8th $2+8+5=6$	Feb. 9th $2+9+5=(16)7$
$\underline{5-2}$	$\underline{6-3}$	$\underline{7-4}$
$\underline{3}$	$\underline{3}$	$\underline{3}$
3	3	3

All during this month there is a final *seven Pinnacle* and a *three Challenge*. This month demands deep thought, understanding, and a scientific approach to any undertaking. It is not a good time to begin something, unless all is in perfect readiness, even though the three Challenge permits activity which encourages personal self-expression and social interests. February in 1958 is a time for intelligent action, understanding of what is to be accomplished, combined with creative thought and courage to dare to exercise the latent talents. The *over-all seven* does not allow for careless or extravagant impulse.

Each day, however, brings its own special opportunities and peculiarities, and during some personal months the Challenge will vary almost day by day.

THE TIMING

As the final Pinnacle is *always the same* as the *monthly* vibration, it is not considered in the timing of the day.

The other *three Pinnacles* cover the twenty-four hours of the day, eight hours to each period.

The *first* Pinnacle, accompanied by the first Challenge, covers the first eight hours of the day—from midnight to 8:00 A.M. The *second* Pinnacle and Challenge influence the trend of events from 8:00 A.M. to 4:00 P.M. The *third* Pinnacle and Challenge cover from 4:00 P.M. to midnight. Most of the day's work is done during the second period.

REFER TO THE CHART

One of the interesting days in February of 1958 was Feb. 7th, a *five* day. The second and third periods were under the *three*, the same as the main Challenge of the month. During the early morning, something came to a head and brought changes (the *nine* Pinnacle and *five* Challenge) which could have rearranged all plans for the day. From then on, from 8:00 A.M. to 4:00 P.M., the creative interests and the inspiration of the *three* directed all activities. It was a good day for trips, entertainment, artistic endeavor, concerts and for all inspirational activity. It was a good time to pack up and take a long trip—with lots of money in hand, for the three can be very extravagant, and there is a three Challenge. There was nothing practical about the day. It was a good time for conferences, talk, the thrill of presenting ideas, and for gatherings where others were to be inspired and persuaded to buy.

Compare this day with the 9th of February—a *seven* day with the *seven* first Challenge and *seven* third Pinnacle. It was not a good day for a trip unless of secretive or scientific nature. Because of the karmic (16) there is a suggestion that plans might not go forward as fully as expected. This was a good day for education, quiet thought, study, and intellectual pursuits.

Note—From the beginning of the United Nations the (16) *seven* has been prominent on the days of action and decision. The (16) *seven* is called a karmic number because much must be paid in the way of truth and righteousness as well as skill and intelligence to hold and maintain the plans of the (16) *seven* activity.

Your Own Personal Day runs parallel with the Current Day. It is not always necessary to figure the Pinnacles and Challenge. However, if what you plan to do is very important, it is advisable to figure them to find the right *time* of day to carry out your personal plans.

Your knowledge of the meaning of the numbers as given in Chapter Two and the meaning of the Pinnacles and of the Personal Years in Chapters Twelve and Thirteen will enable you to read the days and to know what to expect at any given time.

At first it may seem difficult for you to synchronize the different points of analysis, but this will come to you as you keep the meaning of each point of analysis in mind.

CHAPTER XV

THE RACE CONSCIOUSNESS—THE
HUMAN ELEMENT

Clients will consult me and then never act upon the advice given them; or they will go out to do the very same things they have been doing and for which they sought help and counsel, unchanged by the description of their talents, characteristics and future possibilities as written in their names. It often seems impossible for the individual involved in unhappy love affairs or domestic relationships to change his or her ways. "I am just like my mother." Or, "I have my father's temper," and strangely enough they seem to enjoy the classification. Others lacking financial or business success will continue to accept their situation, even when told of their field of opportunity and how to meet the challenges and obstacles in their affairs.

We are all human and have definite responsibilities simply because we belong to the human race. These human responsibilities are told by *how old we are* and are called the Race Consciousness or the R.C. Since civilization began, mankind has followed traditional ways of acting and thinking and built upon them until they have become the accepted ways of life. The seven stages of man have influenced all endeavor and thinking by the human race from youth to the latter days of life. It is only in this modern day that strong souls are getting out of the thought of useless old age and daring to live to the full possibility of their individuality. There are some yet who will not ride in an automobile, or go up in an airplane, while others are planning to go into space and to other planets.

253

How old are you? This is your R.C., found by adding the digit of your present age to the digit of your next year of age.

For example: If you are 35 now and will be 36 in a few months, add these two sums together, after reducing each to a single digit. This final digit will be your R.C. for the present time. Naturally it changes every time you have a birthday.

$$\frac{35\text{--}36}{8+9}$$
17 or 8 R.C.

So if your R.C. is an 8, along with the expression of your talents and abilities shown by your name and birth there is a need for you to take part in the organization work of your community or civic undertakings. There is a suggestion also to pay attention to your business affairs concerning property matters and to be on the alert to meet worldly affairs which might affect your position and holdings.

The R.C. is a subtle force, not always felt or perceived, but is a guide to the outside influence of the moment in meeting the experiences written on the Table of Events, your next lesson.

The Race Consciousness is easily read. The meaning of numbers, as given for the Pinnacles and the Personal Years, can be used for interpretation.

The following chart will give you an insight into the way the general experiences, according to age, will present themselves.

Age:	19–20	20–21	21–22	22–23	23–24	24–25	25–26	26–27
	1 2	2 3	3 4	4 5	5 6	6 7	7 8	8 9
	3	5	7	9	(11)2	4	6	8

	27–28	28–29	29–30	30–31	31–32	32–33	33–34	34–35	35–36
	9 1	1 (11)2	2 3	3 4	4 5	5 6	6 7	7 8	8 9
	1	3	5	7	9	(11)2	4	6	8

Between the ages of 19 and 23, the R.C. is always an odd number. Between the ages of 23 and 27, it is an even number. These will alternate this way every four years during your lifetime.

The odd numbers are introvert in tendency and indicate that during this period the thought is concerning the self or some project that is important to the individual at that age. The even numbers are extrovert. During this period, others and associations are important to the success, or, in other words, getting on with others is important. This could save a marriage or prevent a divorce. Many problems can be understood through the R.C.: why an individual may want to be more alone, or again need the help of others.

While the R.C. repeats the digits over and over, the age does not. Naturally an eleven (two) R.C. in the thirties will be different from the R.C. of the forties. When we are in the teens the thought is for the self. In the twenties the desire is for marriage, family, and business. In the thirties the desire is for creative work and a career—also to enjoy life. The forties are practical and the time to place life on a practical basis. Often in the forties, this seems hard and not desired, especially after the creative and inspiring thirties. This is the time to make sure that the foundation of life is established to provide for the freedom, life, travel, change, progress, and public contact of the fifties. The sixties should give the reward of service and a life well-lived, bringing money, family pride, and service to humanity. The seventies should be the time to retire, and would be, if men and women did not strive to reach the goal of success too soon and scatter their health and vitality. Life and traditions are changing, however, and this modern world is recognizing the value of age, allowing the so-called senior citizens the right to usefulness and even a career.

CHAPTER XVI

THE TABLE OF EVENTS

The Past, Present, and Future as Revealed by the Sacred Symbols of Numbers

"Let no man enter here with impure hands."

A road map of your journey down the highway of life, the direction you will be traveling, the associations you will make, the stop-overs, the detours, and the pleasure of the journey now lie before you in the Table of Events of your life.

From your Table of Events, you will be able to figure and interpret any given period of experience at any given time from the year of your birth far into the future.

Your Table of Events discloses the experiences you have taken and those which are still ahead. It enables you to look backward into the past and forward into the future. It will reveal the highlights of your journey of human experience—the turning points in your endeavors, your love affairs, your business activities, and the reasons "why" for happenings you have failed to understand. Your Table of Events is also the grand opportunity your soul chose to meet when it came into earthly consciousness to give you the privilege of spiritual growth and awareness.

Just how you will meet these experiences depends upon you, your character, and your understanding of yourself. You have gained this understanding through the instructions given in this book. You are now prepared to move forward into the wonders of the future.

Your Destiny will be fulfilled as you meet the new experiences.

Your talents will develop.

Your Heart's Desire or Inner Nature will gain in strength and confidence.

Your Personality, your Temperament, and your Type will find outlet for expression, and your Ultimate Goal will be successfully attained.

The art of Divination has been practiced by wise men throughout the ages. The Table of Events is presented to you in this Twentieth Century as guide to a better and happier life. It is a method to transcend the sorrow, unhappiness, and lack —too often the way of life—for those less informed and unaware of the better things provided for mankind when God first created the world.

The "fortune teller" has no place in the world of worthwhile and respected service. The "counselor," who reads and then teaches all who seek his aid, takes his place among those who serve and enlighten humanity. As you read the events for yourself and others, do not fall into the "pit" of negative interpretation. You only condemn yourself and, in the end, lose your ability to help those in deep need of counsel and direction.

When reading the Table of Events for anyone, it is your task to point out the requirement or the opportunity, perhaps hidden for the time being, and to show the way up and over the hills of opposition to the obligation and the awakening, symbolized by the letters and numbers. All numbers are good. You have learned this long ago. There are no bad numbers and no negative experiences. Discord and disharmony arise from the "way" the experience is taken and lack of understanding of its true purpose.

There is no lasting sorrow, no loss or failure when the

light of understanding is turned on the event or experience and wise interpretation presented.

Your Table of Events is a moving picture of your life. You are the star, the events written there are the plot and the action of the play you are enacting.

You and your Table of Events are companions. You belong together. You can never be separated. Together you prepare a place for yourself in the world of satisfactory accomplishment and for that Ultimate Goal to which you were born.

The following instructions and method of setting up a chart were presented to the California Institute of Numerical Research, Inc. by Valyre Judy of New York City. The interpretation of the letters represents twenty-five years of research, statistics, and compilation. Through the faith and repeated effort of Valyre Judy, the word "Numerology" was placed in Webster's New Collegiate Dictionary.

The meaning of the letters was first given in the book *Yi-King, Tao*, by Violeta Parke Boyle, published in Chicago in 1929.

SETTING UP THE CHART

Timing: Each one of your names and each letter of each name given at birth represents a definite period of time and activity. Each name is like a tape recording telling of conditions you must meet and tasks to be accomplished for personal advancement. Each name repeats its theme over and over again. Each name operates separately. However, all three names (or four or more) work together, something like a chord of music.

The *letters* in each name represent the nature of the event taking place and also the length of time the event or experience will hold forth.

The period of time which a name records is according to the *sum* of the letters of that name before being reduced to a digit. At the end of that name, it is then repeated over and over again throughout the lifetime.

For Example:

Robert

962592

  33

Robert will be *thirty-three* years old when he has lived through the experiences of the name—the *first time*. He will be *sixty-six* when he has completed the experiences the *second time*, and *ninety-nine* at the end of the *third period*, if he lives that long.

THE VALUE OF THE LETTERS

1—A–J–S   represents a *one*-year period.
2—B–K–T   a *two*-year experience period.
3—C–L–U   a *three*-year experience period.
4—D–M–V   a *four*-year experience period.
5—E–N–W   a *five*-year experience period.
6—F–O–X   a *six*-year experience period.
7—G–P–Y   a *seven*-year experience period.
8—H–Q–Z   an *eight*-year experience period.
9—I–R   a *nine*-year experience period.

Therefore, Robert, for the *first nine* years of his life, was under the direction of the "R." For the next *six* years, under the "O," he became involved in the affairs and responsibilities of the family. He was *fifteen* years old when he completed that phase of his life's experiences (9 + 6 = 15).

The next *two* years he was under the directon of the "B." The next *five* years, under the "E," the next nine years under the "R," and the next *two* years under the "T," taking thirty-three years to live through the experiences of his first name the first time.

He then began again the *nine* years of the first "R," moving forward, letter by letter, into the future. Each one of the names given at birth is analyzed in the same way, all names running concurrently. You will understand this when you study a full chart.

When properly set up, the Table of Events is mathematically correct and accurate. It will prove itself by coinciding with every other timed position, such as the Pinnacles and the Personal Year, making it possible to do the right thing at the right time.

THE CHART

First—Figure the name and birth and all its divisions as you have been instructed for character analysis. Be sure to figure EVERY point of analysis. This will point out the reasons for many of the experiences later, for hidden in one of the divisions may be the reason for the experience written on the Table of Events. This is important, for two or more people may have the same combination of letters on a Table of Events; but what it will mean and how the experience will be taken will depend upon the personal reactions of the individual. As a counselor or in reading for yourself, you may make sad and regrettable mistakes if you fail to do this.

Also be sure your mathematics is correct. It is easy to make mistakes in setting up a complete Table of Events. Try to keep both the Character Chart and the Table of Events on one sheet of paper for more accurate interpretation of character and events. A bookkeeping or ruled paper is helpful.

Below the Name Chart rule off nine horizontal lines.

On the *first line* write *Date* or calendar year of birth. Progress forward up to five or six years beyond the present date and your present age.

On the *second line* write *Age*, followed by the abbreviation "Br" for born. Place the "Br" under the first calendar date. This is very important, as a child is not one year old until the next year. It takes twelve months to become one year old. Think this out and do not be confused. When a child is born it must have time to become one year old. Otherwise your timing of events in the future will not be correct.

On the *third line* write *First Name,* and, as was explained in the name of Robert, give each letter its time of influence according to its numerical value.

On the *fourth line* place the *second name* and progress forward according to the value of the letters.

On the *fifth line* place the *third name* and progress forward. (Do the same with all *other names* if you have a long name.)

On the *sixth line* write the *Essence.* This is the sum of the letters year by year. Underneath the sixth line mark a double line to mark the completion of one part of the chart.

On the *seventh line* write *Personal Year.*

On the *eighth line* write *Universal Year.*

On the *ninth line* write *Pinnacle.* Again underneath the ninth line mark a double line to indicate the completion of another part of the chart. You may add your mother's maiden name from birth if you desire, under this line, but this is not of importance. Her influence in your life is already present in your given names.

Observe that the Personal Year at birth and the Universal Year are placed uner "Br."

The first *Personal Year at birth* on all charts is the same as the Birth Force.

The Universal Year is always the current year the person was born. A complete chart is given below. It is an arranged name. Make this an *unfailing rule:* Never separate the Character Chart from the Table of Events. It is not conducive to clear-cut analysis to have the Name Chart on one page of paper and the Table of Events on another. You will miss the finer relationships which result from the combined charts. Remember— *you* and your *Table of Events* are one and the same thing. You belong together.

CHARACTER CHART

(19)1	+	1	+	(11)2	= 4 Heart's Desire
9 9 1		1		6 5	

W i l l i a m   C l a r k   D o y l e
5 9 3 3 9 1 4   3 3 1 9 2   4 6 7 3 5

     (34)7   +   (18)9 +   (25)7   = (23) 5 Destiny

(15)6		(17)8		(14)5	= (10)1 Personality
5 3 3	4	3 3 9 2		4 7 3	

Type		Traits	Pinnacles	
Phy.	4	1-2-3-4-5-6-7-8-9	9	(11)2
Ment.	2	2-1-5-2-2-1-1-0-3	3	Reality
Emot.	7		9 + 3	

Int.   4   March   6th   1932
     (17)8   Pt. of Security   3   +   6   + (15)6 = (15)6 Birth
                                                     Force

                                 3 –   0
                                     3
                               3 Challenge

     1962–1963
     30   31   March   6th   1962
      3   4   3   +   6   + (18)9 = (18)9 Personal Year
R.C.   7
(Race Consciousness)

TABLE OF EVENTS

Date of Birth	1932	33	34	35	36	37	38	39	40	41	42	43	44	45	46	47	48	49
Age	Br	1	2	3	4	5	6	7	8	9	10	11	12	13	14	15	16	17
First Name	Br	W	W	W	W	W	l	l	l	l	l	l	l	l	l	l	l	l
Second Name	Br	C	C	C	l	l	l	a	r	r	r	r	r	r	r	r	r	k
Third Name	Br	D	D	D	D	o	o	o	o	o	o	o	y	y	y	y	y	y
		12	12	12	12	14	18	16	24	24	24	25	25	25	25	19	19	12
Essence		(3)	(3)	(3)	(3)	(5)	9	7	(6)	(6)	(6)	7	7	7	7	1	1	3
Personal Year	6	7	8	9	1	2	(3)	4	5	(6)	7	8	9	1	(2)	(3)	(4)	5
Universal Year	6	7	8	9	1	2	(3)	4	5	(6)	7	8	9	1	(2)	(3)	(4)	5
Pinnacle	9	9	9	9	9	9	9	9	9	9	9	9	9	9	9	9	9	9

Continuing pattern

Date	1950	51	52	53	54	55	56	57	58	59	60	61	62	63	64	65	66	67	68	69	70
Age	18	19	20	21	22	23	24	25	26	27	28	29	30	31	32	33	34	35	36	37	38
1st N.	l	l	l	l	l	l	l	l	l	l	l	l	l	a	m	m	m	m	W	W	W	W
2nd N.	k	C	C	C	l	l	l	a	r	r	r	r	r	r	r	r	k	k	C	C
3rd N.	l	l	l	e	e	e	e	e	D	D	D	D	o	o	o	o	o	o	o	y	y	y
				17	17	17	17	15	22	22	22	22	16	19	19	19	19	13	14	15	15
Essence	8	9	9	8	8	8	8	(6)	4	4	4	4	7	1	1	1	1	4	(5)	(6)	(6)
Per.Yr.	6	7	8	9	1	(2)	3	(4)	5	6	7	8	9	1	(2)	(3)	4	5	(6)	7	8
Uni.Yr.	6	7	8	9	1	(2)	3	(4)	5	6	7	8	9	1	(2)	(3)	4	5	(6)	7	8
Pin.	9	9	9	9	9	9	9	9	9	9	9	9	9	(3)	(3)	(3)	(3)	(3)	(3)	(3)	(3)

The above Table of Events chart is figured from his birth in 1932 to the age of 38 in 1970. (A chart may be figured to any future date.)

William Clark Doyle is 30 years of age in 1962. He is completing a *nine* Pinnacle (36 minus his birth force = 30). He will begin his second or *three* Pinnacle in 1963—operating until he is 39 years old. At this age his third Pinnacle, again a *three*, will take over, guiding him until he is 48. At the age of 49 his final Pinnacle, a *nine*, becomes his signpost for right action.

On the Table of Events, at 30, he is under the "a" of William—the fifth "r" of Clark—and is beginning the first "o" of Doyle, the second time. He is in a *nine* Personal Year. The Universal or Current Year is also a *nine*. It is often helpful when the Personal Year and the Universal Year are the same number. The personal affairs work together with the general activities of the world, and there is less opposition.

His present table of experience is:

Date	1962	The "a" and the "o" show a new direc-
Age	30	tion of affairs; the "r," some of the old obli-
1st Name	a	gations still to be met. However, the rest of
2nd Name	r	the Table shows marked completions and
3rd Name	o	endings due to the *seven* essence, the *nine*
	—	Personal Year, the *nine* Universal Year, and
	16	*nine* Pinnacle all in one column. If he was
	—	not prepared for this big change in his life,
Essence	7	he could have experienced a loss and been
Per. Year	9	unprepared for the new events to be met and
Univ. Year	9	taken advantage of.
Pinnacle	9	

His major numbers do not appear at this time, only the *seven* R.C. which indicates that, at 30 years of age, he should do some deep thinking, exercise great self-control, and consider his part in the Divine scheme of creation. The *nines* not only show he is through with many of the circumstances and associations of the past but that he must express forgiveness and compassion for those who were part of the loss or seemingly responsible for what happened.

All the numbers of the Table for 1962 are introvert in feeling and action, forcing him to turn to his own inner power and not to depend too much upon others. This may not be too easy for him, as he has an extrovert Heart and Birth Number.

His name at birth prophesied this experience at 30 years of age, so it is in no way a tragedy. It is only a lesson to awaken him to a desire to help mankind and give him a more philanthropic approach to life. He has three *nines* on the Points of Intensification, so he will be able to meet the experiences and move forward into the new life, new work, and the more creative opportunity of the *three* Pinnacle.

READING THE CHART

Each Name reveals conditions, events, and activities in the affairs. Each name works in unison with the other names. Each letter represents an experience and a *time* of operation and influence. Beginning at one year of age, move forward to any age desired by giving *each letter* its allotted time according to its numerical value. When the time of a name has been completed, begin again, timing events in the same way as illustrated by the name Robert. The conditions represented by each name add up to the general circumstances in which the individual is living and from which he is to gain experience and fulfill his life.

The *Essence* is the sum of the letters on a Table year by year. It is the platform or stage on which the events take place. It is the field of endeavor—the way events of the Table must be and will be worked out and directed for best results.

The *Personal Year* is a clue to the personal obligation for the time being and the right approach to events as they appear.

The *Universal Year* represents worldly affairs as they influence the thinking of mankind, sometimes assisting and sometimes limiting personal accomplishments.

Now observe the chart *carefully* as the following delineations are made.

To make it easier to observe happenings, events, and changes in the affairs, draw a straight line down the chart at every change of letters on the Table and at every change of Essence. Observe the frequent changes, some long, some short.

Watch carefully for every change of Pinnacle. (The end of a Pinnacle will always coincide with a *nine* Personal Year. If it does not on your chart, you have made a mistake somewhere in your figuring.)

Next encircle any Essence, Personal Year, or Pinnacle that is the same as any one of your major numbers. This will show what the event means to you or the one for whom you are counseling. Notice in this chart the second Pinnacle is his Challenge, indicating he will have an opportunity for a career in art, but with a challenge to meet—perhaps his own emotional nature or lack of application when he should be on the job; for he has a *seven* Total on his Emotional Plane of Expression. However, the reserve of the *seven* Total should give fine technique or subtlety to his work. When you read a Table of Events, bring every part of the character to play on the Events.

Always look for changes in the Table. For example: When William Clark Doyle was four years old in 1936, he completed a four-year period of *three* Essences. Then between his fourth birthday and his fifth, the "W–l–o" of the next Table began to get under way, ending when he was five years old. It was a one-year period, active from his fourth birthday to his fifth birthday.

He completed the "W" of his first name when he was five years old, and, from that time until he was 14 years old, a nine-year gamut under the "i" made him impressionable and sensitive to an authority in his home, which he might have resented. This changed at his fourteenth birthday, and the four years of *seven* Essence were completed, changing to (19)1, giving him more courage and self-determination. At the same time he was under the "y" of Doyle, which began when he had completed his tenth year of life.

In the same way observe all changes of any nature at any place or time on the chart, for each name carries its own influence and determination.

Read the letters of the name from birthday to birthday. They begin with the date of birth. The Personal Year and the Universal Year are read from January to December. A year is always already under way when a child is born.

THE SHORTCUT

It is not necessary to make a complete life chart every time. The events of the present time are of the most importance. A short but complete chart can be made, covering a few years into the past, the present age, and for a few years ahead. Set up the character chart in the usual way.

Figure another name as an example:

CHARACTER CHART

$$\frac{(20)2}{(23)5} \quad + \frac{1}{(10)1} \quad + \frac{(12)3}{(24)6} \quad = \frac{6}{3} \text{ Heart's Desire}$$
$$= 3 \text{ Personality}$$

$$\text{E l i z a b e t h} \quad \text{A n n} \quad \text{A n d e r s o n}$$
$$\underline{5\,3\,9\,8\,1\,2\,5\,2\,8} \quad \underline{1\,5\,5} \quad \underline{1\,5\,4\,5\,9\,1\,6\,5}$$
$$(43)7 \quad + (11)2 + \quad (36)9 \quad = (18)9 \text{ Destiny}$$

Type		Traits	Pinnacles	
Phy.	8	1–2–3–4–5–6–7–8–9	$\underline{7}$	(14)5
Ment.	6	4–2–1–1–7–1–0–2–2	3	Reality
Emot.	4		$(10)1 + (11)2$	
Int.	2		March 25th 1921	
(20)2		Pt. of Security	$3 \quad + \quad 7 \quad + (13)4 = (14)5$ Birth	
			Force	

$$\frac{4 \quad - \quad 3}{1}$$
$$1 \quad \text{Challenge}$$

$$\begin{array}{cc} 1961–1962 \\ \underline{41 \quad 42} \\ \underline{5 \quad 6} \\ \text{R.C.} \quad (11)2 \end{array}$$

March   25th   1962
$$3 \quad + \quad 7 \quad + \quad 9 \quad = (19)1 \text{ Personal}$$
$$\text{Year}$$

TABLE OF EVENTS

Birth Date		1958–59–60–61–62–63–64–65–66								
Age		37	38	39	40	41	42	43	44	45
1st Name		h	h	h	h	h	h	h	E	E
2nd Name		n	n	n	n	n	n	n	n	A
3rd Name		A	n	n	n	n	n	d	d	d
		14	18	18	18	18	18	17	14	10
Essence		(5)	(9)	(9)	(9)	(9)	(9)	8	(5)	1
Personal Year		6	7	8	(9)	1	2	3	4	(5)
Universal Year		(5)	6	7	8	(9)	1	2	3	4
Pinnacle	(11)	2	2	2	3	3	3	3	3	3

Chart of experiences from 37 to 45 years of life, showing her experience for 1962.

This is easy to understand if you figure it yourself. The method is the same for the shortcut in all cases.

RULES FOR THE SHORTCUT

First Name—The sum of the name *Elizabeth* is 43. This is a long name. It takes 43 years to complete the experiences of Elizabeth. At 44 she again takes up the "E" of the name. She will be 86 when she has lived through the name the second time, when she will again begin the "E" of Elizabeth.

However, at present, she is only 41. Therefore she has two more years under the final *h* of her first name.

Now move forward into the future with the five years of the *E* of her first name, then backward into the past with the *h* for four or five years. She has been under this *h* for six years.

Second Name—The name *Ann* is a short name. It sums up to 11. She will experience the obligations of this name many times during her lifetime. She completed *Ann* the first time at eleven years of age, again at 22, again at 33, and will complete it again at 44 years of age, repeating the pattern again and again into the future.

On the chart place the *n* in the 41 age column and move forward with this letter to 44 when she completes this name for the fourth time.

Place the *A* in the column for 45 years of age.

She is under this *A* from her birthday in 1965 to her birthday in 1966.

Then the first *n* begins again for five years, followed by the second *n* to the age of 55.

Third Name—Anderson sums up to 36. Elizabeth had lived through the experiences of her last name the first time when she was 36 years old.

Between 36 and 37 she again took up the experiences of the name *Anderson* under the letter *A* for a one-year period.

(All names carry on together but have different beginnings and endings.)

She is now 41 years old and has moved forward through the *A* and five years of the *n*, completing the *n* influence at age 42, when she takes up the four-year period of the *d*.

At the age of 41 she is under the letters

$$\frac{\underline{h}}{\underline{n}}$$
$$\underline{n}$$
$$(18)9$$

with the Essence 9. It is interesting to note she has been under this 9 Essence since she was 37 years old and has one more year of its influence. She then moves forward to the table of

$$\underline{h}$$
$$\underline{n}$$
$$\underline{d}$$
$$(17)8;$$

the following year to the table

$$\underline{e}$$
$$\underline{n}$$
$$\underline{d}$$
$$(14)5$$

The past period has been very active, but slightly disappointing because of the 9 Essence; at the same time it was rewarding in the opportunities presented for deeper realization and for work among those who carry on the cultural activities of life.

The 9 Essence represents her Destiny and the opportunity to round out her life with many rewards through philanthropic work and interest. However, should she have lived a very selfish life, thinking of personal love and living in jealousy and conflict, she could have found this a very hard period with discord in home and family life and many nervous conditions. (Study the meaning of the letters carefully to interpret the Table of Events.)

Her Personal Year in 1962 is a 1, so she is beginning a new cycle of experiences.

Her Pinnacle has changed from the testing and demanding (11)2 to the more personal 3. She can make much personal progress now and will feel an urge to use her talents. She will have a desire for more popularity, leisure, and romance. If she is true to herself she will have help and assistance from life and friends. If she is too restless (notice the seven 5's in her name) she could scatter her money and waste effort.

On the whole she will find this one of the pleasant times of her life, with travel and money and something of the eternal triangle.

At the same time the four years of the *d* coming up indicate a work to be planned, to help keep her feet on the ground and to build her career for the future. She has only one 4 in her name and does not like routine work; but there is an obligation to family and economic conditions, even though a more personal opportunity is offered through the 3 Pinnacle.

An easy way to set up a "short period" chart is to start with the present date and age. First, place the letters of each name, corresponding to this age and date, into line with the column, going back into the past a few years and then into the future a few years ahead. It is not advisable to try to understand the future too far ahead. The future is still to come and cannot be experienced at this time. Instead try to understand the present and the past. These experiences build up the future.

To prove this chart, figure her name from the time of birth up to her present age.

CHAPTER XVII

MEANING OF THE ESSENCE

The Essence represents conditions and circumstances demanding attention and shaping the personal efforts shown by the Table of Events. On every Table, it is the final digit of the Essence that directs the efforts—modified or strengthened by the numbers forming the digit.

NUMBER ONE ESSENCE

All *1* Essences represent forward movement—toward improvement. The affairs of the life tend to change. A *1* Essence calls for initiative, leadership, executive action and forces a decision about the past and the present and the future. It introduces new interests, new contacts, new ideas, and new occupations, all leading in a new direction. It is a beginning even along old lines of endeavor.

The *(19)1* Essence gives tests of character and brings experience calling for decisions discriminating between right and wrong. The *9* of the *19* demands high standards and the experiences will demand unselfishness. The period can bring strange experiences, sometimes due to resentment and resistance on the part of the individual, born of a desire to be independent and

272

to think and act according to personal desires and ideas. It brings a struggle for independence and to break away from old conditions. Efforts should be made to improve the thinking and to meet conditions with more understanding. It is possible to be led into wrong associations through the emotions and a desire for change. A *(19)1* Essence is often found covering several years. Big lessons are learned during the period.

NUMBER TWO ESSENCE

All *2* Essences represent a period of growth, but "haste makes waste." Partnerships, associations, and the affairs of others bring opportunity. There is little to be gained through trying to avoid the help others can give. Also there is much demanded in the way of cooperation and peaceful coexistence with those met in business and domestic affairs. In fact, Cooperation is the keynote to success. Many little things are to be taken care of and to be well done. A good disposition is part of the progress of the period. There is much help through others, social activity, trips, pleasure and popularity. A feeling of subordination should be avoided, as delays only mean more time is needed for growth and worthwhile, lasting accomplishment. There is no real hurry under a *2* Essence.

The *(11)2 Essence* is a very important Essence, which is apt to be a *learning* period in the affairs, causing a crisis—a sudden break in association, coming as a shock to the emotions. It represents a needed awakening to the desires of others in partnerships and domestic affairs. It may disrupt old ties and for the time being can be very disturbing, causing delays and misunderstandings, feelings of loss, and separations. It is a period of subordination unless there is willingness to cooperate and share, even when at the head of undertakings. There could be sudden marriage, sudden separation. Through spiritual thought there is the opportunity to gain an inner peace. Then all changes and hurts will take on a new order and bring an awakening of worthwhile importance.

NUMBER THREE ESSENCE

The *3* Essence represents creative endeavor and personal opportunity for advancement. It is a time for self-improvement and to advance along the lines of the talents. It offers personal expression with the help of friends and loved ones and encourages the pursuit of personal interests. These should be constructive and in art, music, literature, religion, and the more cultural aspects of living. Whatever the interests, more imagination and optimism should be cultivated for a wider and broader contact with the world. Selfishness and critical attitudes of mind should be avoided. Being an emotional number, it brings love affairs and emotional experiences which can be lovely and bring great happiness. The desire for pleasure, fun, and social activity, apart from useful endeavor, will bring scattered forces, loss of money, foolish action, resulting in gossip and regret. It can also mean loss of position and standing unless the emotions are constructively expressed. Ideas expressed in words or speech can advance the career; and if there has been limitation in the expression of the feelings and abilities, it is important to make the effort to find useful interests rather than to retire within the self or live in repressed emotions. Children bring interest and mutual happiness. Trips for business and pleasure widen the horizon. Make new friends, enjoy old friends, and express the spirit of friendship.

The *(21)3 Essence* brings emotional tests and the possibility of emotional confusion, through too much feeling and worry about what others do. Generosity may cause a sacrifice and a hurt through those trusted and loved. Be generous but businesslike in all undertakings under any *3* Essence.

NUMBER FOUR ESSENCE

The number *4* Essence is a practical period; it is a time to put the affairs in order, on all planes of living. The health, economic conditions, property matters, in-laws call for attention. An effort to place affairs on a better and more orderly level of living is called for. Good management in a matter-of-fact manner is important. There is work to be done which cannot be escaped. This is necessary in order to place a better foundation for growth and attainment. Facts come to the surface, showing the situation as it really is, but forcing the individual to make the effort to better material conditions. This is a time for building a home or business, but accompanied by effort, with need of economy and good judgment. Old conditions may be broken down to bring about the practical improvement. Conditions may seem slow and to hold one down, but results will be accomplished in the end if the responsibility is taken. Relatives make demands and health matters also call for efforts towards improvement, or a check-up. A new order of things and way of living is the result of the *4* Essence if the work is done. Avoid feeling held down. Get things done.

(22)4 Essence. This is an important Essence, for a spiritual force is present, seeking to add religious and spiritual thought to the thinking and interests. There are two activities or two people to be considered (22). Others may be dominant and trying. Quarrels and disagreement bring sorrow and loss. The way should be found for agreements, even if the association is to be broken up. Self-realization must be gained, even in the midst of confusion; to run away while discord exists brings delay and little happiness. Avoid the feeling of subordination. When attention is given to details and willingness to share is expressed, also willingness to wait awhile, a better relationship will be established and the freedom desired will be attained. This is a sensitive period. Resentment and dislike can lead to illness. The *(22)4* Essence appears on a chart to direct the individual to a better understanding of *himself* and others. It is a signboard calling for more harmonious living—a transition from one level of living to another, economically; bills must be paid up.

NUMBER FIVE ESSENCE

In the *5* Essence—a very progressive period—the unexpected is likely to happen, with changes, often not expected, but of beneficial nature in the long run. It is a time to move forward. Accept the opportunity to gain more freedom, prepare for new experiences, and add resourcefulness and new ideas to the undertakings. A very active period, it brings new contacts, worldly interests and public activity, travel and up-to-date affairs. Sudden happenings clear the way for improvements, even in the midst of what at first may seem to be confusion and uncertainty. When the changes are met and worked out they represent a stepping-stone to a new life. It is a period of excitement and social life. Many irons in the fire can scatter the forces and lead to confusion or loss. Nervousness, impatience can defeat the purpose of the period and bring legal affairs. Quarrels bring little satisfaction, delaying the progress and freedom the period represents. Old conditions may be broken down, but at the same time open the way to a more interesting period of activity. A *5* Essence at all times offers a fine opportunity to move forward, or to get free from old conditions. It takes down boundaries and limitations, at the same time demanding law and order and attention to rules and regulations.

(14)5 Essence—This Essence gives excellent opportunity to carry out the requirements of the letters on the Table of Events accompanying it. Trouble with others in business and employment may arise, to be overcome by agreement, based on rules and regulation and governmental procedure. It is wise to avoid personal demands based on impulse, hasty action, or speech. There is not a dull moment, but movement forward. Do not stand still.

(23)5 Essence—There may be long journeys. Others or many people must be considered. Different or odd lines of work may be taken up.

NUMBER SIX ESSENCE

The affairs of the home, family, children, loved ones, and all that stand for ideals and emotions of love and marriage are to be worked for and maintained during the period of the *6* Essence. Business affairs can be improved and stabilized and financial security be realized. The welfare of mankind, unselfish thought and action add to the responsibilities and are part of the financial security. Children and their relationship to the family are of much interest and importance, but may also be the problem and the discord under the *6* Essence. A dominant, possessive, or selfish individual may cause unhappiness. The responsibilities must be taken with good grace. The reward may come through inheritance or financial gain and through love and admiration of the opposite sex. A "care" is present through parents, relatives, doctor bills, expenses, and money paid out to take care of others. Interest in animals brings responsibility and pleasure. The affairs of marriage, even separations, may be problems if love is not true and selfish interests are followed. Popularity, social life, recognition, and standing in the community are the rewards of service and ideals maintained.

(15)6 Essence—There may be many admirers, but problems through the opposite sex. Duty and responsibility must be taken and ideals maintained. A successful business career comes through efforts to help others find joy and inspiration through beauty, art, and the lovely things of life.

The *6* Essence always gives the opportunity to enjoy and experience what the standards of love and romance stand for on the highest level of home and marriage. When love is betrayed or standards broken, many emotional problems mar the beauty of the period.

(24)6 Essence—There is less personal freedom than under a *(15)6 Essence* and more involvement in the affairs of family and associates. The experiences of the Essences are influenced by the numbers behind them as with, for example:

(15)6   *1* and *5,* more will and independence.
(24)6   *2* and *4,* called upon to cooperate and manage affairs.

NUMBER SEVEN ESSENCE

This Essence opens a whole field of intellectual interests, training, and advancement for a better way of living and finer use of the talents. It is a time to look to the more subjective levels of living, to try to understand the principles of Being and thought, to turn aside from objective interests for the time being. It is a time to plan for better emotional and mental control of the thoughts and actions and to try to understand what life is all about. The number 7 is the thinker and the seeker and demands this way of living when it appears as an Essence. It is a time to "delve" into the occult and higher sciences and their principles and laws—to study them, to use them, to write about them, and to make them a means of progress and advancement in business and in all associations. Strange occurrences, unusual circumstances and happenings may force a new look at what life is. Psychic experience may bring awakenings. Research and scientific investigation can bring business improvement or a new career. Literary and educational pursuits bring results. As the *4* Essence is a transition from one level of living to another in an economic manner, the *7* Essence brings a transition also through interests and activities never thought of before, with help in the end or at just the right time. There is a mental test to take; there can be loss and separation, but these force the thoughts and interests in a new direction. Depression, limitation and separation, with the feeling of being alone, are to be put aside through faith and realization. The number *7* is the number of attraction and seeks to reward, in quiet ways, when poise and inner tranquility are maintained. Health matters should be taken care of. Marriage may be delayed or troubled. However, marriage can take place when the interests are on the same level of thinking.

(16)7 Essence—The whole structure of the life can change, with something to pay up or give up, even a feeling of humilia-

tion. This is a karmic test, coming out of the past, even past incarnations. But when it is over, the debt is paid and a new life will open up. The troubles of a *(16)7* Essence never last too long.

A long period of 7 Essences offers a period of study, mental development and scientific work or discovery. It can bring retirement from social life and place the individual among those who are doing the scientific and educational work of the world.

NUMBER EIGHT ESSENCE

The number *8,* being a number of organization and authority and recognition, offers these privileges when it appears as an essence. It places the individual in the midst of many responsibilities but with the opportunity to advance in the affairs of the community, through executive ability, initiative, and understanding of governmental and civic affairs. It has much to do with property, buying and selling, and exchanges. It gives many interests, professional standing, and business opportunity through directing, supervising, and managing personal business affairs, family business interests, and community agricultural projects or large governmental projects. Better results are attained through working with groups rather than alone, and good judgment is necessary. There may be opportunities to judge and direct in an official manner. Money can be made, but with constant effort and endeavor. The expense often equals the gain, not always giving the expected reward for the effort expended. However, a business or activity can be built up to last a long time if the management is of a high professional or trained nature. There may be trips on account of business, with opportunities for printing, publishing, dealing with periodicals and commercial advertisement. Love affairs and marriage are not of a domestic nature, as business activities are always present. Fine marriages can be made and position and recognition be given through marriage, but love is often businesslike rather than romantic. Meet all delays, frustrations, and financial strain with efficiency and good judgment to follow through to the end.

(17)8 Essence—This Essence is a good business force, but demanding constant attention to business to balance the budget. Property to take care of is important.

(26)8 Essence—This Essence has much to pay out for others with little for the self in the way of self-indulgence.

NUMBER NINE ESSENCE

This is an important period and brings many blessings in disguise but demands a broad, compassionate, and tolerant attitude of mind. It gives unlimited opportunity to reach out for a wide scope of activity along any line of endeavor—business, professions, art, drama, music, and religion. A loss may be experienced, for it is necessary to let go of an old condition to clear the way for a freer and more useful life. People or even loved ones may go out of the life, as they are no longer a part of the future or the pathway ahead. This should not be taken as a sorrow of long duration; instead an effort should be made to turn it into the ways and means for a more useful life. Some phase of the life under the *9* Essence may be disappointing and the period may not be truly happy, for *9* is the number of deep feeling and drama; but there are assets and privileges to be taken advantage of. There may be many emotional experiences through romance and love affairs. These can be interesting but also disturbing if love is personal and clinging. Love affairs for personal vanity break up easily. Even deep and lasting love may have to be given up to teach the lesson of understanding and that true *love* simply loves; it does not seek to hold or limit. Under the *9* Essence experiences of many kinds take place and life is an open book to enjoy and study. Big business finds opportunity under the *9* Essence and the scope is unlimited when the welfare of mankind is considered. Money and the best things in life belong to the *9* and can be made and retained. Even with loss of money, more can be gained. Legal matters and lawsuits may enter in when there is lack of honesty. Others may try to take what is not rightfully theirs. Quarrels gain very little and lawsuits can be long drawn out. Where the purpose is right and the good of all concerned, the *9* is the winner.

(18)9 Essence—This Essence has much to do with large corporations and gives positions of authority, but often a legal struggle. Be sure you are right and put up a good fight, with tolerance and compassion as part of the effort.

A long period of *9* Essences calls for attention to the health. The condition and circumstance will hold during the period, to be met in a good spirit, without repeated feeling of disappointment. A lot of good is working through it. Keep in touch with those doing the work of the world which softens the hearts of humanity and improves its welfare.

MEANING OF THE LETTERS

Each letter describes the nature of the events to be met during that particular period of time, worked out under the direction of the Essence and Pinnacle and guided by the Personal Year. All letters and numbers represent the actual experiences taking place, but when understood and used as one would use different tools in a workshop, a stepping-stone to the future will be opened up and a better grasp of the affairs will be gained, giving an opportunity to express the individuality in worthwhile manner.

When a Table of Events presents a group of letters which seem hard, do not read it negatively. Remember—all numbers and all letters are good and represent privilege and opportunity in their special way. The Table of Events is to help one find the "best way" to walk life's pathway. Difficult periods occur in everyone's life, but by knowing what to expect and how to take advantage of the opportunities present or seemingly hidden in each letter and number, life becomes a pleasure and a *victory*.

The meanings of the Essence and the letters have similar influences, as a number never changes its meaning, only its position and its timing.

A J S

Each letter represents a one-year period and points to the future.

A—A decision, new opportunities, new contacts, marked changes in living conditions, moves, trips, and new activities, often without previous preparation. Success and advancement through taking action and moving forward with initiative and determination. Take the step; use good judgment. However, pay close attention to the Essence and Pinnacle.

J—A new direction of affairs, as for *A*, but through the desires and efforts of the individual. More daring shown and changes through the individual's own efforts, surprising to others because of the initiative expressed. More authority, the possibility of a promotion or a trip by necessity. More recompense—a new location. Much effort required. Will and determination open the way to opportunity.

S—A sudden impulse along creative lines will take place, with the opportunity to do what has been desired for some time. A general improvement will result once the adjustment has been made to the unexpected emergencies. However, sudden happenings may cause loss or great changes in family relationships, with loneliness for a time, or lack of social life. Sudden love affairs, not quite the ordinary—in fact, sudden happenings in many ways—occur under the *S* and are interesting and thrilling, even if startling and sometimes disrupting.

When these three letters appear, look for the new idea and the indications of a new way to get ahead.

B K T

These letters represent a two-year period concerned with partnerships and associations.

B—This letter represents professional advancement, artistic and scientific accomplishment. Many details to attend to accomplish the desires, and time is needed to get satisfactory results. A change of location of a temporary nature may be necessary to gain the advancement. The talents are awakened and quickened and opportunities are present, coming through others and because of a better use of the emotional faculties. Do not force issues; try for something to do of a constructive nature. Avoid living in the emotions and being too sensitive. Make living conditions attractive, comfortable, and cooperate to bring about more happiness. *B* tends towards sweet and lovely love affairs and home life and to improvements in the home. Separations and discord and hurts may result if there is little cooperation and desire to please. Do not blame others. Find peace through spiritual thought. Take care of the health. *B* represents a high-strung period.

K—An exciting period of activity. A windfall of some sort during the period. Strange experiences, strange friendships, strange and sudden love affairs. A long trip may be associated with this or change of home and locality. Involved in the affairs of others; a possibility of being misled due to deep feeling, or cheated due to lack of truth or honesty on the part of others. Caught off guard due to headstrong action, nervousness and emotional feeling. Illness but recovery. *K* is a letter of extremes but gives outstanding opportunity to advance financially and for general improvements when the efforts are wisely directed.

T—Progress in business. Money to be made. Partnerships, associations and groups bring mutual advantage, also the problems of the period. Many things to think out calmly, and an effort should be made to find the best way for all concerned. Others may try to interfere in business and personal affairs or try to take over and cause separation. Self-control is important. Nervousness leads to mistakes and delays. Love affairs are important, bringing marriage or, if truth is not there, separation. Love affairs may meet with opposition. It is advisable to look into the background of those with whom partnerships, business dealings, or marriages are considered. Take care of the health and save the nervous system by avoiding emotional intensity. Apt to be glad when the period is over, but many lessons learned about others and the self.

C L U

These letters represent a three-year period concerned with personal advancement and creative endeavor.

C—A strong desire to improve personal affairs and financial matters follows the letter *C*. An optimistic period, giving self-confidence, self-will, and determination to follow personal interests regardless of the opinions of others. A desire to branch out, to do something different and on a broader scale, changing the old living conditions, sometimes breaking up old activities. A tendency to extravagance or not to count the cost may lead to regret in the end. Activities, interests, and studies which improve the personal talents, the personality, and business affairs are to be undertaken. The impulse and desire to change the present set-up may lead to marital differences, but may be adjusted when the desire is not for the self alone. Unwise love affairs, the eternal triangle, careless and high life gain little reward and can lead to loss of position, character, and money. Success comes through more creative activity, added inspiration and imagination.

L—This is a pleasant period, among friends and loved ones. Individual progress and emotional expression along the lines of the talents, with pleasant associations and help through friends. Efforts should be made to perfect the talents and to resist the opportunity to live in ease and pleasure, depending too much on others to make life easy and pleasant. Much can be lost in the end through carelessness and thoughtlessness. *Self-improvement* is the keynote for both *C* and *L*. Those in power and influence give assistance through friendship and admiration. This period gives love and friendship, opportunity to build the popularity, gain through the charm and loveliness of the character; a slight sacrifice through loved ones, but love and appreciation give much to be thankful for. *L* attempts to give the best life has to offer when the finer things of life are made part of the life. The emotions are apt to direct the activities for advancement and sometimes for sorrow. Social activities, entertainment, and artistic interests add pleasure and advancement but should not be the most important way of life. Trips and journeys open channels for romance and business.

U—Many advantages along the lines of the career and intellectual lines of interest. Like the *C* and *L*, it gives opportunity for more personal expression. Generally more than one outlet for expression, combining business and financial activity, also along artistic or professional lines of endeavor. An emotional interest may be hidden for personal reason. Failure to grasp the opportunities present may lead to loss in the end. This may be due to lack of well-directed effort and too much emotional feeling. Unconventional love affairs, not always resulting in marriage, unless love and business are combined in a well-directed plan.

D M V

Each of these represents a four-year period, with work which cannot be escaped as a basis for future growth.

D—Activity concerning property, financial affairs, and family needs and interests. A practical period, and the responsibilities hold one to the undertakings. Steady application to get concrete results is necessary and must be worked out during the period. Many things come to the surface to be faced and acknowledged. This can bring problems, surprises and facts that have been overlooked or neglected for some time. Now is the time to get roots down, make the practical changes necessary or dreamed of. A time to build and to place a firm foundation for the future. Little is gained by efforts to escape the situation. This may lead to disagreements, quarrels, and many family problems. However, *D* gives time for pleasure, pleasant friendships, and family life. Restlessness and lack of application bring loss and regret, even illness. A change of opinion and a new attitude towards life may be gained, often of a religious nature. Trips and much activity. Make sure all papers, contracts, and agreements are understood and properly signed and taken care of.

M—A four-year practical period as with the *D*, but more mental than physical. At the beginning of the period it is necessary to give time to serious thought about the future. A plan or idea can be worked out and much can be gained by the end of the *M* period to establish security and good management of the affairs. Property matters bring interest and problems; all business affairs can be built up for success and general improvement if the work is done and responsibility taken. The period may seem long and hard, giving the feeling of being held down. Opposition may be felt through the desires of others, relatives, and business associates. This opposition demands a conscientious effort to accomplish the results desired. Quarrels gain very little. A stronger mental attitude, quiet determination, and a carefully planned endeavor bring help and assistance in the end, and the reward of having accomplished results in spite of problems. Money can be made and accumulated. A building period in business, home, and family matters. In-laws must be understood and assisted. Health matters are to be given attention. Have a physical check-up at the beginning of the period to avoid chronic conditions later on. Young children bring interest and unusual experiences. The *M* period brings its own reward, more so than some of the other letter experiences. Be businesslike concerning all contracts and papers.

V—A time for serious thought about conditions as they now stand. Practical affairs must be faced and the emotions controlled. Otherwise mental confusion may be experienced and possessions slip away. A better understanding of the self is important. Self-analysis and a better expression of the character bring many rewards. The *V* is similar to a *22* Essence. Financial affairs must be placed on a better business basis. There may be debts of long standing to pay up. At the same time the money owed for a long time can be paid. Gifts, love, and admiration from others help make the period interesting. Business responsibility of a surprising nature may have to be taken. This may seem a letdown but in the end helps place the affairs on a better level, brings out the talents for management and application and helps strengthen the character. Success through building up old lines of business rather than new interests. A desire for travel, luxury and ease may lead to extravagance and regret, for there is a practical work to be done under the *V* as well as under the *M* and *D*. Spiritual and philosophical interests add to the strength of the character and enjoyment in life.

E N W

These letters represent five-year periods. Experience is the teacher; progress is the opportunity.

The number five represents the stage where life is acted out.

It is the arena where life's battles are fought.

It is the forum where all people meet.

It is the world and its ever-changing rehearsal for freedom and progress.

It is activity, never ceasing, constantly moving forward for growth—otherwise stagnation would end the world.

E—Occurs in names many times. When it appears on a Table of Events it represents all that is stated above. It is a five-year period of experience with constantly changing conditions, repeated opportunity, exciting circumstances, the opening of new lines of endeavor, the urging of the individual to accept changes, public activity, and to keep up-to-date. Problems of the unexpected are apt to happen. Many experiences and problems are due to haste and impulse. It is wise not to quarrel with business associates, neighbors, or loved ones, for this can lead to separations, quarrels, or legal troubles. The affairs of the government and law enter into the experiences and are not to be disregarded. A strong desire for freedom may bring breaks in association. Freedom should not be considered a chance to break all rules and regulations. Resourcefulness will overcome many difficulties. It is a time to move forward to renew and renovate the activities at home or in business. Public contact will bring fun, travel, interest, and help to promote business. Marriage is slightly uncertain when freedom is taken carelessly. Sudden marriages or separations may bring legal matters. Good for all lines of work which need the support of the people. Money today, not as much tomorrow, but there when needed if the efforts are for the good of the people. Worldly living and breaking of conventions give little security.

N—Carries all the activity and progressive interests of the *E* but with more mental control. A very progressive period and a good time to gain position out in the world along with lines of the talents. Money can be gained and financial interests move forward if routine is not resisted. There will be interesting experiences and an active life, but home conditions must be considered. This may be slightly unsettled with some unhappiness under the surface. This is a time for husband and wife to grow together and to take a real interest in each other's work or career. Enterprise and new mental interests make this a fine period of the life.

W—Calls for the same progressive spirit as the *E* and *N*. It may appear to be a bumpy road, as the letter *W* has heights and depths in its form. Sudden happenings bring surprises, even the feeling of shock, but are necessary for the individual's growth to break up old conditions. This is to quicken the individual's efforts, to prevent slowing down or becoming fixed in ideas and ways of living. Life must move forward. There is something to be dug out of the consciousness to prevent self-satisfaction or egotism. Business may call for travel or being away from home: Mining interest, underground activities as oil or natural products. Real estate gives opportunity, also transportation or travel. Take good care of the health. Avoid nervousness or resentments toward others. Take care of legal activities with good counsel. Get a grip on things and seize the opportunity the "break up" brought about. Depression or self-pity gains very little. After many ups and downs a way to cross over opens up.

F O X

A six-year period of experience representing the ideals of love and marriage, the home and community service.

F—The practical and physical care of the home, family, children, and domestic responsibility are the concern under the *F* period, but may bring restrictions to some degree, even though service is willingly given. The *F* period, even though one of responsibility to others, seeks to lift one out of the seeming difficulties when the period is over. Time is needed to accomplish the tasks, as *F* is a six-year period of growth and development. The right method, the right emotional attitude towards others must be gained. In this way, financial affairs are built up and the character developed. When the duty is taken as a privilege and not as a burden, the position and success of the undertakings will be promoted. Loved ones, members of the family and children, even adoptions or separation in marriage bring peculiar circumstance. The good of the children is important and a clue to happier relationships. Loss may be taken if there is too much emotion expressed of a selfish nature. Through interest and service to the community, financial gain will be made with social standing. Association with big firms, industry carried out on a broad scale, produce, farms, and the many artistic services give business opportunity. Do not take on too much duty. Do not drudge. Serve willingly. Have more faith in yourself and what you are doing, and appreciate the tasks you are carrying out. Health, when disturbed, will be improved through less worry about little things. Keep an interest in charity. Support welfare endeavors. A plan for the future is waiting to be revealed and discovered during the *F* period.

O—Affairs connected with financial improvement concern the *O*; banking, trust funds, legal activities, and old established business; medicine, teaching, music, artistic professions, and professional sciences. There are many duties; and much work to do regarding the home, family, and children, but with less physical care than under the *F* period. Financial gain and general improvement follow the willingness to accept these responsibilities. The *O* period offers the opportunity to settle down, establish a business, and enjoy the ideals of the home, garden, estate, and the luxuries accompanying the service given in the community. The love of home and family is strong. There are decisions to be made regarding children, often connected with trust funds and inheritances. There is little gain through disagreement and discord. Harmony, beauty, quiet association are needed for wise judgment. Disharmony, loud and unlovely environment can cause illness and much unhappiness in the affairs of love and marriage, resulting in doctor bills, health problems, and much expense. There is recovery when more love is expressed. Dominance is not a good rule. The true desire to help others brings a finer reward. Religious and artistic associations bring pleasure. It is not a good time to lend or borrow money unless security is established. Friends, clubs, and good fellowship at home and in business are enjoyable experiences during the *O* period. Good for investments, but not speculation.

X—Family ties and interests are strong and may develop strange relationships between mother and son or father and daughter. Children may go out of the home, breaking ties, and causing problems between loved ones. The right to freedom of action is the privilege of each member of the family. To seek to possess and hold may bring regret. A great loyalty exists between children and family, and when there is need of assistance this will be given. Financial progress is good through lines of business which serve the public and supply goods and materials for everyday needs. (The letter *X* is found on many commercial products.) There may be a sacrifice made for the sake of others, as the *X* crosses out the personal desires. This may lead to poor health if the emotions are too dominant and not for the good of others. Under the *X*, life must be lived on a high level of thought and feeling, touched with spiritual and religious purpose or the ideal of service for humanity. In this way, personal rewards are received plus the good things life has to offer. Discord and argument gain very little. Schools, education, music, entertainment, radio, television, commercial art, hospitals, and welfare institutions are part of the professional and business opportunities for the *X* period. Honesty is the best policy. Ideals of service, love of humanity assure the *F* or *O* or *X* money, love, and usefulness.

G   P   Y

These letters represent a seven-year period of experience. Knowledge is power. Intellectual training and education are the springboards to sucess.

The letters *G P Y* in the names of children or adults call for a good education and encouragement of the desire for knowledge, books, scientific investigation, mathematical pursuits, and interest about the hidden or subjective levels of study. Music, rhythm, sound, and time interest these naturally studious minds. The experiences under the above letters will be along these lines.

G—The letter *G* is a very influential period. Business can be carried out on a broad scale: big contracts, large firms, and money made through enterprise dealing with many people over a wide area of activity. This is not necessarily humanitarian, but for the betterment of the standards of living and to maintain the industry of the community. The *G* tends to place the individual in a position of influence. The progress may start slowly, then suddenly bring changes in home and living conditions or travel. It is well to study all propositions carefully and not to overestimate the personal ability or the validity of the proposition, to avoid slight disappointment later on in the seven-year period. The advancement will give position and authority but should not be taken with too much self-assurance. It is necessary to measure up to the undertaking. A slight limitation runs through the period with opposition through others, not originally expected. For this reason, make sure, year by year, to avoid any unexpected turn that might disrupt the plans and bring confusion and turmoil. The *G* period is a good period on the whole, with love and pleasure in the home, although illness of a loved one may bring some anxiety. There is opportunity for wealth, a fine home, good friends, along with the mental responsibility and need for wise and careful enterprise. Unusual friendships and love affairs are connected with emotional interests. There is social activity, but a natural selection in friendships in the midst of public and broad acquaintance.

P—The opportunities under the *P* are also through scientific, educational, and specialized lines of work and thinking. It directs the experiences, with some limitation, to an awakening of the mind and for cultivation of the mental and scientific talents. It gives recognition for knowledge and skill but does not always bring the large financial reward or the return deserved. However, through patience and perseverance, the position is maintained, resulting in authority for the skill and knowledge, later on. Application to the tasks which present themselves at the beginning of the period lead to skills and awakened talents later on in the period. It is not a period of luck—the grass is *not* greener on the other side of the fence. Too many changes and restlessness cause delay and missed opportunity. Travel is enlightening, but for the purpose of gaining knowledge and information to add to the original plan or undertaking. Any feeling of lack of education or fear of the self will be overcome through study, reading, observation, and the courage to follow the mental interests which are deep in the nature. Through this, an idea or a skill will be developed to give a financial return, perhaps later on. The mental energy should not be wasted. Too much caution, moods, fear of others or of the self lead to inertia and lack of accomplishment. A certain amount of will, drive, and positive thinking take away any feeling of repression or limitation. Dare to follow, investigate and to use the talents along any line of science and education. Take an interest in the occult, the spiritual, and the subjective phase of mental science. From this idea, formula, or theory—a book or a teaching may be born. There is money to be made, but often very little for the self. Partnerships and marriage bring problems and need of understanding, generally because the letter *P* is not always as companionable as love and romance demand, or as generous. Build up the health through periods of rest, being alone, and right diet. Diet is important at this time. The *P* period brings an awakening to higher levels of living. Faith overcomes the problems and helps make the period interesting, very active, and successful. A close tie with the female side of the family is often realized.

Y—This is a period of spiritual unfoldment, gained through knowledge and mental pursuits and interests. It is not like any other period or letter. There is a desire to know more of the purposes and laws of being. The individual will be aware of changing interests—seem to outgrow old associations and activities with a desire to study and to live on a higher and more intellectual level. This may bring problems in marriage relationships and misunderstandings and give a feeling of being bored with crowds and the "fun" life, and to be more alone, to study and read. Health matters may bring travel or unusual methods of healing. The financial position is good enough to allow this to be taken care of. There may be psychic experiences but these ought to be placed on the mental plane and not allowed to be an emotional upset. It is an interesting period, not deeply happy until an understanding of the influences of the *Y* is achieved. In business affairs final success is often gained through former efforts and activities having to do with intellectual interests of the public.

The *G P Y* periods are busy ones, with many irons in the fire, interesting associations, and future opportunity carrying one over the seven-year periods.

H   Q   Z

These letters represent an eight-year period of experience in which the individual is placed in control—in business, industry, and personal affairs.

H—This is a busy, active period, giving opportunity for advancement in business and financial affairs out in the world of trade and enterprise, with the reward of public recognition and prestige. A definite effort towards improvement is the personal opportunity and requirement throughout the period. Repeated effort, good judgment, and efficient methods gain the reward and freedom desired. However, many problems will come up, making it difficult to maintain and hold the position and to retain personal possessions, adding physical and mental strain. All enterprise, personal or connected with large concerns, must be placed on a secure basis. This means constant attention to the undertakings with an eye to the future. Results may not be attained as quickly as desired or as seem possible at the beginning of the period. There is money to be made, but expenses are high due to the need for examination and growth —also to demands of the family or the care of a loved one, willingly taken or suggested. Civic and community activities afford an outlet for the executive ability, and the talents for directing, supervising, and organization will be developed and called upon during the *H* period. This will bring personal credit and contact with people of importance. Ability to judge human nature is an asset and should be cultivated to avoid mistakes in business dealings or in evaluating individuals. A philosophical attitude of mind will give pleasure and association with groups or secret societies. It gives splendid opportunity for writing, public speaking, travel, research, printing, and publishing. Property matters are often the problem and the asset. Buying, selling, exchange, sports, games, hotels, and politics open avenues of business activity.

Q—This letter is not commonly found in names. It gives an interest in activities, different than the established methods of procedure in business or thinking. It stimulates attempts to begin a new work or to extend the activities in a new way or out of the ordinary. Odd or unusual interests attract the attention and, as with the *H*, call for good judgment and understanding of human nature. New lines of thought and endeavor may lead to the expression of peculiarities of temperament which could be a drawback and bring misunderstanding and conflict in home and marriage—also in business. When reason is combined with emotion and each plan or idea carefully investigated or understood, the new line of interest can bring success and personal credit. Carried too far without thought to the future, it tends to unprofitable associations. Two lines of work may be carried out at the same time—as business and religion. Interest and association with young people bring benefits or become a care as to education and training. Personal advancement comes through literature, teaching, travel, speaking. Diplomatic undertakings give opportunity.

Z—A definite purpose should be established and well-directed effort be made to fulfill this purpose during this eight-year period. A new slant concerning the beliefs will be developed and an effort made to find what truth is in personal experiences regarding the laws and principles of being. The ability to discover hidden purposes in business and on the level of intellectual thinking brings business opportunity and personal satisfaction. As with *Q*, there is an interest in mysteries from a spiritual, psychic, and occult level of action and human behavior—also in the actions of those on the unlawful levels of living. The environment may be different or the wrong environment may be experienced through marriage or associations not fully understood or thought out, leading to repression and opposition. An unusual marriage may be made due to a mutual interest, different from established methods of thought and feeling. Through mental effort, study, and personal effort the chance to rise to recognition and authority runs through the period. There is an ability to bring others together for different ways of thinking and believing that may be touched with the occult or philosophical. Travel can be a source of business success, of discovery or research which helps strengthen the position and finances. Intelligence work, governmental affairs requiring special knowledge offer opportunity, but call for cool reason and emotional discipline. Success comes through languages and foreign associations. Correspondence, writings, and knowledge not possessed by others open many doors.

I R

These letters represent a nine-year period of experience. The drama of life is acted out here. The scope of opportunity is limited only by the character and desires of the individual.

I—Under this letter there is an opportunity to attract wealth and financial protection. Ability· to understand the needs of the people opens the way to success and money. Failure through mistakes or over-optimism can be changed to fortune and wealth when the creative talents are cultivated and the intuition awakened. When a consistent effort is made, luck follows and the desires are attained. Under the *I* the power to attract help and influence necessary to get results is always present. The feelings, emotions and impressions are very strong and must be controlled. Moods and depths of feeling can lead to loss of opportunity and scattered forces or to unreliable traits of character. Sensitiveness and impressionability are the guides to success, but may also lead to a very disturbed life, especially if allowed to control the attitudes, words, and feelings. A strong desire to improve the home and environment give opportunity for use of the imaginative talents and love of the beautiful. A desire for perfection leads to beautiful creations and work. Country life is the true environment rather than the crowded city. A desire to be alone and to get away from confusion and noise brings this about. A dominant character in the environment or business activities may cause unhappiness and lead to sorrow and separations. Many troubles are brought about by others, often exaggerated in importance by sensitiveness. Jealousy and resentment result when the individual responds to others and the environment with uncontrolled emotion. It is necessary to think and act with more love, tolerance, and compassion. There are no limits to the use of the talents, from the very practical to the heights of music, composition, and drama. Influence and affluence flow throughout this period. Keep physically fit.

R—This is an important period and brings many experiences, both rewarding and disappointing, and many emotional tests, but tends to give prominence and position. It demands character and high principles with rewarding personal accomplishment when the heart is warm for humanity. Under the *R* it is necessary to develop the spirit of the brotherhood of man; this gives the opportunity for philanthropic undertakings based on tolerance and compassion for all peoples and all races of mankind. It is not an easy period when intolerance or race prejudice remain fixed states of mind. The letter *R* is the last letter of the alphabet and represents mankind's last initiation. During an *R* period the lesson that all life is one and all people are included in the divine order of creation must be learned. It is a period of great responsibility but of unlimited opportunity in association with those doing the world's work, and it seeks to reward the efforts with the best life has to offer: love, attainment, and the financial means to accomplish broad and universal undertakings. These must be earned, however, and maintained by personal effort. States of mind which ask for selfish reward bring many disappointments, losses, and separations and much personal unhappiness. The letter *R* is forgiving and when the talents and efforts are turned to making the world a better place for all, it helps overcome all difficulties, replaces all loss, and gives the personal love which is so greatly desired during its period. It is an emotional period, for the feelings are impressionable but deep, and reason may be lost in the dreams and visions that fill the mind, much like the *C L U*; but *R* gives more self-control and self-discipline than the *I*. Marriage and love affairs are on a high level, true and lovely when the purpose of the period is lived up to. High living and self-indulgence, "wine, women, and song," and negative habits may break up the home and separate man and wife. Egotism and strong desire for popularity, without good works, end in loss and regret. The promise is given for success and attainment in any line of work which promotes civilization or has to do with art, literature, foods, methods for right living, and all creative endeavor. Problems may arise in partnerships and associations. The dishonesty of others may bring legal matters to be adjusted; or they may be long drawn out. Honesty is the best policy at all times and will bring the assistance necessary to win. Sacrifice of principles will result in deep disappointments in the end. The names of many musicians have the letters *I* and *R* repeated in their names.

CHAPTER XVIII

VOCATIONS AND TALENTS

Every number and every letter in the name at birth is an indication of talent and vocation. From the first letter of the name and the first vowel, to the final number or "Ultimate Goal," the vocation opportunities of the individual begin to build up.

Some people have outstanding talents and are destined for a specialized line of work. On the other hand, most people seem to have many talents and can do many things, but fail to realize their true worth or capabilities. They go from one line of work to another until, by trial and error and many disappointments, they discover they do have talent, often too late in life. Many good and loyal workers could advance to a better position and gain their heart's desire if they would take time to "know themselves."

Vocational analysis is a matter of synchronization—to bring all the traits of character, the abilities, and the destiny into simultaneous alignment. As all points of analysis are studied, they will describe a picture of the strong and weak points of the character, the latent possibilities, the place of power for accomplishment, and the talents which go with these indications, all working together to direct the efforts towards a successful and useful place in the world of business and human endeavor.

The Birth Force gives the natural talents.

The Destiny indicates the place to look for opportunity.

The Heart's Desire or inner nature shows what the individual wants to do.

The Planes of Expression show the personal response to experience and responsibility. Also they support the Birth Force or natural abilities.

The Points of Intensification are the tools to work with to support the natural talents and to fall back on for specialized work. Talents of more outstanding nature will be shown by repetition and emphasis of numbers on the Points of Intensification. (The first letter of the name and the first vowel give strong traits of character and personal intention.)

The Pinnacles and Challenge show the overall direction for present and future successful action; or sometimes may act as a deterrent to sidetrack the endeavors unless understood and made a part of the pattern of accomplishment.

All these indications taken together will direct any young man or young woman to the "way" to make life a success, giving him confidence in his undertakings and future. This knowledge will give an inner satisfaction and add the quality of enthusiasm so important to lasting success.

Whatever your work in the world may be now—whether artist, writer, salesman, politician, scientist, electrician, aviator breaking the sound barrier, lawyer, housewife, servant or office worker—rely upon the endowment of talent as shown by the number of your month, day, and year of birth.

A good way to become expert in vocational analysis is to study the names of successful people in the "Who's Who," to be found in all public libraries.

Method:

Depend upon the talents of the *Birth Force*.

Find an outlet for the likes and dislikes so positive in the *Heart's Desire*.

Make contacts out in the world according to the privileges of the *Destiny*.

Then look for special qualifications through the *Points of Intensification*, and be prepared for the temperament and type shown by the *Planes of Expression* which may be cultivated and trained for special advantages.

Prepare for changes in experience and opportunity as shown by the *Pinnacles* which may, surprisingly, turn the talents into unexpected directions. (One of our famous movie stars, not a true actor, gained a successful artistic career because his *Pinnacles* were *3–3–6–2*.)

Consider the *Challenge* as a possible weakness, turned to a support and talent when recognized and developed.

Study the meaning of the numbers as described under the Birth Force.

SPECIAL FEATURES

House Numbers—Cities and Towns

Naming the Baby—Changing Names
—Signatures

Health—Color—Music

Marriage and Companionship

World Events

Important Questions and Answers

CHAPTER XIX

HOUSE NUMBERS—CITIES
AND TOWNS

A red lantern placed along a highway signals "Danger ahead." Naturally, if you are a careful driver you will avoid the danger spot.

It is not the red lantern which is the danger. It simply signals danger, describes the situation and gives advice as to what to expect and how to act. A number, wherever found, defines a situation in the same way and gives exact knowledge as to what to expect under the circumstances.

HOUSE NUMBERS

I am often asked, "What is a good number for a house or residence?" I ask in return, "What do you want in a house or residence? And, if you get it, can you live up to it?"

All numbers are good, friendly, cooperative, and helpful. At the same time they have firm convictions and definite methods of action, which they live up to at all times. If you move into a house that has nothing of yourself there and fail to read the signs represented by the number, you may experience confusion and unhappiness. Numbers do not set up conditions, however. Their duty is to accurately describe what has been established and what is taking place at that particular time or place.

A church calls for the spirit of reverence from those who enter in. A theatre invites one to pleasure and amusement. In the same manner a house or home, already established, calls for a "response," according to the number describing it.

A house, represented by its number, naturally wants to be itself. If the story it is telling is not to your liking or is foreign to your nature, do not move in, unless you are willing to share with the house. The house will show its true colors, but even so, it may not be a problem if you are intelligent and cooperate with its intentions. If you do so there may be more good there than you think. On the other hand, if you do not care for its vibrations and move in, do so without blaming the house for certain experiences which take place under its roof.

A professional woman, who had worked steadily for many years, moved into a *seven* house. She knew what the number *seven* stood for. She wanted to be alone, to rest and study, to get away from people and the public. Two years later she moved out. She said she had never been so alone in all her life and did not like it. She did not blame the house or make herself unhappy about it. She simply moved.

A great deal of expense, unhappiness and unrest can be saved by understanding the nature of your house. A young couple bought a new home. The landscaping had not been done, and, almost immediately, friction arose between the two. The husband would not do the work to put the place in shape—it was a number *four* house—and the wife felt embarrassed by the unfinished condition of the place. They had put all their savings into the home and could not move. I advised her not to be unhappy about it; to get down to work herself, try to adjust to the situation, and to prove she could be a good manager until her husband's interests were also aroused.

Sometimes, if we put our shoulders to the responsibility and according to the requirements indicated by the number, we take a big step along the pathway of our Destiny and get free from the problem without future trouble.

If you feel you are not in the right place and cannot be happy there, try understanding the house, just as you would try to understand a child or an associate you had to deal with.

What is its type? Landscape it accordingly, at least to some degree, even if it is a rented house. Then, inside the house, be yourself, live up to your Destiny, your Ultimate Goal and your Type and talents; in the end you may be surprised to find many unexpected good things have come your way and it is your "Dream house" after all. Do not allow the house number to dominate your whole life. You are "you," remember, and have the need to "respond" to the story in your own name at all times, in any situation and under all conditions. You and the house together, guided by your numbers and the house number, can accomplish something worthwhile if you will try. I emphasize this, for so many people, when they discover the number of their house or home stands for something they do not want and do not care to live up to, live there in unhappiness and a sense of defeat.

It is illegal to change your house number of your own accord. It is better to sell or move if you cannot make the grade. An article appeared in a Los Angeles newspaper telling of the confusion caused by Numerologists who were changing their house numbers. Once a number is given it cannot be changed, for it is a legal matter.

The full meaning of your place of residence is in the number of the house and the numbers of the street, combined. However, the house number has the strongest vibration and influence.

If you are living in an apartment, your apartment number tells what is expected of you personally under the conditions represented by the apartment house number.

If you are living in a court or in a group where the numbering is ½ or ⅓ or ¼, you will be required to be the tactful and cooperative dweller under the ½—the friendly one under the ⅓ and will find many tasks or situations of a practical nature to be met and taken care of under the ¼.

A NUMBER ONE HOUSE

Independent, individualized people will enjoy this place of residence. It encourages originality of purpose and development of creative ideas. Will, determination, integrity, and strong character are necessary to live there. These qualities of character will be developed by those living under this roof by the many eventful happenings which will take place here. Dignity of manner, personal pride, and intelligent interests are the keynotes to success and attainment. Self-confidence is required, but egotism should be avoided, for dominance, selfishness, or eccentricity bring disappointments and antagonism. Sudden and hasty friendships not based on worthwhile interests are not advisable. Take time to get to know people and to make your own interests known. Many peculiar experiences will take place to make life interesting. Live up to them with courage and mental stamina. Here, you have the opportunity to be at the head of things in your community.

A NUMBER TWO HOUSE

A home for gracious refined people who are socially inclined and like to share what they have and to join with group activities. Religious interests, spiritual principles, and simplicity in living are the keys to happiness here. The aggressive spirit does not bring good-will and could result in confusion and discord. Difficulties are smoothed out through tact, diplomacy, and patience. To be small in thought and action, careless of the needs of others, or to be overly exacting in little things does not bring true happiness. Interesting experience will be taken through partnerships, both in marriage and business. Willingness to cooperate and to go half way will get the right results. Success is gained here through accurate knowledge and by careful attention to the details. Give things time to grow in friendships and business and in all undertakings. Haste makes waste. Keep things neat and clean. These are important to the charm of this home.

A NUMBER THREE HOUSE

A happy, cheerful and obliging atmosphere radiates from this home when its number is lived up to. At the same time a strong feeling of self-importance is present, but a fine spirit of friendship modifies this and attracts happiness and builds for comfortable living. Imagination and creative talent are the keynotes to progress and can lead to a career for young and old alike. Dwellers here should guard against extravagance, for a strong desire to enjoy life without too much physical effort scatters the resources. Impulsive action in the search for romance leads to unhappy experiences and often to the eternal triangle, which can bring gossip and unhappy emotional experiences. Romance loves this house, but expects truth and loyalty. A good place of residence for those who entertain and engage in artistic pursuits.

A NUMBER FOUR HOUSE

A serious atmosphere characterizes this home. Qualities of loyalty, courage, steadiness of purpose, and application to duty bring recognition and worthwhile accomplishment. Practical planning, the use of well-established and accepted methods offer the best opportunities for lasting security and continued success. Family matters, the affairs of relatives demanding practical management are present and may bring problems, but repeated effort and good common sense lay the foundation for growth and security. There is a spirit of fun and good nature underlying the serious nature. A wholesome approach to the needs at hand and in the community makes for popularity and business opportunity. Order, system, and economic living lay the foundation for lasting financial accumulation. At the same time do not allow too much caution to narrow the life. People living in a *four* house can be the steady, well-liked, and respected families of the community. Work well done and "according to Hoyle" will give personal satisfaction.

A NUMBER FIVE HOUSE

This is a home for progressive, active people who enjoy life and get a thrill from worldly interest and constantly changing conditions. Routine is hard to establish and hold in a number *five* house. Interests outside the home and many irons in the fire prevent a smoothly running domestic life, but give many opportunities for usefulness in public affairs. The coming and going of many people, sudden and unexpected happenings keep life from being dull, but at the same time promote growth, enterprise, and resourcefulness. Variety is the spice of life here and living is sometimes hectic, unless this kind of living is enjoyed. Conditions never remain the same over a long period. Impatience and haste are not the best methods. Take time out to rest and relax from time to time.

A NUMBER SIX HOUSE

Domestic and family interests mark this home. Strong family ties, love of children, relatives, and family traditions radiate from this home. Established methods, respect for the ideal of the home and family make this a place of love, beauty and service. Money, comfort, and the good things of the world are attracted to this home when good will and the humanitarian spirit are lived up to. Duty will always be present, and responsibility should be graciously accepted. Over-estimation of the value of one's possessions and too much self-importance may bring domestic problems and lead to discord and unhappy relationships. Children and animals enjoy the warmth and generosity of a *six* home. Residents of this home should take part in the welfare work of the community.

A NUMBER SEVEN HOUSE

Those who enter this home should leave their problems outside. This is a place of repose, quiet, refinement and of fine mental thought and interest. Pride and dignity mark its expression. Self-realization and self-control are needed. The strength of character which gives self-reliance and dependence upon the inner powers of mind and soul grows here and should be the purpose of the residents of the *seven* home. Education and learning form the foundation for attainment. Educators, scientists, writers, and those who are interested in the intellectual side of life find this an enjoyable home. Success is gained through knowledge, skill and specialization. Not a home for those who cannot live alone.

A NUMBER EIGHT HOUSE

This is a home of importance and for those who have gained some degree of self-mastery and have a well-defined goal in life. It is often a place of business activity as well as that of the domestic phases of living. It is not truly domestic in nature, for many interests having to do with broad business undertakings, which keep the world moving forward, are attracted to its vibrations. Situations that call for good judgment and efficiency in management of affairs and money are likely to be experienced. Eventually these bring recognition in the community and respect for the good works accomplished, backed by strength of character and repeated effort. Sometimes this is more of a showy home than an easy-living, comfortable one. Living here, it is best not to strain after success. Instead, have faith in one's self and take time to develop the project in mind.

A NUMBER NINE HOUSE

If you love humanity, have no race prejudice, and can meet all classes of people, you will love this home. Compassion, tolerance, charitable feeling, and philanthropy are the keynotes to happiness and have an amazing power to bring money and love to those who live here. Lovers of art, drama, beauty, and philosophy can grow, produce fine works and give inspiration to the world. Many emotional experiences and disappointments teach that life is not just a personal matter of likes and dislikes, but that of a universal cause in which all people are included. Giving something beautiful to the world, colored by a broad understanding of the needs of others, can bring the personal love that might be lacking otherwise. A happy home for those who have the understanding of the brotherhood of man.

When the number of your house is the same as that of your *Heart's Desire*, you will find an inner satisfaction there if you will follow its dictates.

When the number of your house is your *Destiny*, it will be a background from which to work in reaching out for the opportunities defined by your Destiny Number.

When the number of your house is the same as your *Birth Number*, you should make every effort to develop your talents. Together, you and the house can take your place in the world and by your own efforts.

A house with the same number as your *Ultimate Goal* gives you many opportunities to direct your life to this goal. Be sure you know what your Ultimate (Reality Number) Goal is.

If the house number is your *Pinnacle Number*, it will support you in working out the experiences the Pinnacle is demanding for *that* period of your life.

If the house number is your *Challenge*, you will find it easy if you will dig deep into your character to cultivate and round out that particular side of your character.

Names and Numbers are guides given to direct, protect us. They do not compel; instead they explain, uncover, and through their language, urge us on to a better and happier way of life.

CITIES AND TOWNS

If you are planning to move to another locality, the basic rules are the same as for homes and residences given above. What do you expect to find there? What does the city have to offer you? Can you live up to its requirements?

Each city or locality has its own purpose and destiny and these will be shown by its numbers. Does the locality you are moving to have any of your numbers—your Heart's Desire—

your Destiny—your Talents—your Ultimate Goal? The problems of living there or making a new start will be easier if you understand its purpose and needs.

When you get your city's numbers and understand its general requirements, it may be you will not need to make a move, if you are doing so because of restlessness or the feeling you cannot make a success where you are. In this way you will know what you have to give to gain the opportunities it has to offer and discover why you have not been benefiting.

Begin by figuring the Destiny of the *State* to learn the overall requirements and general influences it represents. A new realization of what it is asking of you may open your mind to lead you to new opportunities. Then figure the *City*. You may like it better than you do now, and feel better acquainted with it. Or you may discover it has nothing to offer you and is very different than your type or make-up. However, if your lifework is there and established, cooperate with it as you would a business partner; gradually some of the barriers to your success and happiness will be removed, and, suddenly, new channels of opportunity will open up to you.

CHAPTER XX

NAMING THE BABY—CHANGING NAMES—SIGNATURES

NAMING THE BABY

From the insight you have gained into the future from the name and date of birth, you can realize that the challenge of naming a baby, changing a name, or arranging a signature belongs to a trained Numerologist. Yet names are changed, babies named, and signatures arranged by even a casual reader or student of Numerology, sometimes successfully, more often for slight improvement, and frequently for even a greater challenge in life.

After years of experience and observation of the lives and destinies of people in all walks of life, I now refuse the responsibility of naming a newborn baby. The child's destiny and its purpose in life are already written in the Lamb's Book of Life by Divine intent. Naming it is the responsibility of the parents it has chosen to be the channel for its birth and life on earth. We all come from the Infinite, and a birth is not just a physical law or happenstance. It is part of the secret of creation and in the hands of the Infinite.

312

There is a purpose, a privilege, and an opportunity for a wonderful life on earth for all souls; and there is a pledge which should be recognized to help carry this out between the child and the parents. To the parents, alone, is given the final decision, guided by the laws of the child's own determination.

When I am asked to name a baby I request a list of names that appeal to the parents. In arranging a name for the baby from these suggestions, the influence of the parents is present. A name given to a newborn child as a cold calculation leaves out the love and warmth necessary for happy growth and future harmony.

The final selection of the name should not be decided upon until the birth of the child, when the date of birth is established. Then, using the surname as a key to the family background and family inheritance on the father's side, the birth force as natural talents which are like a kit-bag the child brings with it into the world, I select the mother's choice for the given name, leaving the middle name as a matter of choice agreeable to both parents, or for special traits and characteristics, to form a balanced name.

When a mother comes to me to name her baby before it is born, I teach her to sit quietly each day and, in imagination, rock the baby in her arms, singing to it, asking it its name, and listening until, in her own mind, she thrills to the name she wants to give the baby. It will come to her, a message from the soul she is bringing into the world, and it will be the right name for the child.

If no name has been decided upon and the child has already been born, it is then a matter of good relationships and understanding of the rules used in figuring a name.

All names are good names—your own name and the one you have given your child. Whatever life holds in store is written there by divine consent; sometimes it is for an easy life, sometimes for one of strange experiences, but for a purpose which, on the surface, may not always be apparent. Whatever your name is, make full use of its qualities and faithfully follow the design it sets forth.

The following are advanced instructions. There are *three* relationships to be considered in naming a child:

1st—The type and nature of the numbers.
2nd—The balance of force.
3rd—The intervals between numbers.

FIRST RELATIONSHIP:
THE TYPE AND NATURE OF THE NUMBERS

Not much has been said in your previous instruction concerning this phase of reading character. There are two types of numbers—the *introvert* and the *extrovert*.

The true introvert is inclined to be reserved, reticent, selective, and very strong in likes and dislikes, which are not easily changed. He likes a few people but does not like crowds or noisy groups. He can become withdrawn when not pleased, and very silent, and is capable of living alone or having a retired life. He may sacrifice for others but finds it hard to forget. He can at times be very moody and go to extremes. He is a student, a thinker, and observer; he likes to know and to be sure in all his undertakings. He is capable of staying in the background at times of success or acclaim, seeming to care little for recognition. Behind this quiet manner, however, is a belief in himself, for he gains success by believing what he is doing is important and that he has done his part to bring about the accomplishment. He does not like to fail. Many of the world's greatest works in art, science, literature, invention, and education have been the projects of the introvert. If the introvert is found moving about in the world of material pleasure, it is due to a desire to escape from the sense of unfulfilled desires or from pressure caused by others, preventing him from being able to follow his own creative interests.

The extrovert, on the other hand, loves people, is unhappy if compelled to live alone, and needs companionship for his best growth and happiness. He loves to be part of what is going on out in the world and is socially inclined. Because of this the extrovert is often misunderstood, as he appears to be forward or without tact, taking unnecessary steps to attract attention or to get recognition. He is a likable person and gives out warmth and good-will to others; he is, therefore, found among the social and welfare workers, taking care of the helpless, sick, and poor. His own need for sympathy and understanding gives him understanding and sympathy for the needs of others. The extrovert likes to share, for his own personal interests are not overly important. He likes life and fun and is filled with overflowing energy and enthusiasm. This is one of the reasons why an extrovert seems, at least to the introvert, to put the wrong foot forward most of the time.

The extrovert is not a deep student like the introvert, for his love of being with others and social activity often tab him with the slogan: "wine, women, and song." In reality, the extrovert is the salt of the earth.

The introvert numbers are the odd numbers: 1–3–5–7–9.

The extrovert numbers are the even numbers: 2–4–6–8.

When reading names, you will find that almost every one is a mixture of introvert and extrovert. Most of us are more introvert than extrovert, which is a good thing, for the introverts are more inclined to turn to the deeper, more subjective or hidden phase of life than the extroverts. Now and then you will find a name completely introvert in all of its divisions and positions, but seldom one fully extrovert.

This mixing of forces enables people to get on together and to work together out in the world of human affairs.

$$\frac{7}{1\ \ 1\ \ 5}$$

W a l l a c e   An introvert name, even in the inner nature
5 1 3 3 1 3 5   and in the sum of the name.

    (21)3

$$\frac{1}{1\ \ 9}$$

D a v i d   Strongly extrovert, although introvert at heart.
4 1 4 9 4

    (22)4

Interpretation of the introvert and extrovert tendencies in a name reveals many surprising human traits; a man may have an introvert Birth Force and an extrovert inner nature or Heart's Desire. Many of his habits will be understood from these facts. He may desire to work in his own way but be very unhappy without close human association.

A man with an extrovert Destiny must meet people and be able to get on with them; but having an introvert Heart or inner nature, he may not care about people, or it may be hard for him to go out in the world to make public contacts.

The force of the introvert and the extrovert working against each other will account for the tangles in human relationships, either within the self or out in the world of public endeavor.

In the same way, before arranging a name for a baby, study the names of the parents. This will help to place the baby in harmonious relationship with the parents.

SECOND RELATIONSHIP: THE BALANCE OF FORCE

The second consideration in naming a baby is the *Balance of Force* shown between the main positions of the name. This is vital in reading all names. It often tells why one may have an easy life and another a struggle most of the lifetime. A new set of terms will be used in describing this point of analysis, but it need not be confusing.

The Heart's Desire . . . . the Consciousness
The Destiny . . . . the Environment
The Birth Force . . . . the Talents
The Reality . . . . the Ultimate Goal

The *Consciousness* is the inner awareness—the urge of the soul and the Grace of God in the heart of each individual. It is a strong, directing and compelling force, active throughout the lifetime, of which the individual may not be consciously aware. If this is the largest number in numerical quality (and it should be), it is helpful and may add the necessary strength to the character to succeed without apparent reason.

The *Environment* is the working ground, the field of opportunity and point of contact with the world. It needs to be supported either by the Consciousness or the Talents to help the individual maintain and take advantage of the contacts. It should be next in numerical value.

The *Talents* are the tools to be used to carry out the urge of the *Consciousness* and to help support the opportunities of the *Environment*; they should be equal or close to the *Environment* in numerical value.

The *Ultimate Goal* is the channel through which the desires, experiences, and talents are ultimately worked out and consummated. It is helpful to have this a larger number.

The strength of the *Talents* has much to do with the ease or the difficulties of the life. However, many people without marked talent get along very well in the world, especially if the *Consciousness* is strong. Surprisingly, many people with marked ability or a large number on the *Talent* position have a hard time, many tests without the "breaks" which the other positions receive. They succeed by their own efforts, pulling themselves up by "their own boot straps." They do fine work in the world, often unrecognized for many years, but in the end establish lasting results and useful works, born of experience and hard work.

There are many combinations and arrangements in names of these four degrees of activity. You will find them easy to read and very revealing if you keep the *meaning of the positions* clearly in mind. Examine your own chart. How is it set up? Have many charts before you as you read the following instructions.

For Example:

If the *Environment* is the *smallest* number, the individual may not know how to reach out for the opportunities desired, unless supported by the strength of the *Consciousness*, or at least, by a *larger* number on the *Talents*.

When the *Environment* is the *largest* number on the four positions, many opportunities will be received, and as often lost, especially if lacking the support of the other positions. Inability to value the opportunity may be the problem.

There are names that have the *same number* on *all* positions. The life may be fairly easy but without positive direction. Some degree of opposition between the positions gives more of a challenge and need for personal effort to succeed.

Or again, the *Consciousness* and the *Environment* may be the *same number*. In this case the desires and the opportunities are equal, which is very helpful, even without marked talent.

Often the arrangement of the name at birth shows the *Talents* and the *Environment* to be equal or even the *same* number. This gives fine opportunity for material success even though the *Consciousness* may not be a very active part of the accomplishments.

If the *Consciousness* and the *Talents* are the *same* number, this is good for general success. The *desires* and the *abilities* are equal and a fine team for success in the world.

THIRD RELATIONSHIP: THE INTERVALS BETWEEN NUMBERS

The *third relationship* is, in some ways, similar to the second, but the approach and analysis are different. It deals with the interval or stretch between the numbers on the different positions. This also helps to read the indications of a hard or easy life.

Study this chart:

3	6	9
2	5	8
1	4	7

On the vertical columns the numbers are one and two degrees apart (in mathematical value).

On the horizontal columns the numbers are three degrees apart.

Diagonally, from 1 to 5 and 5 to 9, the stretch is four points or degrees of value.

From 1 to 9 the interval is eight degrees.

When the numbers on the positions of your name are one or two degrees apart, with little stretch between them by count, your life will not be too hard and not too much effort will be required of you. You will get along.

If they are three degrees apart there will be many problems and probably a long, hard pull.

If they are four degrees apart a helpful arrangement is present; there is a surprising ease of accomplishment with little struggle—sometimes too easy to bring out the strength of the character.

If a number on one position is more than four degrees apart from any other position, the experiences are not easy. It may be hard to keep the affairs on a steady foundation. The wider the interval or stretch, the more confusing the life can be—like crossing a narrow footbridge without support in the middle.

These rules are advanced work, but when understood, they will give a deeper insight into the construction of names and expert character analysis.

Example (an arranged name):

```
    5    +    6    +    6    = (17)8 Heart's Desire (Consciousness)
  Henry  Lincoln  Keeler
  85597  3953635  255359
  (34)7  +  (34)7  +  (29)2  = (16)7 Destiny (Environment)

  July      17th      1912
    7    +    8    +  (13)4  = (19)1 Birth Force (Talents)
                               8 Reality (Ultimate Goal)
                               (Destiny plus Birth Force)
```

Here the *Consciousness* and the *Environment* are close together, showing that the inner urge or *Consciousness* and *Environment* or Field of Opportunity are near in agreement. He has every opportunity to carry out his desires and to find his place in the world. However, the stretch or degree of interval between *"these two positions"* and his *Talents* is very great.

Even with the initiative, will, determination and executive ability of the number one as his *Talent* number, he will find many personal problems. Self-will may be his downfall. As the *Ultimate Goal* is his highest number and his Heart's Desire, he should accomplish a great deal in the end to find the satisfaction of having his ideas and work organized and established with recognition and authority in his latter days of life.

NEW NAMES

This question often arises—"Have we the right to change our names?"—mostly asked by religious people. Or, "Does it really do any good to change a name?"—asked by doubting people. Or—"Will I get rich if I change my name?"—asked by ambitious people.

The Bible says, "Which of you, by taking thought can add one cubit to his stature?"—Matt. 6:27.

* * * * *

Some time ago I read an article on the nature of sponges. An experiment was carried out in which three sponges were dyed—one green, one yellow, and one red. They were then chopped fine, mixed all together and placed in a tank. Gradually each sponge drew its own color particles back to itself and returned to its original shape and form.

It is not a question of right or wrong; it is simply a matter of convenience or personal desire.

There are many levels of living. There are many trades, talents, fields of endeavor and lines of activity to be experienced, contacted and enjoyed. These are open to all who can qualify for them. Just as we choose a costume to fit a certain occasion—for sports or formal presentation—it is sometimes an advantage to use a literary name, an artistic name, or one for easier pronunciation.

But the original pattern described by the name given at birth, even though under peculiar circumstance, remains the same. A woman may bleach her hair and enjoy the experiences and the new contacts which it may bring her. At the same time, she is never quite free or safe from discovery, for the original color keeps growing in and *must be rebleached*.

As has been stated in your first instructions, it is the name at birth that tells the true story of the life and its opportunities. Your highest success for the present or the future is written in its scroll if it is lived up to with pride, dignity, and respect, and if a real effort is made to read the story it has to tell.

Even so, the use of a new name for a special purpose is often an advantage. It can give opportunity for the natural talents and be a means or vehicle for greater usefulness. However, behind this new name is the "you" who must live up to the set of vibrations which it will open up and catapult you into. A new name has no active value without "you" behind it. You may drive a jalopy or a Lincoln. In either case "you" are the driver, just as you may become a blonde or a brunette but cannot escape the original shade of your hair.

Take a new name if you desire, for whatever purpose you have in mind; but realize it is simply a tool for a better use of your own capabilities and consciousness. But at all times remain true to yourself. *You* are always *you*, even with a different name, and have a special part to play on the stage of divine and human action. You were named for that purpose.

Many people change their names, but soon drop them for they have not developed their own natural ability enough to live up to the requirements of the new name.

If you take on an artistic name you will not necessarily become an artist, unless there are artistic talents in your own name. You may find you are led into artistic association by the new name, to gain many benefits, which may be of little value in the long run, unless at the same time you continue to live up to the requirements and obligations of your name at birth. Eventually you may find you are not happy under the new name and feel an underlying uncertainty, because subconsciously you are aware it is not your real self.

I read an interesting article by a famous movie star who

had been given a career name. She was very successful, for she had talent. Gradually she came into a period of emotional unrest, realizing she was not truly happy under its influence; she had the courage to go back to her own name and wrote of her happiness, peace of mind, and feeling of being herself once again.

NICKNAMES

The repeated use of any name will bring a personal response to that vibration, just as your daughter or son may call you "mother" or "mom." A friend or loved one may respond to a certain characteristic in your character and give you a nickname. This nickname, however, is only a garment you are wearing for the time being or for a certain accomplishment, undertaking, or responsibility to that individual.

SIGNATURES

Pick out your best qualities when you arrange your signature. However, I advise men to use their full names as often as possible, if not in the business world, at least on private papers and belongings. Have you noticed that when a man reaches the top in his work or profession, he is known by his full name? He may be Jack as a boy, or Jack L. Smith in business, but when he reaches his goal he is known as John Lester Smith (an arranged name).

Women, also, should use their full names as far as possible, even though they are married. Every woman should have a personal signature for her daily activities, using her first and second names or her first name and her maiden name with her married name, except for formal occasions, naturally. Often there is a stronger financial arrangement of numbers in the wife's name than in the husband's, or at least an equal degree of financial attraction to help gain financial success for both.

This question has been asked me many times—"Should I have my new name legalized?" In most cases this is not necessary, especially if you make it known at your bank or to the family. On legal papers, everyone must sign his legal name, even movie stars who have been known for many years under a public name.

Even though a name, difficult to pronounce, has been changed and legalized, the old name lingers on, holding its influence.

A young man asked me for a change of name to help him get ahead in the movies. He was determined to have the new name legalized. He wanted to forget the past and an old family embarrassment. I asked him to wait awhile. There was so much talent written in his own name. Soon after taking his new name he met a rich girl. They were married under his original and true name, at her special request. He was glad he had taken my advice.

This question is often asked by the children of foreign-born parents who have changed their names or the spelling of the family name on coming to America: "Should the original name of the parents be used, or the new name or arrangement?"

If the child was born in America, after the family name had been changed by the parents, the present spelling or arrangement is the name of the child. Its destiny is different from that of the parents. It is "heir to the age's gain" and need not go back to the old circumstances.

However, in reading a name for anyone born in a foreign country, I use the foreign name given at birth just as it was written or spelled at *that* time.

An act of Parliament, written over 600 years ago, stated: "Giving a new name does not take away the old name. A new name only gives permission to use."

CHAPTER XXI

HEALTH—COLOR—MUSIC

HEALTH

Temperament and disobedience to the rules of procedure written in the name will tend to produce illness or poor health. Problems and trying experiences written on the Table of Events may be confusing, unless understood, and bring emotional strain to the physical body. An over-intensification of one quality of thought, as shown by the Points of Intensification and on the Planes of Expression, may drain the physical energies.

Each number represents a certain part of the body. Often the day of the month alone will give a *clue* to a fundamental physical condition, especially if little attention or care has been given to the physical well-being of the individual.

Number One—Corresponds to the head and lungs. With many ones in the name an inferiority complex may result in illness due to lack of opportunity to make use of the original ideas. Specialized instructions in deep breathing are very helpful and can change the whole life.

Number Two—Corresponds to the nervous system, brain, and solar plexus. The physical body is sensitive and is easily affected by noise, harsh conditions, and coarse associations. The feelings are easily hurt, leading to illness and poor health. The health is improved by food which builds up the nervous system and by instructions in self-realization. Periods of rest are helpful in a harmonious environment.

Number Three—Corresponds to the throat, tongue, larynx, and the organs of speech. With many threes, illness is frequently due to emotional disturbances, the feeling of lack of popularity, and problems through friendships and worry about the self. A more hopeful disposition should be cultivated and less time spent in worry about what others may say and do.

Number Four—Corresponds to the stomach, the right arm, and the upper side of the body. Overeating rich foods causes high blood pressure and overweight. Long periods of hard work wear out the fine endurance of the four. A too serious attitude of mind can bring lack of circulation and energy.

Number Five—Corresponds to the liver, gall bladder, the left arm and upper left side of the body. With many fives, overactivity, restlessness, inner dissatisfaction, and critical states of mind bring nervous tension which upsets the whole physical coordination. This also leads to accidents and physical hurts and long periods for recovery.

Number Six—Corresponds to the heart, blood, and skin. With many sixes, heart trouble may be organic and not the sudden heart condition so common today. These belong more to the four and five. A well-planned order of living and eating prevents breakdowns. Domestic problems, affairs of children, and lack of love and approval can lead to chronic conditions.

Number Seven—Corresponds to the spleen, white blood cells, and the sympathetic nervous system. All sevens need diet and are naturally selective in eating. Periods of quiet, relaxation, and escape from strenuous public life are important. Repression of the emotions and feelings gives poor physical health. The lower left side of the body and left leg are easily affected.

Number Eight—Corresponds to the colon, eyes, and lower bowels. Nervous indigestion, nervous headaches, and ulcers result from overintensity, strenuous living, and too much ambition. The number eight has the most physical endurance of all the numbers, and wonderful ability to recover. An inner poise, regulated endeavor with outdoor sports and normal physical exercise keep up the fine body strength and endurance.

Number Nine—Corresponds to the kidneys and generative organs. Also, diseases hard to control can be brought about by high living, self-indulgence, and wrong habits. The number nine should never indulge in alcohol or drugs. Health is a matter of not being too impressionable and not living too much in visions and dreams.

COLOR

Each number has its characteristic color, according to its rate of vibration.

#1—Flame, crimson, apricot.
#2—Fire, gold, salmon, garnet, white, black.
#3—Rose, ruby, amber, russet, snuff, blood.
#4—Green, blue, indigo, coffee, silver.
#5—Pink, strawberry, cherry, claret, wisteria.
#6—Orange, henna, mustard, scarlet, heliotrope.
#7—Purple, brick, pearl, magenta.
#8—Opal, ivory, canary, buff, tan.
#9—Carmine, lavender, olive, smoke, red.

Number nine *is* all color: Color = 36369 or (27)9.

Wear the color of your Heart's Desire for friendship and social life.

Wear the color of your Destiny to widen your scope of activity.

Wear the color of your Birth Force to help you demonstrate your talents.

Wear the color of your Ultimate Goal for deeper power and future attainment.

Wear the color of your Personal Year to help you make the grade for the time being.

Many clients have said to me, "But I do not like that color." It is not necessary to wear a complete outfit in any one color. A handkerchief, a tie, an accessory—a pen or pencil in your purse or a bit of colored paper in your wallet—if you keep in mind what it represents and why you are using it. A vase or an article of decoration in the home or office intensifies the thought.

Black is the color for formal wear. It is rich and dignified; but if too much black is worn, it represents sorrow and loss. It closes in and confines the emotions. It does not attract loyalty and true love or represent the ties that last and endure.

If you must wear black, wear colorful undergarments or a definite touch of color in some way.

MUSIC

Your name is your theme song. It is the instrument you are playing in the orchestra of life.

The sound of your name may surprise you. At times it will be harmonious. Again it will show discord and a keynote almost too high to reach with harmony and beauty until, through experience and many tries, you learn to reach up and strike it true and clear.

Each number has its keynote on the musical scale.

```
1-2-3-4-5-6-7-8-9          1—A-J-S    middle C
C D E F G A B C D          2—B-K-T    . . . . . D
                           3—C-L-U    . . . . . E
                           4—D-M-V    . . . . . F
How does John sound?       5—E-N-W    . . . . . G
                           6—F-O-X    . . . . . A
How does David sound?      7—G-P-Y    . . . . . B
                           8—H-Q-Z    . . . . . C (High C)
                           9—I-R      . . . . . D (High C)
```

Draw a musical scale. Place the notes corresponding to the numbers of the name on the scale.

Figure a birth date the same way.

In meeting the experiences of life and in working out the destiny as shown by a name and birth, the experiences are not all easy and there are periods of stress and strain. The life song will show just how great the effort is at times and how difficult it is to reach up to the opportunities ahead, especially as the letters and keynotes change on the Table of Events.

Most musicians and composers will not consider the themes as shown by the Life Song. "The intervals are not correct," they say. One musician would not accept the instructions or even listen. His Destiny was the number 9 (High D), and his Heart Number 1 (Middle C). But I could read the story of his life from that relationship—the conflict between his desire for self-importance and this need of his life—to fulfill his Destiny, the broad philanthropic field of endeavor.

Many years ago at the summer school of the Church of the New Civilization in Colorado Springs, where Dr. Julia Seton was Leader, Mrs. L. Dow Balliett was guest teacher. She taught us how to write our Life Songs. One of the students, a clever musician, harmonized them for us by playing the songs with the base chords in the *minor keys*. The songs were fascinating and very unusual.

A song writer, searching for themes for songs, can discover outstanding short themes in the "Life Songs" of his associates. Using the chords of the modern song writers will add charm to the song.

How to Write a Life Song

Each name is a verse, followed by the birth numbers, called the chorus. Repeat the chorus after each name or verse.

Form another verse from the numbers making up the Heart's Desire, followed by the chorus. Write a single chord for the Destiny and a final chord for the Ultimate Goal or Reality, a triumphal note pointing to the future. Time it in any way you like; but Mrs. Balliett taught us to play and sing our "Life Songs" in the timing of an anthem, before meditation, to tune in on the deep purpose of our births. She did not approve of harmonizing the intervals, as this overcomes the true sound of the name.

CHAPTER XXII

MARRIAGE AND COMPANIONSHIP

PAID IN FULL

I wonder if the love you gave to me

    Was worth the price we paid to have and hold;

Now that the years have set our senses free,

    The scroll of hidden music can unfold.

You were a burst of magic in my strife,

    And I? Well, it is strange that I should go

Across the flaming portals of your life

    Into the shadows of our afterglow.

Yet, after all, why burden our today?

    The years brought us our rapture, come what may.

                  —JULIA SETON

"I love you" is God's theme song. We are the children of God, born in His love. To love and be loved completes the plan of divine creation—in heaven and earth—and breathes the music of the spheres upon all souls. The dream of an ideal love, a happy marriage, a home, and children is the deep, divine urge in the heart of everyone from youth to old age.

330

Our magazines, periodicals, and television repeatedly present articles and instructions on "How to Get on with Your Husband"—"Can this Marriage Last?"—"What's Wrong with Men?"—"What's Wrong with Women?"—"Is Marriage a Failure?" From these reports it would seem this dream of true, loyal, and lasting love has gone out-of-date.

It need not be so; there should be no lonesome hearts. Love and marriage could be lasting and harmonious through the years if the hearts and minds of lovers were also warm with understanding.

My clients seeking marriage counsel have asked: "Will I ever get married again?"—by those who have lost love or are living alone. "Will I ever marry?"—by those who have never known love. "Why have I never met someone I could love?"—by those of high ideals. "Is this man right for me?" —by those seeking a true mate. And many more by those who have been hurt and disappointed in love and marriage.

One of the most pleasing phases of my work as a Numerologist has been counseling and guiding young people engaged to be married, earnestly seeking to make their marriage a happy one and to understand each other. This is building on a sure foundation and the give-and-take of true understanding. Problems in marriage *will* come up, but these are the fun of living together for accomplishment and mutual respect.

My first thought as I read for them is: What have they in common in character and in practical, mental, and emotional stamina? What is the point of attraction that brought them together? What numbers and what positions in their names are similar?

To find this answer, a complete chart must be set up for each one and read, step by step, from the Heart's Desire through each part of the analysis, according to the rules presented in this book, down to the final point of study—the Table of Events.

The happenings of human destiny bring people together for many reasons. Sometimes true love is the attraction, brought forth from past lives. (Many numbers in common.)

Or the marriage may be one of experience, with love to be earned through tests and trials, then ending in happy companionship and the joy of being together. (One or two numbers in common.)

Other marriages ending in divorce court have seemed to be wrong from the start; the reason for the attraction based only on a temporary position as a Pinnacle, Personal Year, or Table of Events, all changing experiences.

For intelligent and well-meaning people, the way to solve a domestic problem is a simple analysis of character from the numerical charts of each one.

RULES FOR MARRIAGE RELATIONSHIPS:

First—Look into the *inner nature* of the two people. What number is there? What is its meaning? Do both have the same Heart's Desire number, or is it different?

What is the nature of the Heart's Desire number in each name—introvert or extrovert? This can make a great difference later in life. Is the Heart number a "Go-getter," a "Carry-outer," or an "Easy-taker"? From this analysis alone, the possible problems of the future can be read. This is not always easy to point out to two young people in love, but it may reveal which one will be boss or the dominant one and how the personal interests will be expressed.

We human beings, even when in love, seldom change deep down in our hearts. "Where the heart is, the treasures are." However, time and experience may teach a more constructive or happier way of expressing this urge and of allowing others the same privilege. The Heart's Desire, when it is the same number for both, is a strong emotional tie. Love and interest can remain a lifetime through, even though problems and separation come about for other reasons. The tie between two people with the same Heart's Desire is a spiritual one.

Second—compare each *major position* in the same way. Do they have the same numbers on all positions? This is most unusual. This attraction would be similar to being affinities.

But far too often there is little real accomplishment when two people are so much alike. I have met my affinities in four different people, both men and women, during my years of counseling. We have become good friends and like each other very much; but, generally, I found in them my own weaknesses, which they could not help me overcome.

When two people have the Destiny number in common, the marriage may be comparatively happy, as they live on the same level of activity. They may have grown up together in the same environment, or met through association on the same level of living. Many marriages, comparatively happy, come about in this way because of common interests from birth; but there should be other points of attraction in common to bring the lasting fire of romance.

When the Birth Numbers are similar, this may bring two people together in love and marriage through association at work or social interests connected with the work. This marriage can be generally happy because of a mutual interest. This is usually built on the commonly accepted traditions and standards of home and marriage. Now and then, this tie is strange and intense, with many problems of temperament brought over from past incarnations. This attraction can lead to marriage but not to smooth waters.

The tie between two people with the same Ultimate Goal is a pleasing one, but does not always lead to marriage until later in life, unless there are other points of attraction in common.

Two people may be attracted to each other by the Personality. This is not enough for a happy marriage.

However, most love affairs are based on mixed relationships. Two people may have two or more numbers in common, but placed on different positions. The Destiny number of one may be the Heart's Desire number of the other.

Or the Destiny number may be the Birth Force number of the other.

These relationships occur in many ways. The one having the Heart Number will be attracted to the one with the same Destiny number, finding interest in what the other is doing.

The one with the Destiny number may be attracted to the

one with the Heart number because of the inspiration and inner charm it expresses, encouraging the one with the same Destiny number to greater effort.

Do not allow these comparisons to confuse you. Keep in mind the position, what it means, and what the number means, then line them up side by side. This will show you the outstanding relationships and the nature of the interest each has in the other and to what degree they can get on together for a happy marriage.

To gain a deeper insight into each character for whom I am reading, even if there is a great deal in common between the two on the major positions, I study the *Points of Intensification* or Traits very carefully. From the Traits, what we think of as human nature begins to show up—and the little things which bring the rub in marriage and companionship. An over-intensification of a strong trait of character in one may become an aggravation to the other, leading to argument, anger, and even jealousy. On the other hand, one may grow tired of the seeming weakness in the other and eventually find the relationship intolerable. It is here that true understanding is needed in the marriage relationship. The right of individuality is vitally important. It has gone out of style to try to reform one's mate. When love is there, and understanding, different traits of character will be admired: "John is like that," or "Mary always does things that way," means mutual understanding. *Love* is always tolerant and sympathetic. True love never speaks words of censure.

The *Planes of Expression* have *very* much to tell about a marriage and its outlook for continued happiness. With nothing more in common than a similarity on one or more of the totals on the planes, two people may be attracted to each other because of similar attitudes of mind and ways of thinking. Later they may find they are very different and cannot agree, having nothing in common in the major positions. One may be extremely practical (physical) and the other may respond to experiences from the emotional level of living; or, in another association, one may be very mental, cold, and systematic and finally become impatient with a partner responding to life from the intuitive level of feeling.

Another example—one may show a well-balanced temperament with physical, mental, emotional, and intuitive qualities harmoniously expressed; the other may lack in one of the phases of temperament, physical, mental, emotional, or intuitive, making it very difficult for them to live together, even though there is much in common on the major positions. A willingness to compromise is very important. An effort to understand each other may save the marriage. When this is done, the difference in temperament may add charm and deeper love to the marriage, seeing husband and wife safely through stormy periods.

In reading for two people about to be married, the trend of events as shown by the Pinnacles may indicate harmony and peaceful events for the time being; or suddenly change the order of living to the point of disagreement later in life. A change of Pinnacles may bring a period of concern and unrest, or again, a different Pinnacle may benefit and smooth out the problems in marriage and business for a married couple.

In reading for a married couple contemplating divorce, I especially look for any change of Pinnacles; I have saved a marriage by reading from the Pinnacles alone.

This question is often asked by a troubled wife about her husband—"Will he ever change and settle down to real work and think of his family?" Recently this question was asked by a wife whose husband had a three Pinnacle which told the nature of his actions and interests for the time being. Luckily, he had a six Pinnacle coming up in one year, so I promised her he would. Had he had a five Pinnacle ahead, there would have been doubts.

One client who had given her youth and her time in the care of an invalid mother asked, "Will I *ever* have the chance to marry?" Looking ahead to her final Pinnacle, the number for her latter days of life was a *six*. I assured her she would. She had confidence in my promise and immediately began to prepare a hope chest—not for herself but for her husband-to-be. I have always been sorry that I never learned whether or not she married, but I am sure she did.

To answer the question asked by those who long to marry *again*, I take the Destiny number into consideration (if it is an introvert number, especially the number seven, there is some doubt), the Pinnacle number, and the Table of Events; and then look for partnership and domestic numbers in the future chart.

In reading marriage relationships there is much to take into consideration. Most of the time a compromise must be made to ensure a marriage of lasting happiness and to hold the dream of love and companionship. Knowing one's self, and willingness to accept the marriage partner as he or she is (as shown by the numbers in each name), brings a rich reward and saves years of discontent, unhappiness, and possible separation.

There is one more point of study—The Table of Events. Many marriages have been made by people taking the same experiences shown on the Table of Events, or because the experiences one is taking bring an attraction to someone who represents the purpose behind the experience.

A young woman client was attracted to a man whose Heart Number was the same as her number on the Essence of her Table of Events. The marriage lasted only a few years and was very unhappy. He divorced her just as her chart changed, for the experience was over. He knew nothing of numbers and would have scorned any information written in either chart, but the story was described by the numbers on both charts.

Another client brought me the chart of her friend, feeling he would ask her to marry him. I did not think he would marry her or anyone else at the present time. They had a Destiny interest in common but very little more that was outstanding. She lost confidence in me as a Numerologist right away, for she had studied Numerology, and according to her thinking, there were many points in common. But I had read his Table of Events. He was just entering into a seven period of i-i-y (25) or 7 Essence. Later she wrote me that he had gone away.

To the one who asked me, "Why have I never met anyone I could love?" I answered, "Love is eternal; it is ever present; it never seeks to possess or hold; love just loves"; and advised her to love more, love life, love children, love herself as a wonderful being, a child of God, and to cease to judge or criticize others. True love will walk in, for the way to love is written in every chart. Be true to yourself.

Follow the above pattern for writing a Numberscope or for counseling others.

CHAPTER XXIII

WORLD EVENTS

Cycles of nine run through all the events of history. They interpret action and point the way to peace or war.

There are century cycles, major cycles, intermediate cycles, current cycles, and directive cycles. All these work together to describe the trend of events down through the centuries and to chronicle the progress of mankind. They point the way to the future and explain the experiences of the present time.

Each cycle brings an obligation, a requirement, and an opportunity. Upon how well these are carried out depends the progress or retrogression for mankind.

When the law of the cycles is not heeded, war, conflict, and confusion follow. On the other hand, any time mankind reads the signs of the times and follows their instructions, the way to good times and worthwhile endeavor for all opens up.

The signs of the times ahead, according to the century cycle, are encouraging and open up a new way of living. Mankind is catching a glimpse of this at the present time.

He l l		Li g h t	
8 5 3 3	1900, the present	3 9 7 8 2	The coming 2000
19	Century Cycle.	29	Century Cycle.
10		11	
1		2	

Thus we read the signs of the times.

As the 100-year cycle of 1900 opened up, life began to change. It brought a new age for mankind. Amazing progress has been made in science, invention, manufacturing, education, and building. *New* materials, *new* methods of construction in homes, and every possible way of making life more worthwhile have been promoted, awakening the spirit of adventure—even into outer space.

At the same time, it has been a period of terrific events, and many of the earth's creatures have walked through hell. Attitudes of mind have changed in business, politics, and social life. Old standards have been left behind. There have been wars and strife and struggles for supremacy, born of the desire for leadership which is characteristic of the number one.

But underneath, another force has been making itself felt. Graft, wrongdoing, political strife are being revealed and brought to public attention. LIGHT from on High is being turned upon the affairs of mankind. This is due to the approach of the calendar century of 2000 and to the vibration of the number *two* of the 20th Century which we are now living in, even though the calendar date is in the 1900s. As the force of LIGHT becomes stronger with the approach of the 2000 century, the struggle will be even greater; and unless the peoples of the world begin to open their minds and hearts to the influence of the oncoming vibration, humanity could lose out to the forces of evil seemingly so strong at the present time.

However, just as the 1900 century cycle brought new things the century of 2000 will make its force felt, and a new way of living will gradually come about. Those who can measure up to the spiritual purpose which the 2000 represents will live in a wonderful world. Those who cannot, will gradually lose their power, for the LIGHT of finer things and spiritual awareness will be so strong that crime and wrongdoing will gradually lose their hold.

The trend of events ahead is shown by the efforts put forth by the leaders of countries who have worked and planned for "peaceful coexistence." This is the trend of events which cannot be escaped. This will carry a stronger influence the nearer mankind approaches the oncoming century cycle. The upward climb will not be easy, for the struggles now being experienced between the wrong and the right are like a period of housecleaning—spiritual housecleaning. It is a period of *renovations* of minds and souls as well as of methods and practices.

How old are you? Are you prepared to live in the 2000 century cycle? Have you thought about what it might mean? The new age demands the ability to share. It is not the age of selfish individualization of the 1900s. There is likely to be a leveling of privileges and more benefits for the common man. "Blessed are the peacemakers for they shall be called the children of God." During the 1900 century cycle, men and women had the privilege of self-expression, the right of personal initiative. This will not be lost in the new cycle; individual rights will be strong and recognized, but *good character, culture, beauty*, and *faith in higher things* will be the *force* that will make the coming years worthwhile.

During the rest of this eventful 1900 cycle, begin to renovate your attitude of mind about life and the way to success. Even the businessman should find the way to make his efforts more worthy and to be willing to have the searchlight of the coming spiritual century shine upon his work and his methods. Spiritual attitudes of mind are often scorned by those in business or in the world of affairs. According to the signs of the future, every man and every woman must be able to stand the searchlight of spiritual things; this means to live by the qualities of the soul more than by the power of the mind or the energies of ambition. The "Fires of the Spirit" will burn away the resources and limit the opportunities of those who cannot.

See yourselves through the coming years without fear or regrets. Hang on to the good in the old and head towards the new with open minds and courage. In times of uncertainty ask for spiritual guidance; try to be in the vanguard of those who believe in the promises and love the "Light" rather than the dark.

For those who like to do research, the following chart will be helpful in reading the signs of the times. In 1962 the world *closed* another nine-year cycle, directed by the (11)2 of the 218th major cycle. 1963 was the *beginning* of a time of human Destiny, demanding a vital effort towards peace. The measuring rod of spiritual living is being used on mankind; the Light of Peace is beginning to shine more brightly, and men and women who cannot face the "Light" will pass from the platform of authority.

During the cycle 1936 and 1944, the trend showing the number *9* was towards "the brotherhood of man." The war ended in 1944 except for the kickback of the spring of 1945. That period was under the 216th major cycle. The *16*, hidden within the major cycle, was significant. It brought many uncertainties. As has been mentioned before, the number *16* has played its hand during all the big events of history for the past ten years and more. *16* always calls for understanding and demands payment for past services which nations, races, and peoples find it hard to give.

CHART OF EVENTS

The meaning of the numbers, as given in Chapter Two, will enable you to read events and to know for yourself how the affairs of mankind are going or will go without peaceful coexistence, according to the pattern of destiny set up by the calendar, to be lived under day by day, year by year, and century by century.

<u>1899</u> closed the century cycle of the 1800s and the 211 major cycle.

$$\frac{27}{9}$$

<u>1900</u> opened the new century cycle, 212 major cycle.

$$\frac{10}{1}$$

Divide by "nine."

Century Cycle	Major Cycle	Directive Cycle
1900 to 1908	212	5
1909 to 1917	213	6
1918 to 1926	214	7
1927 to 1935	215	8
1936 to 1944	216	9
1945 to 1953	217	1*
1954 to 1962	218	(11) 2
1963 to 1971	219	3
1972 to 1980	220	4†
1981 to 1989	221	5
1990 to 1998	222	6‡
1999 to 2007	223	7

1945 to 1953, the 217th major cycle and a *1* directive cycle, was the beginning of a new turn of events for mankind. Hidden in these years was the opportunity for a new start towards the cooperation the twentieth century demands; there was an increasing accent on spiritual acknowledgment and growth between the years *1954 and 1962*, under the (11)2 directive.

†*1972 to 1980*, under the 220 major cycle and a *4* directive cycle, will be a transition point—a test as to whether nations and people can work together to establish order and organization for all to build upon, or will miss the goal of peaceful coexistence, now definitely underway, written in the numbers of the time calendar by which all people guide their affairs.

‡*1990 to 1998* is, again, a period of big adjustment, under the 222 major cycle and the *6* directive cycle. A wonderful period, if humanity has by now realized that cooperation is the only way to service and goodwill. The Hell (19/1) of the century will be passing away. However, if nations in power at the time of the 217th major cycle (1945 to 1953) have not sensed the trend of the twentieth century, the upheaval the number 2 is capable of when its peace is not respected may be expressed.

CHAPTER XXIV

IMPORTANT QUESTIONS
AND ANSWERS

First—"If Numerology is true, and, as you say, 'God is All,' how do you account for the different names given to God in other countries?"

Truth of the reality of the Supreme Being does not depend upon how mankind regards this Truth or how they worship or pray. There is only One Cause—One Purpose, and God is All. He expresses Himself in various forms of Life—in tone, in color, as the sun, the moon, the stars, and as nations, races, and peoples, all of which describe His love and the glory of His being. The One Life is abstract in the beginning, but does not remain so in its outer manifestations.

If we begin with nations, each one is part of God's creation and His plan for life and expression. Each nation is made up of individuals who are part of Himself and His Purpose. Nations speak different languages, have different desires and spiritual attitudes of thought and feeling. They worship God in their own ways and according to the spiritual urge which characterizes them. This does not change the Supreme Being or limit the Eternal Purpose. The point of view about God varies according to the nature, experience, and traditions of nations and peoples.

An American and an Englishman may stand on a street

corner and see a motor vehicle approaching. The American will call it a truck, the Englishman will call it a lorry. An American may speak of God, a German of Gott, and a Spaniard of Dios, each worshiping in his own way. Each word has a different numerical value, as each nation has a different evaluation, and the numerical equation is the realization of the Supreme Being for that nation, race, or peoples.

Second—"Why is it that Numerologists differ so? It is confusing. Each book I read, and each teacher is different."

After you study, read and figure many names, you will realize there is very little difference in the teachings. Each teacher may use different words or terminology, as a result of many years' experience in use of the principles and fundamentals. A difference in terminology can easily come about. You will find that you, too, will not be able to use the exact words I give in describing a position, after you have become familiar with the principle or phase of character it represents.

Also one teacher may find more interest in one particular part of the fundamental principles, learn a great deal about it, more than other teachers, and use that part of analysis with skill and understanding. During my years of teaching, I have observed the varying interests of the students. One will be deeply interested in the Planes of Expression and pay little attention to the Challenge or Pinnacles.

One student left the class after studying the Points of Intensification. Later she told me, "I don't need any more instructions. I can read people's character just like that!" snapping her fingers. She was counseling and advising businessmen and women just from the Points of Intensification.

The instructions I give for the meaning of the Birth Number seem to differ from those of other teachers. I use it as the foundation and the background for talent and ability. To me it is not a *new* lesson for this lifetime. The *lesson* is in the need to *make use* of the talents shown by the Birth Force as a means of working out the Destiny, indicated by the new name. The big lesson is, in reality, making use of all facets of the character shown by the names and the Birth Force. As you read many names, you will find even the newborn baby is definitely like the qualities shown by the Birth Force.

The final question—My patient and gracious stenographer, Mrs. Betty Douphner, who has found a new and broader understanding of life through the instructions in Numerology she has copied, remarked, "I can set up a good chart, and I know the meanings of all the numbers, but I cannot read it after I get it set up. How do you *read* a chart?"

The final explanation—Listen to this description of an imaginary man. He is tall, dark, and fairly good looking. He has wavy hair, big brown eyes, small ears and hands, but a strong mouth and chin. (No doubt you are thinking this is a good thing, as a picture of him builds up in your mind's eye; otherwise he might appear effeminate.)

It is the same in reading a name. Read each position separately and carefully. Then move on from position to position, giving each one full value and description. Gradually the type of character will be outlined from the description of the nature of the positions and the numbers.

The position is the important thing. Always know from what position you are analyzing. Know what it *means*, what its *influence* is. Then place the number there and describe this and all its characteristics, mentioning its strengths, weaknesses, and opportunities, from the position from which you are reading.

As you go from position to position, always keep in mind what you have already analyzed (synchronizing, I call it); then you will find you have a clear picture of the type and character for whom you are reading.

It is the same when reading experiences. Keep the type of character in mind at all times. (This is very important! Never read the Table of Events as a separate point of analysis.)

For example: A man with a 9 Heart's Desire, a 9 Birth Force, a 9 Destiny and a 9 Reality has just entered a 4 Pinnacle and has an 8 Essence. You will not find all nines on the major positions very often. It gives unlimited opportunity, but also many disappointments. It shows a character with exceptional ability and with excellent creative talent, artistic and intuitive feeling—very impressionable, idealistic, and visionary. However, he is apt to be confused at times, or unreasonable, for he feels things deeply, due to the dynamic force and spiritual intuition of the many nines—so that without understanding of his potentialities, he could scatter his energies, leading to many disappointments and sorrows, at least until he learns to view life and love from the philanthropic level of expression and realizes the truth of the Brotherhood of Man. The number 9 includes all when it is rightly lived.

A 4 Pinnacle, which is a period of practical endeavor, demanding application and steady effort, is not going to be easy for him. Right away look over his character chart again. What balance has he on the Planes of Expression? What traits on the Points of Intensification to help him meet this period? Are there fours in his name? This will help. If not, you know it will be harder for him to settle down and meet his routine economic period of his life. At the same time it gives him an opportunity to put into concrete form some of the ideas and dreams he has had for a long time. Having an 8 Essence, there is a business opportunity present right now, requiring good judgment and executive ability, with the possibility of a promotion if he measures up, and with money to be made and paid out.

Refer to page 71 for the rules for reading a name and then blend each point of analysis into a picture as you would weave a rug or shawl, taking up each thread to color and outline the pattern.

Learn to tell the story of the Destiny and experience in your own terms, based on your training in the fundamentals.

Numerology is the easiest and most interesting of all branches of character analysis. It takes less time to learn and less time to use well and successfully. Once you learn the meaning of the numbers and points of analysis you will carry them around in your head and can put them to work for others at any time and in any place.

The people need those who are trained and have sympathetic understanding to help, comfort, and guide them. Because you have gained an insight into the forces of Being and human nature as shown by the Principles of Numbers, your life will be happier, your problems will lose their power, and you will have a new usefulness and purpose for living.

AUTOBIOGRAPHY
of a
NUMEROLOGIST

INTRODUCTION

FRIENDS AND STUDENTS have often suggested that I write my autobiography. This had never seemed important until recently, when, to my surprise, a woman said to me—in a somewhat overbearing manner—"Who are *you*? Where did you *come* from?" I was startled. I have never given my background much thought. Where did I come from, and who am I? Does it really matter this late in life? Moreover, who can say or question my story, now that I am in my middle nineties, should I decide not to tell the truth, or instead, make up a thrilling story just to please you.

How can I remember all the experiences of ninety-five years of living? The ups and downs, the sorrows, the frustrations, the disappointments, the delays; and the fun, the joys, the rewards, the thrills of attainment, the happy association with those of you going my way in the lifelong search for spiritual understanding and a more useful and happier human destiny. Ninety-five years is a long, long time.

THIS IS MY STORY

I was born on a farm, about 4 a.m. sun time, on June 8th, 1884, near the town of Saville, in the vicinity of Medina, Ohio. I was named *Juno* Belle Kapp, as my mother was reading Greek history at that time. I love chickens, dogs, cats and horses, but am frightened out of my wits by a cow. My father was a strong but gentle country boy, born on a farm also.

My mother was a foster child, living on a farm nearby, but not a farm girl at heart; a dreamer always. Her father was a soldier in the Southern army during the Civil War. Her delicate mother,

349

unable to take care of four children—two boys and two girls—gave them to foster parents, breaking up the family. They were all reunited later in life.

Due to my mother's failing health, we moved to Denver when I was two years old. We stopped over at Topeka, Kansas, and experienced a cyclone, my first childhood memory.

I have no recollections of the farm, but there must be farmer's blood in my veins, for at all country fairs, I seem to be drawn to the farm displays—the chickens, horses, pigs and even the cows. We remained in Denver until I graduated from Dental College in 1905.

During my growing up days in Denver, our lives were pleasant enough, although eventful. I was taught discipline, obedience, the fundamentals of housekeeping, to be on time, to do what I was told to do, and to take responsibility when it was asked of me. Otherwise, I was free to follow my own interests—which I did—with all the gusto of a cowboy.

With a cousin of my own age, we roamed the then widespread and often flooded basin of Cherry Creek, gathered wild roses and johnny-jump-ups, investigated every vacant house or forbidden territory, played Run-Sheep-Run (I was often the leader, for I could holler louder than anyone else), and went to school, as a necessity, in between times.

One of the memories of my very young days, which I cherish and love to recount if anyone will listen, is of father as driver of the horse-drawn street car, the means of transportation at that time. Father was young, enjoyed his job, and stayed with it until he had three stars on the sleeve of his coat. I often rode with him. Later, when he became motorman for the electric streetcars which followed, he frequently received a stern demerit for speeding. He loved to "let go" at the end of the line.

In these modern days, I have learned not to talk of "old times," especially to young people, even when I am hoping to be entertaining. "Days of old" mean nothing to the modern generation. They cannot even visualize a horse-drawn streetcar, not now—with doors that open as you approach, push button telephones, computers, men on the moon, T.V. and satellites.

However, during my long life, I have experienced and taken

in stride many changes: morals, styles, government, architecture, religions, wars, depressions, inflation.

As a numerologist, looking ahead to the year 2000, I see many more changes ahead on every level of living. It is astonishing to realize that these so-called scientific wonders of today will be antique and forgotten too. However, these changes will bring tests for every individual—emotionally and spiritually. It is wisdom to keep alert, whether young or old, and to be ready to move forward, often with speed, as the coming 21st cycle gets underway.

One of the memories of those early days, which no doubt helped to shape my character, is of torch-light parades and marching bands, when the women of Colorado decided to get VOTES FOR WOMEN. Of course, my mother was there, leading the band, a strong advocate for freedom and progress. I was allowed to march with the band and to stay up late. To this day, at the sound of marching feet and a band, I will drop anything and everything and run for a good position on the street. All my life I have been kidded about my love of a parade—which, in a way, shows how early events and happenings influence the impressionable minds of children.

One parade I will never forget. I stood on the streets of London, England, just after the first World War was declared, and watched the first regiment of English soldiers going off to war, marching with perfect timing and heads held high, led by England's beloved General Lord Roberts. Few came back. Sadness creeps over me when this picture comes to mind.

It was during these early days of parades and Run-Sheep-Run, that my tomboy nature got me into trouble. We girls were running from the boys, and one boy threw a packed snowball and hit me directly in the right eye. The consequences did not show up until later—about 1950—when it had to be removed and an artificial eye became my constant companion and handicap for the rest of my life.

This seemingly unhappy event, again, helped to form my character, for I gained sympathy for the handicapped, from whom I had always turned away before that. I realized, now, that they suffered, and like myself, were often embarrassed and unhappy. They, too, needed love, understanding and encouragement. Also, I wondered "why?" Why did these hurtful and unhappy experiences take place? I sought the answer from numbers. Through Numerology, I found many answers to the challenges we meet in life, and especially how to overcome them.

One of the unexpected turns of events of my younger days happened when I was about eleven years old. My mother, in better health now, became a physician. This was unheard-of in those days. A woman doctor? She was a very successful M.D. in spite of all the feeling against women in the professions, which carries on to this modern day. She went on to eventually become known round the world as Dr. Julia Seton—healer, metaphysician, and educator, comforting and uplifting the minds and hearts of thousands of seeking individuals with her story of Eternal Life and "God and Man are One."

My own spiritual training began at about this time, although I was unaware of it. I have had a deep devotion to spiritual living as my inspiration all my life. You often hear me say—"Always keep an aerial to the sky."

As I grew older, about 16 years of age, I went to work in a drugstore. Mother got me the job. She would! "You will learn a lot," she said. I loved it. I enjoyed the public contact and I did learn many things. As a drugstore clerk I did everything—sold cigars and candy and even worked at the soda fountain. My boss, Mr. Clark, taught me how to fill and wrap *seidlitz powders*, and to do them properly; a good training, as I have no fours in my name.

In my leisure time I spent many pleasant hours at Denver's City Park, listening to John Philip Sousa and his band. Curiosity often took me to the cemetery nearby, for in those days, a band might lead a funeral procession. My developing character analysis found me wondering why John's wife had died so young, or why a beloved baby had passed away.

Life went on much the same, day after day, until I was about eighteen, when what seemed like a tragedy entered our lives. My mother got a divorce from my father. My family was broken up and my father went out of my life.

A great deal of publicity and newspaper headlines resulted

from the divorce. I was placed on the stand and forced to make a decision—a deeply emotional experience for me. I will always remember the understanding judge who helped me, and who made it easier for me. However, this disturbing event did not stop my ambitious mother. Shortly afterwards, we left for Boston. My friends, my schooling, and my job were left behind me without notice. Mother took a post-graduate course in nervous diseases and I entered Tuft's Dental College, finding myself one of two girls in a class of eighty young men. Quite interesting! A romantic attachment followed me home by correspondence, but did not last long.

After the first year in Boston, we returned to Denver—Mother to marry "the man," and I to enter the Denver Dental College, where I completed my training and graduated in 1905. Here I was the only girl in the class of 50 young men. After graduation, I married the one I liked best—Roy Page Walton, and together we entered the big wide world, prepared to serve all who had aching teeth, and to make a fortune.

We established a practice in the little town of Holly, in the southeastern part of Colorado, a sugar-beet farming territory, and soon became part of the business and social activities of the town.

We had a fairly well-equipped office and did our own laboratory work. I did my part—made dentures, crowns, bridges, even extracted teeth. I often ran the office on my own while my husband, with a team of horses and a folding dental chair, crossed the Arkansas River, into the dry farming areas where dentists were greatly needed. We felt important. My husband often came home with $300 or $400, which we thought was a big sum of money. Believe it or not, we extracted teeth for 50 cents, made dentures for five dollars and bridges for ten.

These were happy days, for Holly was a small town, quiet and unhurried. We had time for relaxation, a team of dapple grey horses, and a beautiful collie dog named Jim. I often rode out over the prairie on Lazarus, one of our horses, with Jim as companion. One fourth of July, two of my friends and I won first prize as the best women riders in the parade. There weren't any other women in the parade. . . .

We even raised chickens, incubator-born, and had chickens

all over the place. These chickens were a source of training in character analysis to me. They were so "set in their ways." What they do first, they do over and over, and show a bit of temper at any attempt to change them.

About 1911, as Mother was lecturing in London at Caxton Hall, we decided to visit her. We stayed three months. We enjoyed the opera, the art galleries, museums, trips down the Thames river to visit King Henry's castle, and returned home, much to my regret, just as London was cleaning and polishing every building for the coronation of King George V. I would have enjoyed the excitement and beauty of it all.

Back home and waiting. My son Orin Phillip Walton was born March 7th, 1912. When he was three months old, we returned to London. We had learned that American dentists were greatly appreciated. There we established an office in Golder's Green, a suburb of London, gradually building up a good practice as we won the respect of the English people.

This period was an important phase of our lives and very worthwhile until one day—a Sunday in August, 1914. With no Sunday newspapers and no radio, we waited and waited—WAS ENGLAND GOING TO WAR WITH GERMANY?—until Monday, when the *First World War was declared!*

Now what shall we do—strangers in a foreign country!!?

In February of 1915, as we surmised that the war was not to end soon, my husband sent Orin and me home. Fearful of submarines, we sailed on the Lusitania. We arrived in New York safely. On its next journey, the Lusitania went down.

Our arrival in New York will *never* be forgotten. We sailed into the harbor at night—the lights, the noise, the whistles, the flags. After the darkened and restricted months in London with its blackouts, this was too much for me, and I wept. Orin, who had not talked much before this, said "OH! OH!" and has talked ever since. The American Flag is the most beautiful of all flags—"This is my country. Land that I love."

New York proved to be a challenge and a disappointment. Once again my life changed. I made every effort to take the New York State Board examination to permit me to practice dentistry there, but in those days, there was little or no exchange of credits or recognition between colleges. So I went back to Denver to stay with my husband's family until he sold the practice in London and returned to America. At least this is what we planned.

In the meantime, Mother, no longer practicing medicine, had become well known as an outstanding teacher and leader in the New Thought Movement, as it was called then. She ultimately carried her message of Transcendental Living around the world. In Johannesburg and in Sydney, Australia, the people offered to build her a temple or a grand church if she would stay with them, but she said NO! and came back to the United States. In New York she filled the Belasco Theater to the gallery every Sunday as she told the story of mankind's birthright. In San Francisco, at the World's Fair, she talked to a thousand people every noon. The Mayor named a day for her—Dr. Julia Seton Day.

She was a great voice, a dynamic personality, and because of her strong and fearless character, broke down many religious prejudices and opened the way for many metaphysical teachers who followed as "New Thought" began to be accepted. She was active until she was 86 years of age. Her last public work was in San Francisco a few weeks before she passed away. Some of her books are in the Southern Methodist University Archives, with others by teachers of that day, placed there for future seekers to read. She was deeply loved. She was my beloved mother.

On her way home from Australia, she stopped off in Denver and found me doing nothing. Immediately, in her uninhibited way, she proceeded to do something about it.

It always happened that wherever she had lectured, there would be a group of students eager to carry on their studies of the "New Civilization," as her church was called. The same thing happened after her talks in Denver. I was *commanded* to take over. "Juno," she said, "if you have any gumption—begin NOW!"

What a *shock*—ME take over?
Conduct CHURCH SERVICES?
Speak before all these PEOPLE?

What a *laugh* too, especially if you knew me *then*. Even though I was a strong, sturdy young girl and free as the wind, I was very shy, quiet; blushed if a boy even spoke to me. I had been taught, as far as manners were concerned, that "little girls should be seen and not heard." I never expressed myself or talked very much in groups. Others seemed to express their opinions over and above anything I had to say. I was very self-conscious and seldom felt smart enough to express my own ideas.

Now my life began for me in earnest, turning the tide of my future in a direction I had never dreamed of. Gradually I learned the art of public speaking. By hard work and mental agility, I memorized Dr. Seton's talks. How I suffered! No one can know. I look back on those beginning days and wonder why anyone came to hear me.

Gradually, I wrote my own thoughts and memorized them, and public speaking became easier. Today I can talk without notes or memorizing as long as anyone will listen. Believe it or not, I grew better-looking; I was no longer afraid to be myself, and began to take my place on the public platform during those early days of New Thought.

I have written a textbook on "Be a Good Public Speaker—Earn Extra Cash." It is so simple. It is the *Know-How, Step-by-Step*. Anyone can learn. There is nothing so satisfying and self-inspiring as to be able to stand before an audience and talk on any selected subject *well* and be paid for it.

Wonderful days followed! Yearly New Thought Conventions in many large cities when Metaphysical lecturers came from all parts of the country: "Live Forever" Harry Gaze; Mrs. Elizabeth Towne, presenting the *Nautilus* magazine; H. Victor Morgan, a wonderful speaker; Mr. H. B. Jeffery, author of many spiritual books; and many others. The wonder and inspiration of it all will never be forgotten. It was a period of spiritual growth for students, speakers, even the nation.

So I began to teach in Denver and make use of my early spiritual training. While public speaking was difficult for me, the metaphysical teaching came easily. I had been brought up in it. As a young girl, I went to any denominational Sunday School in the morning, with my girlfriend of the moment, and to the Theosophical Sunday School in the afternoon. As I grew older, I went to the spiritualist meetings with my mother during the time in her life that she was investigating psychic research. She eventually taught her students to meet their loved ones in their sleep and dreams.

Often students accuse me of analyzing psychically when I tell them truths about their character and experiences; but I am not! I analyze simply from the numbers of the name and birth. These are definite symbols of Cosmic Consciousness and never tell anything but the *truth* about any condition or circumstance where they are found. We may misinterpret them, which is regrettable, but within each number there is a definite statement of life, love, wisdom and experience.

My first introduction to the spiritual and objective value of numbers came when I was about 20 years old. While attending a lecture by a beautiful woman—Mrs. L. Dow Balliett, who had heard "the Music of the Spheres," and presented numbers as spiritual vibrations—my imagination was keenly inspired. I went on to study them and made them part of my metaphysical work. *To this day, numbers sing love songs for me and for you.*

Experience and problems followed. One afternoon during my early days in Denver, a nice man called and asked about my work, especially numbers. I told him about his name. A few days later, I received an official notice to appear before the District Attorney. He could not find anything wrong with my work—and in those days, numerology was something he had never heard of—and he made no charges. But being very conscientious (I have an 11 (2) inner nature), I discontinued my classes in numerology. About three months later he returned and said: "Make a living if you can!" I wished I could slam the door in his face. I had police inspection once again—in San Francisco, about 1920. This was very annoying and frustrating to me, but no charges were made.

I was in Denver only a short time. I was called to New York, teaching there only a short time, then to Boston for a season (where Dr. Seton had first started her metaphysical work), then to Chicago, where a New Civilization Center was being organized. This was one of the most successful and interesting periods of my work as a metaphysical teacher and lecturer. I had a loyal group of followers and students. Together, after my Sunday Service, we attended the lectures of every speaker who came to town, all of us growing in the realization of eternal life; courageous and self-confident in our determined effort to understand and live by the truth: God and Man are One.

Then in 1918, I was called to San Francisco. The leader there had passed away. This is the *how, why* and *when* I entered upon the scene in California.

*   *   *

One of my personal memories is of the day I arrived. Mother had promised to meet me in Long Beach on the way to San Francisco, but was delayed, so left me a note saying: "Thou shalt be with me, this day in paradise," (she loved California) and my son and I experienced our first earthquake, as we awaited her return.

I loved this period of my life. I really found myself and realized my own inner power and individuality. It was during this time, I began to make more use of numerology to help solve the problems of my clients. I discovered that many who came for advice and help were unable to free themselves from their personal and material problems or to find spiritual inspiration until they would "get themselves out of the way." This is why, today, I am a numerologist. It is all based on my background of spiritual training and earnest and sincere study as to the meaning of our names and the purpose of them as we meet the challenges of everyday life.

During my stay in San Francisco, I obtained a divorce from Dr. Roy Walton. He had entered the American Army during the war and even though the war was over, did not intend to return to the United States.

As Orin was growing and needed more fresh air and room to play, we moved to Los Angeles and have been here ever since, except for the lecture trips to many cities, which were generated by the growing public interest in names and numbers.

So numerology—presenting it to you in all its true meaning —has become my life's work. "Our Names are our Destiny," unfailing in their support in times of anxiety, uncertainty or loss; and even more fulfilling in the blessing they bestow if we allow them to guide us as we tarry here for a while on the grand Cosmic Journey.

In my beginning days as a numerologist, I made many mistakes as I struggled to learn the truth about the use of numbers and names. One woman left my studio in disgust because my analysis was so far wrong. I had used a system someone had recommended, but I had never proved it or considered its source. I could not go on this way, calling myself a numerologist, counseling and getting paid for it. So I called together a study group which eventually became the California Institute of Numerical Research, incorporated in the State of California. Our association gave us the right and privilege to teach and counsel, as well as legal protection and professional standing.

Our purpose was to prove or disprove Numerology and the influence of numbers in the human experience. For twenty-five years, from September to June, once a week, we took up for examination every phase of analysis we had ever heard of. Each member examined and tested each idea and reported her findings until together we proved, and proved beyond a doubt, that NUMBERS ARE SYMBOLS OF THOUGHT, ACTION, EXPERIENCE, HUMAN PURPOSE AND DIVINE PROPHECY. They are unfailing in their purpose and direction. It is only because we, with limited understanding of their direction and influence, sometimes fail to interpret their true meaning, that they seem to be untrue.

Our names are life's love stories.
They are novels of Divine Intent.

During this time, a very fine gentleman came to my lectures at the Eleanor Reesburg Metaphysical Library in Los Angeles. His name was Wallace Bishop Jordan. He asked me out to dinner several times. In October 1930 we were married; we spent 38 years together.

The change of name from Dr. Walton to Dr. Jordan seemed difficult for students to remember, so we compromised on Dr. Juno. Some people, in fact, have never heard my last name.

The C.I.N.R. disbanded when we had accomplished what we had set out to do. I continued teaching and counseling for several years. Time and years passed by. Numerology, which had often been scorned and laughed at, called fortune-telling, gradually became an accepted and dependable means of self-development —spiritually, emotionally and materially.

My classes, my work, and my teachings increased in value and importance to the degree that my students pressed me to put into writing my instructions and method of analysis. So I wrote a book—*The Romance in Your Name*—and from what you tell me, it is your textbook as you read the *Life Story* written in the name of each person who seeks your counsel. This is a great reward to me, for in many ways, I sacrificed other opportunities to continue with Numerology, especially during those days when Numerology was under a cloud. You reward me and honor me by your expressions of appreciation through your letters, phone calls, and public respect.

* * *

Now you know who I am. I hope the story has been interesting and encouraging to you. Surely now, as I am 95 years old, it is time to retire and allow you all to carry on—*but! do not count me out!* I know why one should live a long time and a long life. The rewards of your labors and work have only just begun to show up then. Beginning with my 90th birthday, Maurene Dragone, my brilliant student of many years, and well known in her own right, gave me my most wonderful birthday party. Two other women of the original Research group were there. But now, in 1979, I have outlived them all.

In 1977, I was chosen Woman of the Year (1977–1978) by the Santa Monica Chapter of the American Business Women's Association. In November of 1978, I was sponsored to a trip to Venezuela, South America, to testify as to the identity of a reticent numerologist who had predicted the identity of the next president of the country. This placed me right in the middle of a political squabble, fierce and intense.

The sponsors were two Venezuelan gentlemen. Having heard of my book and my standing as a numerologist, they visited me here in Santa Monica. They brought a film crew, took pictures of me and my diplomas as Dentist and member of the California Institute of Numerical Research. They also had a notary sign copies of the candidates' charts that I had made out, although I refused to make a prophecy.

These Venezuelans then pressed me to go to their country. *I knew* the numerologist who had made the selection for the next president. He was not very well known, as he worked more for his own interest in numbers than for public acclaim. To complicate the situation, the opposition party brought a man from Cuba who posed as a numerologist. It was soon discovered that he had no knowledge of names and numbers whatsoever.

Naturally the Press in Venezuela thought it was all a hoax, until it was learned that a noted numerologist from the U.S. would appear and identify the man in question. My name and my picture as an old lady were in the papers for days. I was interviewed and photographed. Finally there was the press conference. Newsmen and photographers stood poised and ready to pry from me the man's name and my *own* prophecies. When I refused, they left in a huff, though satisfied that at least I knew him.

It was all very exciting, those five days. 100 of my books were given away, and the unexpected happened, for my lecture later was well accepted. Without realizing it at the time, numerology, or the interpretation of names and numbers as we are using it, became *international*. Students there are carrying on with the teaching and intend to take it to other countries and neighbors, who will be eager to learn and study. I had a wonderful time, even though my son and friends disapproved my going away with two strange men at age 94. I have a #5 Destiny.

But this is not all!

When I returned home, I received word that my latest book—*Your Right Action Number*—had been accepted and was going into print, to be on sale in May (published by DeVorss and Co., Marina del Rey, CA).

Life can be beautiful. Keep moving forward.

It has been wonderful traveling down life's highway with you. Always remember—Keep an aerial to the sky.

Sincerely,

Dr. Juno Jordan